AROUND IN CIRCLES
WITH LES ROBINSON

AROUND IN CIRCLES
WITH LES ROBINSON

LIFE, BASKETBALL, AND THE NCAA

W. Thomas McQueeney

Palmetto Publishing Group
Charleston, SC

Around in Circles - Les Robinson: Life, Basketball and the NCAA

Copyright © 2018 by W. Thomas McQueeney
All rights reserved

First Edition

Printed in the United States

ISBN-13: 978-1-64111-190-4
ISBN-10: 1-64111-190-9

TABLE OF CONTENTS

DEDICATION
BARBARA SIMON ROBINSON

This book is dedicated to the extraordinary Barbara Robinson—wife, mother, grandmother, and friend. She was the surrogate mother to a generation of basketball players. This production revolves around coaches and incredible life journeys. The best coaches excel in a multitude of roles. Among them are educator, teacher, mentor, and advisor. In that vein, Barbara Robinson was one of the best.

I first met Barbara in the summer of 1972. Along with my freshman teammates, we had just completed our first week at The Citadel. To say that we were a miserable, homesick group of boys would be a gross understatement. One player had already gone home, and the rest were thinking of doing the same thing. Then we met Barbara—sweet, precocious, warm, and welcoming. In spite of trying to corral her four small children, she gave us her undivided attention, and we knew that we had someone who would look out for us and mother us as needed. She became a second mother for a continuous line of basketball players.

Barbara was more than a coach's wife. She was integral to the team. She filled a role of full-time associate head coach. Her ebullient and uplifting personality provided stability, motivation, and support. In a business where spouses can hinder careers, Barbara helped make Les' career thrive.

It was always Barbara and Les. You never said one without the other. She was a part of everything. Les's favorite pastime at conference meetings was to gather a small crowd within earshot of Barbara, and say, "You know why I brought Barbara with me don't you? So I wouldn't have to kiss her goodbye." After the obligatory laughs—his being the loudest—Barbara would stick her tongue out at him…but always with a sparkle in her eye. That part was true. He didn't want to say goodbye. He always wanted her with him, and she knew that.

When Barbara knew her time was running out, she was at her best. She coached us into accepting her impending death as she had coached us in the past. She made us believe that everything would be okay. She taught us that death was a part of life and that we should celebrate, not mourn. She was truly an inspiration.

Barbara died on the day of the total solar eclipse. It was billed as a *once in a lifetime* experience. How appropriate because knowing her was also a *once in a lifetime* experience.

Richard Johnson
Director of Athletics
Wofford College

AROUND IN CIRCLES
CIRCULARITY

(L) Les Robinson with Bill Walton, 2007, and (R) with David Thompson, 1975.

(L) With President Gerald Ford, 1976, and (R) with Jerry West 1970.

(Top) With Johnny Wooden, 1971, (bottom) and with Mike Krzyzewski, Dave Odom, and Bobby Cremins, 1993

FOREWORD

It's circular on a sphere with a volume of roundness. It's about bad bounces and bouncing back. It could be said that this story is about basketball. But it's more than that. This volume details an incredible journey of a player, a coach, and an athletic director, Les Robinson.

The stories move past the person and the sport into circles of everyday people in their everyday lives. Les Robinson has lived every fabulous facet with the temerity of a Charleston beach developer and the timidity of a West Virginia coal miner. His arch of achievement is dwarfed by his rebound of humility. But this work is not about his achievement—his wins and losses; his accomplishment or his failure. It is about what he is inside. Just as there is air in the sphere, there is *more in Les* than meets the eye!

His circle is wide. His experience bounds. Les Robinson is the real-life *Forrest Gump*. Somehow, by the alignment of the bright spheres that make up our universe, Les gets the award for the best supporting actor to scenes from a past we all recognize. He was there. He was the *You Tube* and the *Web Cam*, the *TiVo* and the *FaceBook* post. He lived it all and we—unknowingly—have it recorded as sports lore.

By example, he was a timely witness unexamined in Tallahassee in December of 2000. As television color commentator of the Florida State University basketball game hosting the University of Florida that evening, he began a story by recalling odd similarities to the contentious 2000 presidential election to play-by-play analyst Chip Carey. He brought up the experience of his most recent coaching-search interview. Les served as Director of Athletics at NC State University. His referenced coaching interview was with the former FSU football assistant who became the newly-hired NC State Wolfpack head coach, Chuck Amato.

Les wedged into the subject by recalling Amato's interview response, "The real war in Florida for recruiters always centers on who controls those football rich counties— Broward County, Palm Beach County, and Miami-Dade County. These comprise the Miami metro area. Who gets the players from there—FSU, Florida, or the University of Miami? That war will determine who wins the head-to-head games between these three powerhouses."

The throngs of the largest media attention the world may have ever known had crippled traffic to and from FSU's Leon County Civic Center that evening. Amato's point had been made a year earlier when AD Les Robinson was trying to find a coach to replace the recently-departed Mike O'Cain. But the comment from that coaching search gained a quick insight from Les. The world media had descended upon the Florida Statehouse in Tallahassee. Florida State University spreads across the metropolitan Tallahassee area. But Les was alluding to a larger determination than who would win the prep recruiting wars or who would win football bragging rights in Florida. Those three counties would determine who would be the next President of the United States.

"Ironically, Chip, that's why there's not an available hotel room anywhere in Tallahassee! It's the control of Palm Beach, Miami-Dade, and Broward Counties by recount that will tell us if we've elected George Bush or Al Gore!" Les deadpanned. "I'm not sure to what *end* that situation has been *tackled*, but I know there are a lot of extra *guards* in Miami right now!" His pun tickled Carey.

Yet another related story had come full circle. Some fifteen years earlier, Les met a new friend and East Tennessee State University supporter John Howren at the popular Peerless Restaurant in Johnson City, Tennessee. Howren owned and operated Howren Oil Company in Johnson City. It was September, 1985, and Les had become the new head basketball coach at East Tennessee State University. Howren, a big burly man who had played basketball at Wofford College, had brought a brash young guest to meet Coach Robinson. As they sat in the privacy of the Peerless's individual booth-rooms eating saltine crackers and drinking beer, the bellicose Howren turned his attention to his quiet guest.

The guest was tall and impressionable. He was seeking approval and support, but had no reason to look over his shoulder. There was no media, no eavesdroppers, no curious minds. They were in a small closed room unto themselves. The tall gentleman was inside the Beltway in Washington, holding a new political office, but did not seem very sure of himself. There was not much opportunity to speak with Howren controlling the conversation.

The tall dark-haired man had served as a U.S. House member from Tennessee's 6th District before becoming a U.S. Senator. Howren broke the silence once the beer was ordered. It was not the usual way that one would introduce a basketball coach to a senator.

"Howren opened up our conversation by asking, 'You still smokin' that weed, boy? You are, aren't you? I can tell by the look. Don't fret, son. Nobody hears us. I know you're on the weed!' Howren then laughed at his subject of choice," Les said. "And I immediately felt bad for the guy. He didn't know me and it was such an odd way to be introduced even if we were in a closed off room."

The young senator demurred. He recoiled. He was afraid to speak. Les noted the tension and quickly changed the subject. The young man having a steak with Les and John Howren that night was the Carthage, Tennessee, gentleman who was finishing his rookie year in the United States Senate, Albert Arnold Gore, Jr.

"Howren liked the kid. I figured that Howren not only was a Gore financial supporter, but also wanted to introduce him to as many people as he could in the Tri-City area—Kingsport, Bristol, and Johnson City," Les concludes.

The introduction tour had to be uncomfortable for the young senator. It is doubtful that Howren would be doing many more introductions after this awkward one was completed.

"Honestly, Senator Gore handled it well," Les stated. "I'm not sure that the event didn't help him prepare for the unexpected."

Les never forgot the trepidation in the young man's eyes. That image came back to Les as he considered the events unfolding in Tallahassee, Florida, at the end of the 2000 presidential election.

"I had no idea that the uncomfortable introduction meeting at the Peerless Restaurant would have me—fifteen years later—sitting in the middle of the Florida capital and wondering like the rest of the world, who would be our president—and that it might be him. Howren, Gore, and I had a few beers that night, but nobody was talking about him becoming president," Les recalled.

The circle had returned unto itself.

Les carried the color commentary for the Atlantic Coast Conference clash just blocks away from where the world seemed to clash. A state attorney general was overseeing "hanging chads" and other disputed ballots. The world watched in awe. The coveted electoral votes of the State of Florida would determine the leader of the free world. A basketball game seemed inconsequential. And what was brought up at the Peerless Steakhouse in Johnson City, Tennessee, just fifteen years prior, seemed like a lifetime in a faraway place. The whole world had come full circle.

Yet the circumstance of Les Robinson being at the epicenter of anything and everything had become a repetitive theme.

Les's journey has hurtled through a world of college sports. There is good and bad. There are moments of craziness, humor, and introspect. Aboard a cycle that measures turns in revolutions per minute, the life and times of Les Robinson deserves another "RPM" category altogether—remembrances per moment.

Les's journey through the commonalities of life is recorded here for posterity and hilarity. From Charleston, West Virginia, to Charleston, South Carolina, his life has come full circle. There is wisdom in his approach, candor in his recollection and, above all, the astonishment of unexpected humor intertwined within it all. But it is not all here by our accident as his audience. It is here by his circumstance of being circular and including our life within the confines of his broad circumference.

Perhaps as fine a storyteller as may exist in college sports, the insights and timing of his experiences are here for a recounting, unlike the afore-mentioned recount in Tallahassee. His recount has very little argument or invective. There are no hanging chads. It is for enjoyment.

Les Robinson is at the center of it all. From these pages, readers will understand why. If he had accompanied this book to sit with you in person, he'd order a beer or a cup of coffee to verbalize the joy of life, basketball, and the NCAA. His recall of events, sentiments, and words spoken—even expressions—helps us all to relive them for what they were within the nur-turing charm of the story told—and lived. Storytelling is a lost art. So, other than a few connecting sentences and some historical context, these stories are Les's life and his observations throughout. Read on, reader!

Les with North Carolina Basketball Caoch Roy Williams at "Les Robinson Roast."

INTRODUCTION

It was mostly the Scots and Scots-Irish who found their way into the new American Highlands of Appalachia. The mountains posed a problem for those pushing westward to the great American breadbasket. The identifying names of the duty-inspired trailblazers intimated their European lineage—Daniel Boone, Davy Crockett, Andrew Jackson, and Les Robinson. There are few from that region that have impacted the modern American way of life, especially sporting America, as Les Robinson has. Like the other trailblazers, he made the Appalachians his foundation of intrinsic values, revealing insights and the mountainous community's penultimate export: common sense.

Les was a war baby, born on September 23, 1942. His mother, Mary Trowbridge Robinson, was another Scottish-lineaged native of the area. She was the guiding force who directed Les, his older brother, and two younger siblings through the exigencies of Post-Depression West Virginia. But Les's outgoing personality and gregarious nature were more the gene provided by his father, A.G. "Inky" Robinson. Inky Robinson was a Union Carbide worker in Charleston, West Virginia. Charleston is a place of trade unions, coal extraction, loud trains, river barges, churches, and basketball. The Robinson family lived a few miles down the river from Charleston in St. Albans. The next town on the river beyond is Nitro. That's a coal industry name, spoken loudly. It is actually where nitroglycerin was invented. Other industries with names meant for growth were incubated there—Monsanto, Union Carbide, FMC, DuPont, and Westvaco.

Inky's Robinson clan was much like other families of the area during the decades before Interstate 77 came near. The Kanawha River, named for the Native American tribe, snakes through the valleys of the Allegheny Plateau and joins the Ohio River at Point Pleasant, West Virginia. There are numerous artifacts extant detailing that ancient civilization the inhabited this area ten thousand years earlier.

Les likes to tell his friends that it would be possible to get on a boat in his back yard at St. Alban's of his childhood years and arrive within a few blocks of his home on Sullivan's Island, South Carolina. Don't doubt him. He would convince everyone in earshot that rivers and streams were first discovered in West Virginia.

To be sure, basketball was not invented in West Virginia. They just perfected it there.Not much farther down the river is another coal and river community of Chelyan. A short creek runs from the river for not much more than the length of a fullcourt shot. Cabin Creek is part of Chelyan, but earned a name of its own as if it were another town because of basketball. When the NBA listed its "team of the century" in 2000, one of the five selectees was Jerry West. West grew up on Cabin Creek. "Zeke from Cabin Creek" is the pride of West Virginia and a trove of NBA highlight films with the Los Angeles Lakers. Officially, Jerry West is from Chelyan. Understandably, the NBA sportswriters did not want to promote him as "the Hellion from Chelyan." Les is proud to remind his ever-growing listener audience that West's silouetted likeness became the emblem for the NBA. That fact establishes West Virginia as a giant star in the basketball universe.

There were so many others that vaulted from the Kanawha River to greatness. Hot Rod Hundley hailed from Charleston. He was the first player taken in the 1957 NBA draft. Others like Hall of Famer Hal Greer and O.J. Mayo are from Huntington. Deron Williams is from Parkersburg. Jason Williams is from Belle. Rod Thorn, who coached and played before becoming General Manager of both the Chicago Bulls and New Jersey Nets, was born in Princeton.

Coach Claire Bee, who went on to win national championships at Long Island University in the 1936, 1939, and 1941, hailed from Grafton. He is credited with the invention of the 1-3-1 zone defense and the adoption of a 3-second lane violation rule. Over twenty years his teams won five of every six games—still an NCAA record. Bee's legacy in West Virginia inspired the adoption of basketball as the state's primary sport.

It was yet another West Virginia basketball coach, Eli Camden 'Cam' Henderson (from Joe), who invented both the 2-3 zone defense and basketball's answer to height dominance—the fast break. After all, the court is longer than it is tall. Henderson famously trained his team to be sprinters for the avalanche of points they could amass when opposing team's players tired late in the game. Henderson coached high school basketball in Bristol during World War I. Bristol's new gymnasium was so poorly built that the rain would dampen the floor. Henderson used a zone defense because of the slick flooring. Considered a major impact coach of the era, he went on to coach at Muskingum College, Davis and Elkins College, and then Marshall University.

West Virginia, "Almost Heaven" according to songster John Denver, seems to have ties to every major American venue through the heroism that sport gains in its hills and hollars. Baseball? George Brett, Lew Burdette, Bill Mazeroski, Steve Yeager and the all-time Major League Baseball RBI season champion, Hack Wilson. Football? Sam Huff, Randy Moss, Lou Holtz, Chuck Howley, Gino Marchetti, Nick Saban, Curt Warner, Jimbo Fisher, and John McKay. Boxing? Jack Dempsey. Gymnastics? Mary Lou Retton.

West Virginia has produced others outside of sport that became household names. Entertainment? Think Jennifer Garner, Don Knotts, Brad Paisley, Soupy Sales, and Bernie Casey. If you're not impressed yet, add in Pearl Buck, Stonewall Jackson, Chuck Yeager, Cyrus Vance, Jay Rockefeller, and Booker T. Washington. Devil Anse Hatfield and Abraham Lincoln's mother, Nancy Hanks, were from Almost Heaven. Place another checkmark beside the name of Leslie G. Robinson. He has spent a lifetime as West Virginia's traveling Chamber of Commerce.

The honor of "writing it down" has befallen me, not as a writer, but as a friend who has known Les for nearly fifty years and is enthralled with the assignment. I would do nothing to betray that trust, so everything written herein has been carefully researched and recorded before it was submitted to the ultimate editor, Les himself. After all, what we enjoy today within the mystical world of sports, the NCAA, and the interaction of its great coaches largely comes from experiences and friendships. Les has been willing to detail amazing sports and real-life connections to us in a most entertaining fashion. If you heard it from him, then the book reference should be identical. If you haven't heard him tell these stories, get that cup of something you like and sit back. These are astonishing reflections, moreso because they have touched so many people we all know across one of America's most fertile landscapes, the world of NCAA sports.

This recounting was a long time in the making. It really started because of Les's 5th grade pronouncement that he wanted to grow up to coach college basketball. From there, his determination took over. He became the voluminous vault of that experience. In 2009 that the idea of "writing it down" became a goal, but getting Les away from his extremely active daily routine became anything but a routine matter. It's not that he is not interested in doing it. It is that he is interested in everything else and busies himself doing those things as well. He loves people. He adores his family. His fifty-four-year marriage to the late Barbara Simon Robinson is as admirable a story as there is in any romance novel. But theirs is real.

Les never runs out of material from his incredibly focused mind that includes the details that would make a government grant writer blush. He knows the weather, the circumstance, the background setup, and the final score. The Google search engine only verifies it in a widening digital world. As Casey Stengel would say, "You could look it up." Research only underscores Les's remarkable abilities of recall.

From here, for the most part, I'll defer to Les. Let Les tell it. There will never be another one like him.

W. Thomas McQueeney

Les reflects upon his career by mentioning the two "Key Wests" –
West Virginia and Jerry *West*.

CHAPTER 1

THE CURVATURE OF THE EARTH

The earth is spherical. The sun is an orb. The moon phases into predictable curves left and right. What we know, we know in circles. Though Les's circle began in Charleston, it was not Charleston, SC.

The suburban hamlet of Saint Alban's is nine miles west of this Appalachian capital city. Here Inky and Mary Robinson raised their four children. The family was truly a reflection of times past. There was Poe, the older brother from Mary's previous marriage to a man who had passed away. He was ten years older than Les. Then there was Debbie, a sparkplug of spirit and energy. She was a level mixture of both parents—with a personality both outgoing and settling. The family caboose, Mark, also rose to heights from the pastoral community outside of Charleston, West Virginia. A bright student, Mark Robinson became the director of Energy Projects at the Federal Energy Regulatory Commission, FERC.

The oldest, Charles Poe Robinson, was born in 1932. Les was born in 1942, Debbie in 1947 and Mark in 1952.

Poe enjoyed the closeness of the Robinson home, but being twenty years older than Mark, Poe was emancipated from the household and serving in the United States Air Force when Mark was born. He had a difficult time after the Air Force, never fully defeating his most difficult demon, alcohol. He would come to visit often enough, enjoying the memories of the home where he was born. Poe had attached his happiest days of youth in the plain and airish St. Alban's house. That old 1920's architecture never lost its attraction to the Robinsons. Mary Trowbridge Robinson never lived anywhere else after her early marriage to Poe's father. It was indeed ironic that when Poe visited from Miami near his sixtieth birthday, he died from a heart attack in the old Robinson homestead. His sudden death occured less than ten feet from where he was born six decades earlier. He had just visited NC State with Les's dad to see Les coach in his second year after returning to his alma mater.

Debbie Robinson graduated from Marshall University and married a fine gentleman from Pennsylvania, Bill Zacharias. Zacharias was an excellent golfer. He graduated from Eureka College (Illinois)—the same college that produced President Ronald Reagan. The Zacharias' four-generation masonry business in East Stroudsburg, Pennsylvania, flourished under Bill Zacharias's keen business management.Eventually, Debbie and Bill were able to build a second home only blocks away from Les's Sullivan's Island residence. The Zacharias's three daughters spent their summers enjoying the quaint island setting and the frequency of the Robinson family get-togethers. Sadly, Bill Zacharias died suddenly while on a cruise through the Panama Canal in February of 2014, just months short of their fortieth wedding anniversary. A kind, caring, and community-invested man, Bill Zacharias left a legacy. He was loved by all.

Before Mark Robinson's rise in a major federal agency, he walked to school daily carrying a bundle of books. He was interested in the world beyond the Kanawha River and felt certain that he would explore much of it. He was destined. Personable and considerate of others, Mark was a stellar student. As a *Summa Cum Laude* graduate of West Virginia University, he found that the vehicle of education, when properly applied, could take any person anywhere.

Mark did not buy a place on Sullivan's Island.

"Why would I need to buy a house when Les already had one?" Mark notes with a wink. "Besides, he and Barbara would open it to my family even if they were away. And Debbie and Bill were just down the street. I always felt like I had a place there whenever I needed it. And I didn't have to pay the property taxes."

Mark and his wife Karen spent much time with their three children and the Robinson clan. He lives in the Washington area, where Les says, "When you go 'inside the Beltway' I instantly become Mark Robinson's brother." Indeed, all of the waterways and gas pipelines in America are under the control of FERC—and Mark Robinson runs the show as its director.

The transition from Charleston, WV, to Charleston, SC, was a process that has brought insights, industriousness, and ingenuity. It also brought the finest set of qualities that could bridge the two Charlestons from Les's childhood to his retirement years—an overabundance of common sense, sincerity, and unreserved acceptance of others. A sense of humor has been the constant. These qualities have shaped his life.

Les's childhood was all about the same sport that would consume his lifetime.

"I was obsessed with basketball. My hero was Jerry West. And since Jery was from just up the road, it made it even more of an obsession to work on my game to become the epitome of that great player. In a way, Jerry West was doubly responsible.

"I first picked up the sport in the fourth grade, but played other sports, as well. I particularly loved playing little league baseball. But basketball had me hooked.

"Our high school had great teams, and it was unusual back then to make the varsity as a sophomore—and I wasn't good enough. But by the time I was a senior I had enough ability to attract coaches from colleges to stop by. And my dad's relationships in the sport had grown because of his promotions of the Sportsman's Club Tournament. That's how I first met Hot Rod Hundley and, later, Jerry West himself."

A visit by Jerry West on Labor Day of 1959 changed his life.

"All the kids knew that Jerry West was coming by the house. It was a big deal that he knew who I was through my dad. But that day, I had this really bad headache—which was unusual because I never got sick. West did come by as promised, and he showed me and the others a few things. Everybody in West Virginia at the time wanted to be Jerry West."

The aftermath of West's afternoon visit was nearly fatal.

"My headache never went away. I had perfect attendance all through high school and didn't want to miss school. There was an academic benefit for never missing back then. You didn't have to take your final exams unless you needed to take one to pull up a grade. That was a great benefit to me because I didn't exactly embrace studying. So I went to school even though my head was still hurting. I even went to the office to ask how long I had to stay not to be counted as absent. The principal let me go home after lunch. I didn't return to high school from that early September day until after Thanksgiving. I had been diagnosed with meningitis. It was contagious, so I was quarantined.

"Because of the meningitis, the rumor at school was that I was going to die. People died from meningitis enough that my mother and father were really worried. Nobody could see me because of the quarantine, so the death rumor grew on its own. But I got better within a month and was able to go outside and shoot hoops.

"The family doctor, Dr. Rodney Harshbarger, recommended exercise, though I was still under quarantine. Doctor Harshbarger was a family friend. Incidentally, he was a 1939 graduate of The Citadel. I knew all about The Citadel through him.

"I played for several hours every day, doing drills that Jerry West had showed us. I shot free throws, dribbled left and right, and went through spot shooting drills. I got better. I also got much stronger. The bout with meningitis kept me out of school, but it was the break I needed to become good enough to attract colleges."

After ten weeks at home and no visitors, Les was cleared to go back to school and to resume his basketball career.

"My coach accepted me back with open arms after the relief of knowing I was healthy. It surprised everyone. The teachers took it easy on me, believing I had barely escaped death. And I did nothing to dissuade them from treating me in a special way. I got away with not doing homework by telling the teacher that my concentration was still not back to normal. They all accepted that and gave me a free pass on assignments. It was a situation that I milked all the way through my senior year.

"In fact, I started the very first game back, though I had missed nearly every practice. I became a 'feel good' story. In that first game, I led the team in scoring and had a good floor game as well. I didn't know it at the time, but the University of West Virgininia head basketball coach, Fred Schaus, was in the stands. I received a letter from him a week later inviting me to visit their campus in Morgantown.

"We had a very good team—and two other players on the team were definite college material, Alfred Bailey and Frank Roy."

Les had befriended Frank Roy, a big and pudgy African American from Amandaville, a minority enclave near St. Albans. He had met Frank while playing pick-up games on outdoor courts during the summer in Amandaville. It was Les that convinced Frank Roy to attend St. Albans and to go out for basketball as a sophomore.

But Frank Roy had misgivings.

"Frank was still heavyset and the other kids made fun of him because he didn't look like a basketball player. He was big and still flabby. The needling from the other players did not help during their tryouts. Frank had become discouraged.

"Frank Roy is maybe the reason I recognized that I could coach. I recognized that he had talent. But after that first practice and the verbal barrage he got from the other players, Frank became disenchanted. He had lost some confidence. He told me that he was not coming back the next day.

"I recognized that Frank was agile, had great hands, and that he positioned himself instinctively for rebounds. He had a soft shooting touch. I thought that he could become a good player. I told him all of these things and more trying to encourage him to not give up. He bought into what I had said—and he stayed. As a result, he and I both made the J.V. team.

"A few weeks later Frank was promoted to the varsity. This was rare for a sopomore at St. Albans. As a big school, we constantly had good talent in the upper classes. Just after Frank was called up to the varsity, he became a starter. The rest is a great story.

"During his senior year, Frank was recruited to play basketball and football at several colleges. He was recruited to go to a junior college in California by Coach Bill Armstrong, a famous coach in Compton, California. Armstrong's Dad was from West Virginia. Frank initially went to the junior college and then on to Utah State. There, he lettered in football, basketball, and track. As a top athlete, he was drafted into the National Football League by the St. Louis Cardinals. He played receiver for the Cardinals.

"Frank and I became great high school friends. In fact, he and his future wife Adelaide double-dated with Barbara and me to our Senior Prom in the spring of 1960. Both couples remained married for more than fifty years!"

The other college-level player, Alfred Bailey, received great advice from Les's father, Inky Robinson. Because of the testing qualifications for NCAA teams back then, the 6'4" Bailey did not qualify for an NCAA scholarship. He was a fine player with a skill set and basketball aptitude that could play in nearly any college. Devastated by the test results, Bailey wanted to go into work force instead of college. But Inky Robinson found an alternative.

"Dad knew the coach down in Buies Creek, North Carolina, at a junior college, Campbell. This is now Campbell University. Dad got him into Campbell. And Alfred did great starting out, but quit suddenly and did not return for reasons nobody knew.

"When my dad died thirty years later in 1991, Alfred came to the funeral home. He came by the casket near where I was standing. He was an old teammate. His life had tumbled into a series of bad turns. I said hello and thanked him for coming. Right then, Alfred just blurted out, looking down at my dad, 'If I would've listened to that man in 1960, I might have made something of my life.' I never forgot that."

There were things that his dad did to help others that Alfred and Les had never addressed. Inky had a good heart and was often there to help others.

"I never knew the story, but I had assumed that Dad couldn't talk him into staying at Campbell Junior College," Les concluded. "He never spoke about it after Alfred left."

Les did keep up with Frank Roy. Les remembers an odd circumstance of meeting up with Roy for dinner in St. Louis in the spring of 1973.

"I was an asssitant coach at The Citadel. All NCAA coaches are invited to come to the Final Four. Since I was in the area, I had called Frank to get together for a laugh and maybe a meal. Frank and I went to one of the top steakhouses in the area and were walking back to the hotel when we saw Bill Walton at an outdoor payphone late in the evening," Les recalled the circumstance.

Walton had played the night before against Memphis State University and played what is considered a near-perfect game in the UCLA Bruins 87-66 win. Walton made 21 of his 22 field goal attemps, scoring 44 points. But he was out late on a St. Louis street trying to call his assistant coach, Gary Cunningham. Les and Frank Roy stopped to chat as Walton was hanging up the phone.

"He had to go to another hotel for a room because where UCLA was staying did not have a large enough bed for him to sleep. So, as he got off the phome, I re-introduced myself. I remembered that Walton played his first varsity game in Pauley Pavailion against The Citadel. He remembered the game, too. It was only the year before. Walton was a junior by this time.

"I asked if he'd do me a favor and say hello to a friend back home. I had been busting on the College of Charleston's head coach, Alan LeForce. So I called Alan. I told him I didn't mean to call him so late, but I was out with someone he'd like to hear from. Now, I knew that Alan had just seen the game and the incredible performance the night before. I gave the phone to Bill Walton to say 'hello.'

"As soon as Walton said hello, he opened the phone for the response we could all hear. You could hear LeForce's response as the three of us were laughing out loud," Les retold. "Maybe it was the laughter that convinced him that the Walton voice was a hoax.

"He yelled through the phone, 'Les, you lying SOB. You thought you had me. Bill Walton, right! I wasn't born yesterday. Are you drunk or something?' LeForce went off on us.

"Even Walton was laughing. Then, Frank Roy got the phone. He said, 'Hey Coach, I don't know you and you don't know me. But I'm Les's teammate from high school and I'm here with Les and the guy you just spoke to was indeed Bill Walton. I know Les pulls a few over on people, but this time he told the truth, my friend. The jokes on you. Say goodnight to Bill Walton!'"

Years later, Walton handled color-commentary for the NCAA tournament and attended the common traditional events that preceded the Saturday-Monday Final Four. Walton often greeted Les with a big smile as the practical joker he first met at a phone booth in St. Louis. There seemed to be some nebulous cloud that kept bringing the big redhead next to Les for a laugh or a reminiscence. Walton is apt to bring up that he played his first college varsity game against a Les-coached team.

Les reverted back to the subject of his high school experience.

"We were good and we had talent and discipline. Our coach was tough and he gave us the tools to succeed.

"My coach at St. Albans also had a connection to The Citadel. His son, Steve Nida, became a professor at The Citadel. He was dean of the Psychology Department. Coach Al Nida was a fine coach that believed in conditioning and fundamentals. He was ultra-disciplined. He could have been a great drill sergeant. He didn't like hot-dogging and showboating. I listened to him and followed directions. I wouldn't cross him because he'd make life very difficult and practices hard. He taught me to go at everything with one-hundred-percent effort. He was structured and was a great coach for me at the time.

"We won games, and people came to see us play. We were a fine team with a rigid coach who knew basketball. It made sense that we were successful."

Home life in the Appalachains was simple. Les summed up the options.

"I had a supportive family, a father who knew how to plan events and sell tickets, a fine high school experience, and a fire inside of me to work hard. I could go as far as I was willing to work. The environment I was in would not allow any other substitute. I could work at basketball as a way to something else, somewhere else. Without basketball, I would have remained there working with one of the big employers in the energy industry. That wouldn't be bad, but I liked the road to becoming a basketball coach much better."

The Robinson home in St. Albans was about basketball.
Les's father Inky Robinson was well-known in NCAA circles.

CHAPTER 2
GREGORY 'INKY' ROBINSON

Les's father was a household name in Charleston, West Virginia. He was considered that capitol city's P.T. Barnum.

"Dad always had something going on," Les's brother Mark Robinson stated. "Everybody knew him and wanted to get into the games. It was better than the circus coming to town because you knew so many of the players. Dad had the two main ingredients of success: energy and imagination."

Gregory 'Inky' Robinson and his business partner, Jim Murray, started the amazing Sportsman's Club Basketball Tournament in St. Albans in 1942. It was before the sport of basketball had hit its stride. Gyms were crude, and the floor markings would not be recognized as what they have become today. There were no lanes, no arches and no "hashes." Possessions were frequently changed by jump balls. Now there is only one jump ball in a regulation game. Inky Robinson found a vein of gold in those hills. The people of West Virginia fell in love with the sport. In time, the place and the players moved to the largest arena in the state, Charleston Civic Center, from its start in the St. Alban's high school gym.

"Dad and Jim Murray worked their tails off to make this tournament a go. They found sponsors up and down Court Street, Lee Street, and Washington Street. They hit the pavement," Les recounted.

It was Inky's promotional mindset and the influence of the early college players that vaulted the week-long tournament forward. The college players who turned pro were invited back. After all, picking up a few hundred dollars in the offseason, given their relatively Spartan contracts, made sense. Inky knew this, but he needed influence. His first great influential West Virginia star who could help him tap into the best of the NBA was Rodney Clark Hundley, a West Virginia University basketball star from 1954 to 1957. "Hot Rod" Hundley was only the fourth player in NCAA history to score over 2000 points. He did it in only three varsity years. As a Mountaineer, he led them to three Southern Conference championships and NCAA tournament appearances. During his junior year he averaged over 26 points and 13 rebounds per game. He later played for the Cincinnati Royals and for the Lakers—both in Minneapolis and in Los Angeles.

Inky knew Hundley, and Hundley knew everybody. Inky appealed to Hundley to help him build a brand. There was a system that Inky and Jim Murray had worked out: optimum game times, bargain-basement game officials, gym floor maintenance, and concessions. Ever the promotion expert, Inky knew how to parson out player payments, even out the team rosters, attract sponsors, and energize the local press.

When Jerry West came along just three years later, Inky's tournament tripled its growth. The succession of stars in the local media from Hot Rod Hundley to Jerry West had to be unprecedented for any small metropolitan area. Others were to follow.

Jerry Lucas, John Havlicek and Bobby Knight, teammates at Ohio State University, came. Hal Greer from the 76ers and Marshall University came. Oscar Robertson came from the University of Cincinnati. Johnny "Red" Kerr from the University of Illinois found it to be a great event. Bill Russell came because Jerry West invited him. Given West's competitive nature and excruciating losses to the Boston Celtics, Russell's invitation was not expected. West enticed Elgin Baylor, as well. The list of players from the Big Ten, the Atlantic Coast Conference and the old Southern Conference was compelling. Players' names read like the history of basketball— Tommy Kearns, Billy Packer, Jim Harrick, Chris Smith, Chuck Noe, Larry Brown, Billy Cunningham and Art Heyman. The youngest player ever to compete in the tournament was a high school guard from St. Albans, Les Robinson.

The youngest coach to ever lead a team in the tournament was the same Les Robinson. It was his first "gig" as a coach.

"Both of those statistical truths are by accident," Les admitted. "Dad had me fill out a roster when a player couldn't come at the last minute. That's really why I covered Jerry West at the end of a big game. Then, Dad had another snafu with one of the coaches. I was pressed into service. That would have been a nightmare had we not gotten into a close game and had a chance to win. That really was my first taste of coaching—making player changes, working the clock, calling time-outs. The only thing I didn't do was cuss at the refs. I was too young to know all of the phrases."

A wide-eyed youngster would not need a program to see who was on the basketball floor in the St. Alban's High School gym in 1960. One might get a look at Dana Kirk, the future NCAA coach who played as a 6'6" rebounder from Morris Harvey College, or maybe Lee Shaffer, the 6'7" bulwark of the University of North Carolina Tar Heels. These and other all-star players were invitees to the tournament, but the kids in town came to see one player in particular, the recently graduated guard from the University of West Virginia, Jerry West. It was the smooth and confident West that every kid in West Virginia wanted to emulate.

To be sure, Shaffer was named a first team All-American and garnered the ACC Player-of-the-Year Award in 1960. John Milhoan from Marshall University averaged 30 points per game for the Thundering Herd. There were starters from Wake Forest, NC State, Maryland, Cincinnati, Xavier, and Dayton.

Les recalled a moment. "I met Adolph Rupp because my father went over to Kentucky to get players. One time he was outside the Kentucky dressing room, and Dad was talking to the seniors about coming to the tournament in the spring. Coach Adolph Rupp was standing by and said, 'Don't go up there, you'll get cheated. Don't go to that tournament.' Of course, some came anyway. Dad never cheated anyone in his life."

"Rupp didn't like his boys going on these tournaments; but once their season was over, for some of them their career was over, too. And those boys wanted to make money. The State and UNC guys saw the opportunity to pick up a few bucks. The Big Four seniors barnstormed every year up there. You had guys like Billy Cunningham who was a gym rat and enjoyed playing games in the small towns. It had become a tradition to go up and make a few dollars from your playing career. They went around Rocky Mount, Wilkesboro, the little towns, and they'd go play just anybody wherever. In fact, I played with Billy Cunningham's All-Stars, that's what we called ourselves that year. He was the big name, and he would pay me good money.

"The Kentucky guys did come to the tournament. My Dad treated them all well. And word got back to Lexington each year. Though Coach Rupp was against his senior players barnstorming, he couldn't keep them from doing what they liked for money that they mostly needed. They went on to win the national championship in 1958. And those seniors came to Charleston, too, because of my dad.

"I've had the occasion to talk about that tournament with a couple of those players since. It was a great experience. Joe B. Hall was Rupp's assistant back then. Joe B. confirmed to me that Coach Rupp didn't like Dad's tournament. Being the assistant, I'm not sure Joe B. liked it either. I never knew why they had that attitude. But Coach Hall knew that the players did come and that they were treated well. It may be because he saw it as an opportunity for an ankle sprain or a knee injury."

The Sportsman's Club Tournament that Inky built would come up in conversations years later from unexpected sources.

"I remember being sequestered in a restaurant with the whole NCAA Selection Committee and with broadcasters Jim Nantz and Billy Packer a number of years back. We had our spouses with us, and the chatter was lively. I was sitting near Billy Packer, a great playmaker at Wake Forest. He mentions to me that he knew my dad way back when and made a good analogy. Packer said privately, 'Inky Robinson was way ahead of his time.'

"I said, 'It's funny you said that because I run across guys everywhere that played in Charleston and were paid a few extra bucks. They all spoke highly of my dad.'

"Suddenly, Billy Packer got up like he was about to make a speech. We're sitting at the same table. He starts out, 'I'm sitting back there with Les and reminiscing. I played at his daddy's tournament. His dad was way ahead of his time. He was doing what the NBA is doing right now. And in the NBA, the big boys, the name players, they get all the money.' Packer motioned up high with his hand. 'And the others get x-amount'—and Packer motions low with the same hand.

"He said, 'I went out there in the middle of West Virginia for peanuts. Meanwhile Jerry West, the Big O, Jerry Lucas and those guys were getting twenty times what I got. Les' dad knew to play the ones that sold out the gym. He gave the rest of them, players like me, just peanuts. But it paid our way there and we all got an experience that lasted a lifetime because of Les' dad.'"

Les gave a follow-up insight.

"I was momentarily taken aback because I didn't know whether he was complimenting Dad or complaining about what he got paid more than forty years ago. But Billy Packer had it just right. Dad knew how to bring in the best players and others who could play, but the pay was all across the board. He knew talent; and he knew how to sell tickets.

"The rosters were exceptional. The guys that went into coaching and even broadcasting like Billy Packer were a 'Who's Who' across America decades later: Dana Kirk, Jim Harrick, Chuck Noe, Bobby Knight, Pat Riley."

Inky Robinson had carved out an event in Appalachia by attracting one of the most amazing assemblages of basketball players the sport had ever known. In West Virginia and points beyond, the best players knew Inky Robinson. They barely knew his son, Les. But that would change.

The Big O, Oscar Robertson played in the Sportsman's Club Tournament.
The long-running tournament was father Inky Robinson's creation.
Photo courtesy Robinson family.

CHAPTER 3

THE SPORTSMAN'S CLUB TOURNAMENT

Jim Murray and Inky Robinson had brought in the best players available, and the gym would be nearly packed for every game.

The tournament started in 1942, the same year Les was born.

Les has a particularly insightful view of what his dad had accomplished.

"There was an identity with big-time basketball in Charleston. Dad and Jim Murray provided that connection for many years as an aside to their regular jobs at Union Carbide. You could say that a community-involved person, like Dad, made a difference by raising money for the poor or providing activities for youth. Dad did it by giving Charleston, West Virginia, the best venue for out-of-season celebrity basketball that perhaps the entire country has ever had. Just that alone makes me proud to have been my Dad's son."

The tournament changed other lives. It also jump-started another career. The Cohen Drug Store team was made up of players from Ohio—mostly from the universities at Xavier, Cincinnati, and Dayton.

A freakishly good 6'5" guard they brought in made a difference. Oscar Robertson was from the University of Cincinnati. The Cohen Drug Team won the tournament in 1960. Robertson had been named tournament Most Valuable Player. His team beat Jerry West's team in the final. Both Robertson and Jerry West left the Sportsman's Club Tournament in Charleston to go to a training camp for the United States Olympic Team. They were named co-captains of the eventual 1960 Olympic Champions.

That Olympic Team, coached by Pete Newell from the 1959 NCAA Champion California Golden Bears, was considered the best amateur basketball team of all time. Their average margin of victory in the Olympics was over 42 points per game. Notably, two NBA hall-of-famers, John Havlicek and Lenny Wilkens, did not make that team. But they did have Walt Bellamy, Jerry Lucas, Terry Dischinger, Darrall Imhoff, Bob Boozer, Jay Arnette, and Adrian Smith. In addition to West and Robertson, Lucas and Bellamy made it into the NBA Hall of Fame.

"When you look at that 1960 Olympic Team and their dominance, the only team that comes close might have been the Dream Team of 1992. But the Dream Team had Magic, Bird and Jordan—so they came with their own press corps. That 1960 team was probably less visible to the entire sports world, but easily as accomplished and mostly overlooked by the media," Les offered. "And you had the two greatest guards that ever developed to that time—West and Robertson—as team captains."

They dominated everyone, including the Russians who had boldly predicted victory over the Americans. But Jerry West had a vendetta issue with the boastful communists. His older brother David was killed in Korea in 1951. West scored 19 in the second half to help the Americans pull away for the 81-57 win. The 1960 team boasted four NBA "rookies of the year," Oscar Robertson in 1961, Walt Bellamy in 1962, Terry Dischinger in 1963, and Jerry Lucas in 1964. Their victory margin over eight games was greater than any other basketball team in Olympic history. The fact that the team was all amateurs instead of seasoned professionals like the 1992 team makes it all the more impressive.

Les saw the great Oscar Robertson play and contended that he was unstoppable. Indeed, Robertson won the Sportsman Club Tournament MVP Award in 1960 and was standing on an awards platform with Jerry West in Rome holding an American flag just a month later.

"I'll never forget seeing the two of them play in dad's tournament. I was so proud to be a part of the event, and to have been known even slightly as the bratty little kid whose dad put the tournament together," Les reminisced. "Because of my dad, I had access. I could walk up and call Jerry West by his nickname, Zeke. I could talk to "the Big O" about crunch time and the importance of making free throws.I took payment envelopes to guys like Bobby Knight and Billy Packer. They all gave me some degree of respect—all because of my Dad."

Les never knew exactly how his Dad and Jim Murray could pull off bringing the best players in America to Charleston, West Virginia.In later years, the professionals came back to play before the NBA season started. They were paid, so coming to town was no surprise. But the early years featured only amateurs who had finished their NCAA eligibility. Since their eligibility was up, they could be paid. Inky Robinson had a system that protected the pay amounts for each player from becoming common knowledge. The stars were paid through another player on that star's team. Payments were made in envelopes. In cash. Inky was careful not to impair eligibility, especially in 1960, when neither West nor Robertson could be paid because of the pending Olympic tryouts.

"In fact, Coach Fred Schaus of the University of West Virginia confronted Dad about the potential of paying either Robertson or West—and ruining their eligibility for the Olympics."Les overheard him pointing at his Dad and saying, 'I'll tear up this tournament if West receives a dime from you.' Schaus seemed to be very concerned," Les related.

Les continued, "Now Dad was a pretty slick operator. He knew the ins and outs of managing the tournament—and he knew the eligibility rules like the back of his hand."

The professionals who came back in later years included West, Robertson, Rod Hundley, Bill Russell, Elgin Baylor, Walt Bellamy, Hal Greer, Billy Cunningham, Jerry Lucas, and John Havlicek. These names appear on every list of the best players of the 1960's.Every one of them made it into the National Basketball Hall of Fame in Springfield, Massachusetts.

The Sportsman's Club Tournament did give the great pro players a chance to play a full week before the NBA training camps started and to pick up a few extra dollars on the side. The NBA had not grown into the mammoth financial sport that it is today. Players appreciated the extra dollars, and the professional clubs seemed not to be concerned. Murray and Robinson had found a niche.

"My Dad was a great promoter. He put together these games and rented the gym for a week. He paid everybody that he could pay legally. He treated everyone well and created the exciting atmosphere for the tournament. He'd find local businesses to sponsor teams and printed programs that sold advertisements. He'd understand the dynamic of having names. He'd pay the professionals like West or Russell $500 with the proviso that they could not tell the other players what they were getting. He brought in the best players at Ohio State one year by attracting Jerry Lucas with a bigger payout, usually $500. Along with John Havlicek, Bobby Knight was on that team. They also had Larry Seigfried. But Lucas got the big pay day for helping Dad get the other Ohio State players to the tournament."

Several of Les' childhood memories grew from the exciting experience of the Sportsman's Tournament. Les remembered when he was a young teen and his dad had to host a player at their home. Inky hosted players routinely to save on expenses.

"Tommy Kearns was the point guard on the undefeated 1957 North Carolina Tar Heels team that beat Wilt Chamberlain and Kansas in three overtimes," Les related. "It was Coach Frank McGuire's only national title. Many coaches considered that 1957 game as the best final game of all time. Kearns was a second team All-American and his jersey #40 hangs in the Dean Smith Center, honored as one of the greats at North Carolina to ever play the game.

"Kearns was a handsome and popular New York kid when he stayed at our home for the week. Dad used to save a few dollars by sending other players to people's homes, and the hosts enjoyed having a top player stay with them. He figured that Tommy Kearns would be a good fit for our home. It seemed like as soon as he got there that he noticed that we had a really good-looking female neighbor. She was a few years older than me, and she was a gorgeous girl that turned heads. I was able to score Kearns a date with that neighbor. They hit it off that week and I had the biggest grin ever because I knew that Tommy Kearns was going to brag about me getting him a date with a real "looker." Sure enough, I had other players asking me to introduce them to other pretty girls in the area. Kearns looked upon me as the coolest kid in St. Albans.I liked playing that role and would have a girl or two in mind when the players came to Charleston each year."

Upon his graduation from UNC, Kearns played briefly for the Syracuse Nationals of the NBA. But he re-emerged on the big screen in 2000 as a basketball coach in a film also starring Sean Connery, *Finding Forrester.*

The players who came did not always move on to NBA careers. But whatever they did beyond basketball always came back to the common denominator of playing in the Sportsman's Club Tournament.

"Here's a piece of trivia," Les started. "It has a basis in Dad's tournament.Dad brought in three players from the same graduating class and from the same team that all made it to the basketball Hall of Fame, but only two were enshrined as players. Can you name them?

"Ohio State University had an exceptional club in the three seasons starting in 1959. Classmates John Havlicek, Jerry Lucas and Bobby Knight came to Charleston, West Virginia, to play in the Sportsman's Club Tournament in 1962. This was a major draw for my dad.

"The answer stumps a lot of people. I still have a notation where I took a payment to Bobby Knight, who paid Lucas and Havlicek from the one envelope. Knight was coaching then because he represented the group. He had great leadership skills even back then."

During their three years together in Columbus, they never lost a home basketball game and won OSU's only national title in 1960. Bobby Knight was a substitute player who went on to win more games than any other coach in NCAA history by his retirement in 2008. His career record of 902-371 included three national championships and an Olympic Gold Medal as Head Coach of the 1984 team. His own player at West Point, Mike Krzyzewski, broke Knight's record. Krzyzewski and Robinson became friends years earlier. The Duke coach broke the Tennessee Volunteer's Pat Summit's Division One men's and women's basketball win record with his 1099th win in 2018, finishing the year with 1100 NCAA wins.

Knight was indeed the "bag man" of the 1962 Sportsman's Club Tournament. Inky recognized his leadership skills and found him to be trustworthy. He could pay Knight the extra money it took to get Lucas and Havlicek to the tournament without giving the money directly to the stars. Knight was a player that few fans were familiar with, but he was the avenue to get the others into Charleston. Inky seemed to know those dynamics instinctively.

It took nearly forty years to corroborate the following improbable (Sportsman's Club Tournament) story that Les' dad told him when he was just a teenager.

Inky and promotion partner Jim Murray were basketball fanatics. Their successful tournament in Charleston brought in the greatest players in America at the highest level—and they took an approach to scout and try to meet top players at every opportunity.

Les retold the story.

"In 1959, Dad and Jim Murray had decided to go to the Final Four without game tickets or hotel reservations. One of the hometown West Virginia kids was in the championship game, Jerry West. The finals were being held in Freedom Hall at Louisville, Kentucky. Nearly 250 miles from Charleston, the difficulty of driving the Appalachian Mountains did not dissuade either of them. There was no good way to get to Louisville back then. They headed there because they had the confidence that they would find tickets and lodging.

"They saw the championship game, won by California over West Virginia, 71-70. It was Jerry West's final college game. His shot at the buzzer did not fall, but West was named tournament MVP—an unusual honor for a player from the losing team. Meanwhile, Jim and Dad brought a story home that few believed. They were both known to tell a tall tale ever now and again to get a laugh. But this story was so unlikely, that nobody took them seriously, especially my mother.

"When they got into Louisville, they could not find a hotel room anywhere. They had tried a dozen places. As dad had just left the front desk of yet another hotel there was some commotion in the street near the front. It seems that a desperate gentleman had decided to end it all. He jumped out of his hotel window from the eighth floor. A crowd gathered. Police came. It was a terrible scene as dad described it. The awful suicide had decent people looking away in sadness. But dad had figured out something from the incident that others hadn't considered. He had just been to the front desk to get a room and was turned away. The suicide changed everything. Dad returned to the desk clerk while the commotion out front held everyone's attention.

"He goes back to the clerk and says, 'I know you said you didn't have a room, but one just became available.' Dad told him. 'I believe that jumper had a room on the eighth floor on the front.'"

Les smiled as he recited what his dad told him. It was too far-fetched and incredible to believe. Les admitted that he had always 'half-believed' the tale as an embellished tale to entertain his friends.

"As he detailed to mom, the suicide jumper's belongings were taken from the room and Dad and Jim had a place to stay. It was all very matter-of-fact. When Dad returned to Charleston and St. Albans, virtually no one believed that story of quick thinking and brash reasoning."

"That story became unverifiable lore that was mostly forgotten. Even Les thought his father was spinning the wild tale to keep a bar crowd in suspense. But when Inky passed away in 1991, a reference to that yarn made it into the local *Charleston Gazette*. Evidently, the story grew, and the newspaper thought enough of it to mention it in his write-up.

"I guess they felt they should mention it since the story was part of his life," Les recalled. "But even I was still skeptical. My siblings, Mark and Debbie, saw it like I did—another of dad's adventurous accounts."

Over the years, Les had forgotten the story. He had filed it away realizing his Dad liked to tell the story to entertain a crowd. Inky told the story on numerous occasions.

When Les became the Athletic Director at NC State in 1996, one of the traditional Director of Athletics' functions was to take the ACC writers to a pre-season luncheon. The band of journalists was treated to the famous Angus Barn restaurant in Raleigh. It was late August. With football season about to start, the luncheon became a convenient way to build rapport, foster social interaction, and enjoy a great meal.

Les was enjoying the event and fielding writer's questions when Bill Brill (1931-2011), a Duke University graduate known as author John Feinstein's mentor, was retelling some of his NCAA experiences.

"Bill Brill was one of the senior writers invited to the lunch. He sat near me. In a conversation I overheard with another writer before we got started, Brill was asked about how many NCAA Basketball Final Fours he had attended. He responded that he had been to thirty-six, in all. The follow-up question was asked of the veteran columnist, 'What's the most unusual thing that he'd ever experienced at a Final Four?' I assumed that he was going to tell a story about a team or a player."

But the colorful Brill had another story to tell.

"What followed stunned me. Brill began to corroborate my dad's story; only he did not know that the guy he was telling it about was my dad. He raised my eyebrow when he began the story by telling about attending a Final Four in Louisville in 1959. I knew, being from West Virginia, that this was the Jerry West final, when Zeke was the MVP, but his team didn't win the tournament. Brill started by telling about the hotel where he stayed and the circumstance of a guy a few doors down the hallway jumping from his window to his death. It was an unexplained suicide.

"I perked up. 'It can't be,' I thought. I immediately realized that the details my father had repeated for years about that trip to Louisville were 100% accurate."

Upon hearing Brill's description of the suicide event, Les interrupted the senior columnist.

"I know who got his room!" Les interjected.

Brill, turning around and unaware that Les had been listening, was astonished that there was a dangling conclusion to this most unusual story. Les then began telling the same suicide story he had heard from his father's perspective over many years. His father had passed five years earlier. The story he told that was undermined as being questionable had finally merited a final vindication. Sportswriter Bill Brill provided it by the circumstance of the AD's luncheon.

"Brill was startled that I knew almost everything about the event from my dad's crazy story. But it wasn't crazy at all. I summed it up to Brill by saying, 'I don't even think my mom ever believed that story, Bill, but it was my dad who went back in to the desk clerk when the crowd gathered to ask for the poor guy's room! And here we are nearly forty years later getting the same story from another witness.'"

Les added, "What are the chances of that? Dad told those details to deaf ears that Bill Brill had not only witnessed but had told it as his best Final Four story for many years.Dad told it confidently, for the rest of his life. But few believed him. And now I knew it for sure but couldn't go back and tell my dad that I doubted him for so many years. There has to be a lesson in there somewhere!"

The Sportsman's Club Tournament fostered many stories by the best players in the game. One player, the University of San Francisco's Bill Russell, would probably have even another insight to the event. He arrived in Charleston for the first time in the summer of 1956, even before there was a cohesive Civil Rights movement. During his career, Russell was an outspoken advocate for racial equality. He maintained admirable principles in his role as a sports celebrity throughout his career.

ELGIN BAYLOR receives the 1961 Most Valuable Player award from Governor Barron.

Elgin Baylor receives MVP award at the Sportsman's Club Tournament in 1961.
Clipping courtesy of Robinson family archives.

Russell is in the argument for the best post player ever to play the game. But there is no argument that he was the best winner the game had ever known. He averaged more than 20 points and 20 rebounds per game as his University of San Francisco Dons won the 1955 and 1956 NCAA National Championships. He led the USA Olympic Team to the Gold Medal in Melbourne, Australia, in 1956. Once Coach Red Auerbach negotiated the rights to Russell from the St. Louis Hawks, the Boston Celtics proceeded to win ten NBA championships over the next twelve seasons. The last two of those titles were achieved with Bill Russell as player-coach.

"Dad knew that there could be issues concerning having the Big O, Bill Russell, Hal Greer, and Elgin Baylor stay in the hotels for the tournament. Those great players being all minorities, the racial issues back then could possibly have surfaced. But the problems that were evident around the country did not seem to be of much consequence where we lived in West Virginia. Dad was surely not racially inclined, and we were far from it as a family. Nonetheless, dad would usually find a home for the players, white or black. When he couldn't, he'd go to the hotels in Charleston and make arrangements for rooms. If there were issues, Dad resolved them right away with the hotel manager or owner. If any one of his players were denied by race or even religion, he would never use that hotel again.

"Not related to the tournament, Jerry West brought the Los Angeles Lakers for an exhibition game. Jerry was concerned that the main hotel in Charleston, the Daniel Boone, could be operated by someone who might not serve Elgin Baylor. This was the best hotel in town at that time. Upon their initial booking, they did as Jerry suspected and it cost them dearly. Jerry took the entire Lakers team to another hotel across town. That incident cost the Daniel Boone a tremendous amount of business even after the Lakers left."

When Bill Russell came, it was another story entirely. Les laid out the situation.

"The issue first surfaced with the great Bill Russell. Dad went to register him for five nights and the desk clerk momentarily balked. Dad asked for the manager. He explained that there would be scouts, sportswriters, and other key people from the basketball world all coming to Charleston. It was not exactly a tourist destination. The hotels had rented rooms by the week for businessmen who came to transact deals with Union Carbide, the railroads, and the coal mining companies in the area.Each hotel competed to get their business from the next hotel. Now Dad was delivering—not only the best players in America—but also the coaches, their families sometimes, the media, and others to see a tournament that put Charleston on the map. If Russell were refused a room, he'd just go down the street and check him in at a competitor's hotel. He then made it clear to the manager, in case he was refused, he would never come back. Bill Russell and the best players in America had rooms, and those hotels thrived on having celebrity players stay there each year."

Some memories are vivid to Les.

"I remember when Bill Russell came, I was a player at State; but I happened to be in the hotel lobby. They had reporters all over the lobby of the hotel—all wanting to interview Jerry West and Oscar Robertson. But then Bill Russell walked in. If there were a dozen reporters with West and the Big O, ten of them immediately moved over to talk to Russell. Russell was news. He had won a handful of NBA championships by then. I watched it to see the reaction from Oscar Robertson and Jerry West.

"Russell came to the tournament as a substitute. Jerry West had his teammate Elgin Baylor coming, but Baylor had gotten injured at the end of the season. Jerry called my dad and told him that Baylor wouldn't make it, but that he could get either Wilt Chamberlain or Bill Russell. My dad posed the question back to him, 'Which one would you recommend?'

"Jerry knew the players and their personalities. He didn't even hesitate to recommend his archrival, Bill Russell of the Boston Celtics. By chance, I listened to the phone conversation on the other line at the house. West conceded that they both would be great choices, but then he said he'd take Russell because he knew Russell would show up. He went on to say that Wilt might tell you that he was coming but forget to make the trip. Based on the Jerry West recommendation, we landed Bill Russell for the tournament."

Ironically, Wilt Chamberlain would later play on what many consider the greatest NBA lineup of all time with Jerry West. Add Elgin Baylor, Gail Goodrich, Happy Hairston, and from the bench, future Lakers coach Pat

Riley. They won an NBA record 69 games in addition to beating the New York Knicks four games to one in the NBA Finals in 1972.

The Sportsman's Club Tournament, which began in 1942, ran its course and ended in 1965. Television and agent-drafted NBA contracts were becoming fashionable. Lawyers were concerned with the liability of a player getting hurt out of season. The senior college players were advised against the tournament for the same reason.

"Dad had something that was both unique and special. He also had the disposition and marketing know-how to pull it off. Had it not been for my dad and especially the Sportsman's Tournament, I'm not sure I would have followed the path to a coaching career in basketball." Les summed it up, "I would have probably stayed and worked for one of the big energy corporations back in Charleston."

Les accepted the athletic scholarship offer to play for Everett Caseat NC State University.
Photo courtesy NC State University.

CHAPTER 4
STATE BOUND

The Sportsman's Club Tournament was the catalyst that moved Les into the highest level of college basketball—the Atlantic Coast Conference. Les wanted to dominate like Oscar Robertson. He wanted to swish shots like Hal Greer, dish it out like Tommy Kearns, electrify a crowd like John Havlicek—and he wanted to be like "Zeke from Cabin Creek." He saw the best to ever play the game. He wanted basketball to be his life. It was so.

At his dad's urging, Les worked daily on skills and led his powerful Saint Alban's team in scoring. He made mistakes in games that he worked on in his back yard. He stayed for extra work in the gym. He became obsessed with the sport with the round ball and the rectangle behind a circle with a net.

"I worked on something every day. If I had worked on my homework like I worked in the gym, I might have had grades like my brother Mark. But I would rather play basketball than eat. I had the fever," Les recounted.

"I would find a pick up game somewhere. We were segregated from the minority neighborhoods back then, but I had black friends over near Jefferson and we got along great. I always knew there'd be a great game there, so that's where I thought I could pick up more skills. Plus, they played tough there. There were not many fouls called. I liked that pace and that toughness. I knew it would make me a better player. I ate, breathed, and slept basketball as a high schooler."

Consequently, Les got looks from the best basketball schools in the East.

Recruited by the bigger schools such as West Virginia and North Carolina, Les decided to further his education and basketball career under one of the best-known figures of Southern Basketball in 1960, Coach Everett Case of NC State. He remembers being recruited hard to play for Frank McGuire at North Carolina, being courted by then-assistant Dean Smith. It was later that year that Dean Smith would take over for McGuire, who left to coach the NBA's Philadelphia 76ers.

"It may have been one of the few times that Coach Smith was wrong about talent," Les recalled. "He had Billy Cunningham in those days. I think he felt that the Frank McGuire-recruited kids out of New York and Philadelphia were ripe for the ACC, and wanted to get another Rod Hundley or Jerry West out of the coal area because he liked our blue-collar approach to the game. Obviously, we didn't have film to study back then, or Coach Smith would have never had me visit Chapel Hill."

Les played in his dad's famous summer tournament. The coaches knew that Les had the advantage of of tutelage from Oscar Robinson, and Bill Russell— not to mention his Cabin Creek neighbor, Jerry West. Much that came of that collection of talent gave young Les stories that have lived many decades beyond.

"West played his last tournament on a team comprised of mostly West Virginia teammates in the summer of 1959. I was about to enter my senior year at Saint Alban's, and Dad put me on a team as a fill-in since the tournament was a player or two short. The team I was sent to as a substitute guard was captained by Morris Harvey College star Jim Harrick. In the middle of a game against the favored team with Jerry West—in a packed gym in front of my high school buddies—one of the college stars on our team sprained his ankle. Since we only had seven players and I was the only other gurad, I had to go in. Only, I didn't really want to go in because I knew I could not measure up to the talent on the floor.

"In fact, I looked down the bench to see who would have to go in, and the only other person on the bench was looking at me as if to say, 'It's your turn.' Jimmy Harrick had been guarding Jerry West to the best of his ability. West was scoring at will, as he would for his entire NBA career. I was wet behind the ears when I hesitated to walk onto the floor. Harrick waved me on and caught my eye. I immediately asked him who I should cover."

"He said, 'Les, you take jersey number 4, and I'll switch to number 2.' Harrick commanded. "Well, number 4 was Jerry West—the living, breathing icon who would become the trademark of the NBA. I was in front of everybody that mattered in my life and just 17 years old, and I was having to match up against the best player I ever saw. They were up by enough points that West took it easy on me, as I recall. But I had never been so nervous on the basketball floor ever before or since. I grew up a lot that day."

Jim Harrick would win an NCAA Basketball Championship coaching at UCLA in 1995, the only banner at Pauley Pavilion not attributed to the venerable. Harrick knew how to get the best match-ups as early as 1959.

"I did just as well on Jerry West as Harrick or a dead man! When he wanted to score, he did. But I think even he felt this was too easy and passed up some easy shots." Robinson would later recall. "I was just glad that Everett Case wasn't there, or I'd have lost my chance at a basketball scholarship to NC State."

But NC State did call. Despite a push from Coach Schaus at West Virginia to keep the young Robinson at the Mountaineer State institution, Les reported to Raleigh, North Carolina, in late August of 1960. He would become a key part of the NC State Wolfpack's future, in ways well beyond his career basketball stats.

Les recalled the choice. "My dad was all excited that I had signed to play for Everett Case. Dad knew who the greatest coaches were and their style of play. He knew how disciplined Coach Case always was and felt that would be an excellent upside for me. Even back then, the Atlantic Coast Conference had the great teams like North Carolina, Wake Forest, Virginia, Maryland, and Duke. State took a back seat to no one."

Les reported and established himself as one of the most promising players on the freshman squad. His stay at NC State would have turbulence ahead—events and circumstances no one had anticipated.

Legendary Coach Everet Case
Photo courtesy NC State University.

CHAPTER 5
EVERETT CASE

Before there were the legends known to the Baby Boomers like Dean Smith, Johnny Wooden, and Bobby Knight, NCAA basketball was dominated by three coaching giants. They were Adolph Rupp, Phog Allen, and Everett Case. The numbers and winning percentage for each coach remain compelling.

Everett Case sprung out of a small post World War II Indiana town as a coach with an impeccable rèsumè.The 1923 graduate of the University of Wisconsin returned to Anderson, Indiana, and coached at several high schools before enlisting in the U.S. Navy at the age of 40. He coached two Navy basketball squads during his service time to a combined record of 56 and 5. He was hired by NC State University in 1946.

Of note, Everett Case never married. His devotion was to the sport, and as such, he changed college basketball with nuances that remain.

"Everett Case was way ahead of his time. He was a guy that insisted on conditioning and worked the fast break as a late game weapon to demoralize other teams that were not as conditioned as we were," Les noted."He saw the popularity of the sport as it attracted the best athletes. He saw the need for bigger gyms and more media. He liked the intensity that basketball required and the small details that won big games."

Les has fond recollections of Case.

"If he liked your effort and your attitude, playing for him was a given. He had a better eye for skill sets than most coaches. And he was so aggressive in attacking other teams that he naturally drew the ire of the other coaches. It was because when you beat an Everett Case team, you had really accomplished something special."

One of basketball's best coaches, Frank McGuire, found that out early in his career. The Case-coached Wolfpack rolled over the Carolina Tar Heels, once winning fifteen in a row. Coach McGuire came to Chapel Hill in 1954 in an attempt to change all of that. But Everett Case matched his team to his advantage too often. Frank McGuire was not used to losing. The Case-versus-McGuire games became wars, no matter which team claimed home advantage. The tide had already turned for the Tar Heels when Everett Case got sick in 1964 with a rare form of cancer, Multiple Myeloma.

His NC State teams won six consecutive Southern Conference championships before the Wolfpack moved to the Atlantic Coast Conference in 1953. He proceeded to win three more ACC championships.McGuire won the NCAA Championship in 1957, beating Wilt Chamberlain and the University of Kansas in three overtimes. Case was never able to accomplish a national championship despite having among the very best teams in the country year in and year out. McGuire also had to weather the 1961 scandal because a Tarheel player was involved. He was similarly devasted by the point-shaving scheme.

"That may have been a reason that McGuire left to coach the NBA Philadelphia 76ers the very next season," Les offers. "And you know he was in a conference that had him going head-to-head with Case twice a year."

Les knew much about the great Everett Case even before he showed up in Raleigh to begin his freshman year in 1960.

"You see a lot of things in college basketball today that would not have happened without Coach Case's influence. He was like my dad in a way. He innovated. He promoted ticket sales by promoting the game and its players. He brought in a pep band for games before anyone else thought of it. His ability to control the pace of the game led to the ten-second backcourt count. He was the first to do pre-game player introductions, and the first to cut down the nets after winning. I think he was among the first to film games and break down the film in preparation for a game or practice. He was an amazing coach who was dealt some bad cards."

Indeed, after the 1961 point-shaving scandal his health was at issue. Case demanded the best conduct and ethical demeanor for his players over his entire career. All had changed. His cancer became worse and it was inoperable. The disease that was detected in 1964 took his life on April 30, 1966.

Knowing that he was dying, Case devised a share system to disperse one-third of his estate among 57 players he selected. A few received half shares; most received full shares. Players whom he felt had brought honor to their own lives and to the sport of basketball got even more. Case placed great emphasis on earning a degree. The estate recognized the accomplishment by ensuring that every degree-holder received a minimum of a full share. Les received two full shares.

A former player, Joe Harand, who started on Case's 1950 Final Four team at NC State, used most of his share on the first color television he and his wife ever owned. With the rest, Harand had a small golden plaque made that read "Through the generosity of Everett N. Case." Harand set that plaque on the TV stand. And although he owned many more TVs, the plaque remained.

Les found out about the estate gift just like the rest of the citizens of Raleigh.

"The players were listed from the start of Case's NC State career in 1946 until his last team when I played.

"Many months past his death and funeral the *Raleigh News and Observer* published his will. It happened that I was the last player listed. It was money that I never figured on, so it was a tremendous surprise. Barbara and I had not been married for long when the attorney sent us this very generous check. We were thrilled," Les recalled.

"Coach Case's coaching legacy was established because he was devoted to every facet of the sport as well as taking care of his players.

"Coach Case started the best basketball tournament in the South—and probably in the country—the Dixie Classic. The Classic pitted the Big Four ACC teams—State, North Carolina, Duke, and Wake against the top four teams in the country. Coach Case won the first four of those tournaments against competition that was the best in the land at the time. In doing this, he elevated the ACC to become, arguably, the best basketball conference nationally. With other coaches, he moved the ACC above them all way back in the 1950s. Even the coaching talent rose because of Case. The other coaches had to recruit and coach to Everett Case's level. Only a few could do so—Vic Bubas, Bones McKinney, and Frank McGuire. But that's a helluva set of coaches. They paved the way for guys like Terry Holland, Dean Smith, Lefty Driesell, Mike Kryzyzewski, Bobby Cremins, Jim Valvano, and Dave Odom," Les continued. "They all owe everything to the best promoter to ever hit the ACC, Everett Case. Even Florida State's Leonard Hamilton, who has won five hundred games, can thank Everett Case. Needless to say, my career became reality because of Everett Case.

"Coach Case was from Indiana, but was really a flash point of the history of the ACC. Much of what the Atlantic Coast Conference was to become can be traced back to Everett Case, a class act by every measure. Here's a guy that went back into the military after he turned forty years old. He was deeply patriotic and wanted to help the war effort in any way he could. And it worked out for him because he learned so many other skills from that experience.

"He thought noise was a tremendous home team benefit and measured it to excite the fans. The pep band addition had never been done before. It built the atmosphere for fans, and then for television, as well.

Les reflected upon his mentorship further.

"I was lucky. I had the opportunity to play for both Everett Case and Press Maravich. The honor of being recruited and signing with Everett Case was something that only about four or five players a year could receive, at best. I was privileged to be one of them. And then when Press Maravich took over, it expanded my experience. Press was like a second father to me.

"I knew so much more about basketball because of my dad. But I got a master's degree in the sport from emulating much of what Coach Case taught. He was the biggest reason that I went to NC State instead of North Carolina or West Virginia," Les reminsces. "To play for Everett Case was a great honor."

GUARD LES ROBINSON   NORTH CAROLINA STATE

Les's ability to defend gave both Coach Case and Coach Maravich latitude in utilizing his contributions to a winning program. Coach Maravich recognized his on-the-floor coaching acumen. Photo courtesy NC State University.

CHAPTER 6

THE WOLFPACK AND THE PREY

Les's career at NC State was a mixed bag. They won. He played. But it was not at all what he had expected.

"I continued to do what I did in high school on the freshman team as a point guard. I had a nose for the basket and a penchant for hustle. But I had no idea that my role would change substantially during the next season on the varsity," Les recalled. "Now, to be honest, I like scoring, but I was a coach's player. Whatever Coach Case and then Coach Maravich wanted from me was fine. I wanted to help us to win."

Les led the freshman Wolfpack in scoring while improving his defense and ballhandling skills. But things were happening outside of Les's sphere in the basketball world. Gamblers had bought their way into the game. Several colleges were targeted by the seamy underworld.

"When I got to Raleigh, Coach Case was nearly 60 years old and winding down his career even before the awful point shaving scandal. Several other programs were implicated besides NC State. There was North Carolina, NYU and St. Joseph's. Everett Case never got over the disappointment when he found that two of his players were involved. Unwittingly, I recall that one of the implicated players did something strange one night, shielding me from the mess.

"I was an innocent backwoods freshman from West Virginia. As freshmen we were not eligible to play varsity the first year. I was having a great year as a player. We routinely hung around the varsity players between games and around practices. One night one of the players and I stopped to get a beer away from the campus. He pulls over to go and buy the beer and he tells me to stay in the car. Actually, he commanded me to 'sit tight, not get out.' The guy goes to a phone booth and writes down some numbers before placing the slip of paper in his wallet. When the story broke the next year, I recalled being there that night and wondering what the varsity starter was up to. Looking back, I became more appreciative of his command that I stay in the car. I could have gotten sucked into that whole mess unknowingly.

"Coach Case took the news hard. He just couldn't believe that he had players on his team that would miss shots or throw passes away at the end of a game to get the point spread right," Les retells. "And I couldn't believe it either. I thought everyone was on the level and that everyone was honest. I was really naïve. It taught me a valuable lesson."

Les details the aftermath.

"As I became a sophomore, Coach Case was both more strict with our time and more lax with some of the old drills. It was as if trust had been lost across the board with everyone. He was more sad than angry, but I think he was never really the same after the point shaving in 1961."

Scandals were not new to the NCAA.

"One scandal, maybe worse than that 1961 affair, had happened a dozen years before at Kentucky. That scandal involved Kentucky basketball under the great Adolph Rupp. He had to be devastated. Two of the three consequential players involved were Ralph Beard and Alex Groza, the NFL kicker Lou Groza's brother—both from Youngstown, Ohio," Les detailed. "They were a year or two ahead of the other guy that was caught, Bill Spivey. Spivey was a seven-footer who was implicated, but not convicted on a mistrial. It was maybe the most shameful period in the great history of Kentucky basketball. It was followed by the Manhattan and City College scandals in New York."

An ESPN chronicle of the past NCAA basketball scandals exposed the impact.

Big time college basketball survived near destruction in 1951. Though another major scandal developed in 1961 and several lesser scandals developed in the '70s, '80s and '90s, the sport became even bigger. Big time betting has also thrived. The amount of money wagered on basketball is staggering.

Eventually, the organized crime-backed point shaving scandal of 1951 involved seven colleges and thirty-two players. But it was the scandal of 1961 was still lingering as the 1962 Wolfpack season began. Les's playing role changed that year.

"When I got to the varsity, my role changed right away as I had not suspected it would. As a scorer in high school and during my freshman season, I anticipated more of the same. I looked for openings to drive to the basket. But Coach Case wanted to use me differently. He saw me as more of a ballhandler and a defensive player. Nowadays, a player would reject that kind of a change. But playing for Coach Case, you did what he wanted you to do to make the team better. I carried Coach Case's penchant for that ideal into my own coaching. Coach knew that it took many parts to make a whole team better. If he needed me to concentrate on other roles, then I would never question it. The man was a basketball genius.

"As my junior year was shaping up, I knew I would be playing behind two starters. We had a tough year, unexpected at State. We went 8-11 after winning four of our first five games. Coach Case was not his old self from what I saw. His intensity was gone. We had no idea that he was getting sick. He was probably still reeling from the player scandal, too. Coach was above reproach. He felt that the association of the players he trusted damaged his reputation. He was still beating himself up for not knowing and not having caught it. He was easily among the most ethical coaches ever. It was a forgettable year. We only went 4-10 in the ACC.

"My senior season began with us splitting games with Furman, a win, and Wake Forest, a bad loss. After the game, Coach Case did not come back to practice. He was sick. He suddenly stepped down. Everyone was saddened. It was both an emotional time for us and an inspiration. We wanted to win for Coach Case. Coach Maravich, who had mentored me all along, had stepped in to take over."

Les recalls the transition.

"Press Maravich had a career record as head coach at Clemson University, an ACC opponent to NC State, of 55-96. He coached from 1956 to 1962 before accepting the assistant role at NC State. But Clemson basketball was much an afterthought to legendary Clemson coach Frank Howard's football prowess. Coach Howard had won multiple conference football championships at Clemson. Clemson had never won an ACC basketball championship."

There was no indication from Press Maravich's coaching past that NC State, under his leadership, would be a contender in the ACC.

The Wolfpack proceeded to win the next eleven games in a row. They went on another streak of six straight wins at the end of the year, including the ACC Tournament Championship game over Duke University, 91-85. They beat St. Joseph's but lost to Princeton in the NCAA Tournament. They had won 21 games, losing only 5. Press Maravich's portion of that record was 20-4.

"In that third game of the season, Press Maravich's first as a head coach, he made a minor change. He sat one of the regulars down and started me at the guard position to play defense on one of Maryland's guards. We won a squeaker, 63-62. Coach Maravich used his roster a little differently than other coaches. He liked to look at his opponent and then match his roster to stop them. I was a beneficiary of that strategy because he liked the way I played hardnosed defense. I knew my role and did what he expected.

"And Coach Maravich would explain things to me as a player when he made a move. It was like he was coaching me to become a coach," Les intimates. "I listened to him and admired the way he moved chess pieces around the board. He was really a fine coach. You could say that because of the Clemson and LSU experiences, he was underated. His abilities on the sideline when the game was played was where he was a smart tactician.

"After my senior season, Coach Maravich convinced me that I needed a Master's Degree to coach top level basketball. He asked me to stay on as the freshman coach. The previous freshman coach had left suddenly to take another job. So I had an opportunity to be a head coach, start on my Master's Degree and learn from one of the best coaches in the game.

"Besides, I got to play ball in the gym with this skinny kid with floppysocks and a hippy-ish hairstyle. It was Coach Maravich's son, Pete, and every college in the country wanted him. "The Pistol" was at Broughton High School and then Edwards Military School. I had to pick him up at school sometimes to bring him to the campus. Not the best of students, Pete was trying to gain the academic eligibility required by his first two college choices, West Virginia and N. C. State."

Pistol Pete went on to become the most prolific scorer in the history of college basketball. In just three varsity seasons, the showman Maravich averaged 44.2 points per game and scored 3667 points. He did this without a three-point shot which was not adopted until fifteen years after he finished college.

Les loves odd statistics. He cites one that few knew about his friend Pistol Pete.

"A lot of people remark that the Pistol did this or did that, and they cite that he never had the advantage of a three-point shot. Technically, that's not true. He played his last year in the NBA with the Boston

Celtics. The NBA adopted the three-pointer that year. Pistol was older and banged up, but he managed to launch fifteen three-pointers that year. Incredibly, he made ten of them. What would he have done had there been a three-pointer back in his LSU days? He'd have shot more from the outside, probably. He might even have scored over 5000 points had he been freshman-eligible."

Les elaborates on the prep star's skill set.

"When we played pick-up, I preferred to play on his team instead of against him. It was simple. With Pete, as young as he was, we usually won. If you worked to get open, he'd usually find you—especially on back cuts to the basket. And because of my role with both State head coaches—Case and Maravich—I liked playing defense. Pete was deficient in that area. But if I had to play defense on him, he'd just make me look silly."

Pete's dad Press Maravich did not disappoint in his second year as head coach at State, either. The 'Pack went 18-9, finishing second in the ACC regular season, eventually losing the tournament title game to Vic Bubas and Duke, 71-66.

It was Maravich's last game coaching in Raleigh before taking the head coaching position at Louisian State University where he had signed a top prospect—his son Pistol Pete. Had Pete Maravich qualified academically for NC State, Press Maravich would have been a household name in Raleigh. NC State already had a penchant for bringing in top players, a condition that was not particularly true in Baton Rouge."

That transition of losing both Maravich men to LSU also meant a regime change. NC State hired a fiery coach from the University of Florida. Coach Norm Sloan would bring in a new set of assistant coaches. Les would need to find another job somewhere.

"Coach Sloan was very cordial, but organized. He knew what he needed. He also had other young coaches in mind and knew very little about me. The handwriting was there. I needed to find a place to coach before the following fall. I had no idea of what or where to turn. I depended upon Coach Maravich's recommendation and a lot of luck."

Les would weigh options as a lame duck assistant finishing his first year in the master's program at NC State. He mailed out resumes and letters. He contacted others who could get him interviews. He and Barbara had eloped two years earlier and a second child was expected. He needed a way forward in the career he had chosen. Surely, he would open a very promising door in short order. Or would he?

Wilt Chamberlain remains the only NBA player to score 100 points in a game.

CHAPTER 7

MY BACK-UP WAS WILT

Les was completing his first-year master's program requirements in Raleigh.Barbara had given him the news of their second child, and he was without a job as June arrived. He busied himself with strategies to develop opportunities in coaching. He would need to find something suitable for the coming season.

It was during the transitional time in Raleigh that Les found himself in Reynolds Coliseum to watch the Philadelphia 76'ers practice.At the professional sports level, heated competition often divides the contenders from the pretenders. The 76'ers ran a very hard practice.

Reynolds Coliseum opened in 1948. It was a state-of-the-art venue for the sport of basketball that was large and loud. Coach Everett Case had the idea to make it even more home friendly by placing an oblong box at the center-court scoreboard he named the "noise meter." It was an effective tool with the fans and the students, and especially used to intimidate opponents.

The 76'ers were practicing at the expansive Reynolds Coliseum for a reason. It was like a major city NBA arena. The coliseum attracted many other teams outside of ACC basketball. The Globetrotters came often. The other NBA teams would make a swing down to Raleigh to have a practice or two in addition to exhibition games. The powerful Philadelphia 76ers were in the gym with a fine team of stellar athletes.

Les told the details. "I was in the gym, dressed casual and wearing loafers when Coach Maravich asked me to referee their scrimmage. At first, I sheepishly backed off, not comfortable with my lack of experience and dealing with the guys I saw out there doing layups—Lucious Jackson, Hal Greer, and Chet Walker. Billy Cunningham was a young addition who was ironically practicing on our floor. He was an All-American the year before at the University of North Carolina," Les remembered.

"And the biggest human being I had ever seen was out there. I was in awe. Seeing Wilt Chamberlain was like the first time you saw a live elephant. You just can't describe the amazing scale of size to anyone. And he was powerful. His shoulders and arms were more muscular than long. I couldn't believe that a team could ever lose a game with this huge player in the middle.

"After a second prodding by Coach Maravich, I consented to officiate the scrimmage. I thought it would just be a run-through and that I would just run up and down and call a few fouls or walks. I had no idea what I was getting myself into.

"The first team usually scrimmaged against the second team. All of the players were top-notch athletes. And they played for keeps.

"What I didn't know was that they routinely scrimmaged with a bet. The winner would get dinner that night from the loser. Now, the NBA back then paid the superstars some decent money, but as you got down the roster, many of those guys hated buying someone else's meal. They played the game as a blood sport. They hated to lose. That fire of competition was hot," Les recalled. "So, the soft position of just running up and down and blowing a whistle every once in a while, went out the window. They wanted to hear that whistle, and they let me know that right away.

"So, I go out and throw up the jump ball and focus on the rules. I don't call a lot of the walks and I start hearing it right away. The three-seconds rule? They never called that in the NBA games I saw on TV, so I didn't spend much time on that either. What I didn't count on was that there were always five players screaming at me in a language that would make a sailor proud. My whistle got immediate results from five players at a time. I was never called by such derogatory names before or since, even by fans later in my coaching career."

Les detailed the situation.

"Philadelphia's team included a 6'7" forward named Jesse Branson, who played ball at nearby Elon College. Branson fit into that category of players who were not paid enough at the deep end of the bench to be buying dinner for Chet Walker or Hal Greer. And Branson was a competitor who kept a salty attitude at all times. He was tough. Like the others, he wanted more playing time.

"As fate usually commands, I made a foul call in the lane on him. I forgot whether the call was close or obvious, but I do remember being out at the area near the coaching box and Branson immediately coming at me.

"He was livid.I was thinking that this big guy was going to deck me right then and there. All kinds of things went through my mind. One of them was 'why in the hell am I doing this, putting my life on the line for nothing?' They weren't even paying me to do this. That thought made me think I should just hand Branson the whistle and leave. But he was barking wildly, and I thought I was dead.

"As Branson got right into my face, Wilt Chamberlain came over. One grab with those huge hands and Branson seemed to be six feet away instantly. The big guy had gotten between us. He turned to Branson and with some other choice words more or less told him to 'back off.' He then told him that the ref was not a real ref and that they all needed to give me some slack. As he was saying it I realized that the biggest, strongest man I had ever met had just stood up as my protector. He had assumed the role of being my bodyguard. None of those guys could mess with me now. They had just seen Wilt jump in front of me. It was like having a guy with a shotgun step in front of a guy with a knife. I was golden for the rest of the scrimmage."

There was a lesson learned beyond the foolish decision to referee the game without pay.

"Well, that incident changed my attitude. The half-hearted calls I had made before were now made with confidence. The whistle got louder. My voice was more directed, and even the way I ran up and down the court was more assured. None of those players questioned what I did for the rest of the practice. Even they had the good sense to not get Wilt in front of them."

Jesse Branson played for the 76ers for the rest of the season. He was traded to the ABA New Orleans Buccaneers at the end of the season. Branson passed away in November of 2014.

"I felt sorry for Jesse Branson after that incident. A great player, he had no place to go on that team. They won it all that year. Wilt Chamberlain may have stymied a lot of good players, even on his own team. He was not just big, but so muscular that nobody messed with him. I do know that I could not have had a better ally to have in the heat of battle. He may have also kept me from having a lot of dental work just out of college!"

Wilt Chamberlain, at 7'1" usually played to a fit weight of 275 pounds. He was admired for the shape he stayed in by playing volleyball in the off-season. He is the only player to score 100 points in an NBA game. He also won 7 scoring titles, 9 field goal percentage titles, and 11 rebounding titles. No one else has ever done that. He even led the league in assists once from his post position. In the high-powered NBA, Chamberlain remains as the only player to average at least 30 points and 20 rebounds per game over the entire course of his NBA career. He died in October of 1999.

Eddie Biedenbach and Monte Towe visit Cedar Key High School to corroborate that Les's descriptions were accurate. The school remains the smallest public high school in Florida. Photo courtesy Monte Towe.

CHAPTER 8

CEDAR KEY: LIKE NO OTHER PLACE

The coaching change at NC State was inevitable. Coach Norm Sloan had coached at The Citadel before moving to the University of Florida in Gainesville. Sloan replaced Press Maravich, who had taken the head-coaching job at LSU so that he would have an opportunity to coach his own son, 'Pistol' Pete Maravich. 'The Pistol' had been accepted at LSU and subsequently, the Bayou Bengals had brought his accomplished father to replace the coach they had released. It was the start of legendary times in Baton Rouge— and in Raleigh, as well.

It was Coach Sloan's first summer camp at NC State in 1966. Les stayed around to help while weighing other high school coaching options. It was during the time of working the camp that he ran into the Florida Superintendent of Schools—who kept his boat at Cedar Key during the winter months. He told Les about the opening in Florida. Les and Barbara had never heard of Cedar Key, believing it to be part of the Florida Keys on the way to Key West. Things worked out and Les took the job—sight unseen.

Les tells the details.

"Coach Case had passed away in late April. Many came to pay their respects at that church on Hillsborough Street in Raleigh. Mel Thompson came in from The Citadel, I remember. I tried to get on there, but he hired someone else. That turned out to be good for me because Mel Thompson was fired the very next year—his coaching years were immortalized in Pat Conroy's book, *My Losing Season*. Coach Sloan had just started at State. Coach Maravich came to the funeral. Of course, he was close with Everett

Case. The funeral is where I first met the Superintendent of Education from Florida. He was also an NC State graduate."

Les was enamored with the idea to coach high school basketball in Florida for a year or two before getting into the door to coach in college. It would give him more practice structure and sideline experience in the heat of battle.

It was the nexus of social times in America, but Cedar Key did not participate. Across the country were the constant nightly reports of the unpopular Vietnam War. There were flower children—the "hippies"—along with war protesters and a wave of new mind-bending drugs. The civil rights movement gained purpose and direction. The South was changing. There was even a transition in music—from Frank Sinatra and Perry Como to the British sound like the Rolling Stones and the Beatles. There was Soul Music from Detroit and the new 8-track players in automobiles that played the Beach Boys. College-aged kids were protesting in front of administration buildings. A women's movement took shape. Bras were burned. A revolution of thought beckoned.

Yet, little of the outside world entered Cedar Key.

The trip to Florida was a dream. Les, Barbara and the two young boys, Greg and Robbie, were packed up the 1965 Pontiac Tempest, that pulled a small U-Haul trailer. It was June, 1966. Coach Maravich had helped Les buy the car in Raleigh for a good price and also assisted him in obtaining the financing. The Robinsons left four days earlier than needed. They took Highway 301 south all the way through South Carolina and Georgia until they reached Highway 24 in North Florida. That two-lane highway tracked from just west of Jacksonville into Gainesville, then continued to its terminus at the small fishing town of Cedar Key.

"It was like going back in time, back to the 1940's or even the 1930's." Les recalled. "The place was really different—but different as in the pace of life and the lack of outside distraction."

Cedar Key, Florida, was a storybook place. There is no other town quite like it. There were less than 900 inhabitants. The school, kindergarten through twelfth grade, had 165 students. The Class C mini-high school was the smallest public school in the State of Florida. The closest other Florida town, Bronson, was more than thirty miles away.

The history of Cedar Key included pirating—Jean Lafitte and Captain Kidd—as well as a Spanish occupation and Indian wars. President Zachary Taylor established a fort there in 1839, making it an important strategic position in the planned coastal defense of the United States. The town was named for what the Spaniards called the cedar keys, in reference to the red cedar tree that was prevalent in the area. There were actually dozens of islands, or keys, that dotted this westernmost point of Levy County. Cedar Key was the strategic port of the west Florida area that precipitated both an early railroad terminal (1859) and a battle over the salt-producing ability of the area during the Civil War. It was occupied by Union troops by 1862. Later years were enhanced by two industries, commercial fishing and pencil-making from the cedar harvesting. Yet, the remoteness of the low-lying islands stunted the expected population growth. Similar to the distant town of Key West, Cedar Key was part of Florida, but not the mindset of Florida.

Barbara and Les were exuberant about the opportunity. Les had turned down other combination teaching and coaching jobs in West Virginia and North Carolina to take the Cedar Key opening, sight unseen. The pay scale for teaching in Florida was among the best in the nation. Les would earn other income as the basketball coach. He would also become the football coach and athletic director. The lone road that took them there would have to–one day–take them away again. But for that summer of 1966, Cedar Key was in the front view of an adventure-in-the-making.

"We knew that getting experience was critical to any future I would have as a college coach. Looking back, it was one of the great opportunities—a small school that was not looking for a seasoned coach, a low cost-of-living community, and a chance to meet some very interesting people," Les recalled. "And the pay was really pretty good."

Cedar Key High School in 1966 had less than 50 students. They were in a little-noticed division of Florida's Class C conference. There was no Class D. The basketball team had essentially the same kids that played on the six-man football team. There were only 23 boys in the 9th through 12th grades. They played against the very few other small high schools across central and north central Florida. The students matriculated from multi-generational families that subsisted from the main industry of the area – saltwater farming. Everybody lived from the abundant sea products: shrimping, crabbing, and commercial fishing. It was a classical southern fishing village. It was a unique place in Florida; almost everyone there was from Florida. There were few "strangers." There was a small post office, a hardware store, a community dock and a one-story school complex. The high school, the middle school, the elementary school, the kindergarten, the gym, the band room, the town library and various other small utility buildings were sequestered on the same campus grounds within the loop of Whiddon Avenue that defined three of its borders. The Gulf of Mexico was the fourth.

Cedar Key had a popular watering hole, the town bar where fishermen, volunteer firefighters and families gathered. The L&M was the substitute for everything that was not in Cedar Key. There was not a movie theater, a bowling alley, an arcade or a convenience store. The town had no stoplights. The minister, Reverend Bill McLemore, did keep regular Sunday services at Christ Episcopal church, but would leave town for a fortnight from time to time as part of his training and commitment to the diocese. The Island Hotel, once a general store, had guest rooms dating to 1860. There was an antebellum anticipation of railroad guests that were circumvented by the spread of the Civil War. The conversion to a 10-room bed and breakfast with a restaurant made the historic tabby-walled edifice a Cedar Key icon. But to be sure, there wasn't much for tourists in Cedar Key. Island residents had few choices for activities to consider. An idyllic life paced in the warmth of the Florida sun became the daily default setting. The breezes and the rich wildlife interacting upon the gorgeous marsh views came with no charge.

The Robinsons had arrived at a place so unique, so friendly, and so out-of-the-way that it became the most unforgettable experience they could have imagined. But their timing could not have been worse. The winds whirred offshore the evening that they arrived at Cedar Key. They were directed to their Spartan rental cottage next to the bay. The rain was beginning to sting from a sideways angle. Hurricane Alma, a category 2 storm, was about to skirt the island. Tides were going to be quite high. A storm recorded a hundred years earlier brought a 27-foot surge. A similar storm, Hurricane Easy, had hit in 1950 and two other hurricanes made landfall in the previous six years. Storms were never routine, and always a threat. Many of the residents had already left to go inland. The locals knew the risks. The Robinsons dropped the U-Haul trailer. Les chained it to a tree. They headed back inland to Gainesville, 57 miles away.

The Robinsons stayed with friend Dick LaLance in Gainesville that evening. LaLance, also a teacher with West Virginia roots, coached at Newberry High School, near Gainesville. LaLance had been instrumental in convincing the Robinsons to take the Florida high school option weeks before.

"I'm not sure Dick expected that he'd be putting us up that night, but he was nice enough to take us in. We weren't sure what we'd see in Cedar Key the next morning. I was supposed to report for work that day at the high school," Les recalls.

The burgeoning storm was simply part of the expectations of a summer in Florida. The night passed. The rain in Gainesville subsided. The headline of the *Gainesville Sun* the following morning announced that Cedar Key was in ruins. The Robinsons had much of their personal belongings still in a U-Haul they had hoped had not washed into the Gulf of Mexico. They headed back with a small prayer not to find it amongst the refuse. They also wanted to begin a new life in a new setting. Fatefully, Cedar Key was not as devastated as the newspaper had reported. And the Robinsons found the trailer right where they had left it. Water from the torrents of rain did not invade the interior of the U-Haul, nor did the tidal surge carry it away. The Robinsons could begin life in the diminutive cottage with all imported resources intact. In a matter of days, electricity and safe drinking water were restored.

"What I remember is that Barbara had concerns, having the two young boys and now pregnant with Kelly. Her first impression was that it would be an impossible place to live. The home we had rented, unseen, was an old fisherman's cottage. It was in bad shape," Les recalled, "and there wasn't any electricity when we got there. The town was in some disarray, but not near what was expected after the storm passed. There was no television or radio, even when the electricity was restored. The station towers were too far away. We read to each other each night for entertainment. Barbara did a better job of reading than I did," Les laughingly recalls.

Cedar Key is a remote fishing village on Florida's Gulf Coast. It is both hard to find and hard to forget. Photo by the author.

Within three months, the Robinsons found a much larger and nicer home on the water with a view of Seahorse Key. With a wide smile, Les remembered that the rent for the bigger and better place was only $75 per month. But the initial cottage with well-worn furnishings and a leaky roof left quite an early impression.

"I went out to get a few things that first day and to report to the school. It was the date and time that I had promised to be there. Barbara was back with the boys trying to make that old cottage livable. I met the principal. But in two weeks, the principal left for another job. The only employees of the school for that entire summer were the school secretary and myself. There was no summer school, and no other teachers there. We would be starting football practice in a few weeks and I had no idea who was going to show up or if I was to help. A new principal would not arrive until September."

Wyath Read, the new principal, arrived later. Read was an LSU graduate and had met Coach Press Maravich there. Les spent both years at Cedar Key doing some scouting work for his mentor, Coach Maravich at LSU. He would make trips into Gainesville to see SEC rival Florida as well as Florida's game opponents. Les became Maravich's eyes and ears in Florida. The association with LSU basketball made the new principal and Les fast friends. Over the two years, Wyath and Mary Read have remained friends with the Robinsons, though both couples moved on from the sleepy-perfect setting of Cedar Key.

Both Les and the new principal were in for an experience.

"The high school was much like the rest of the town. It had character. The gym was fine. My office there was so small that a desk barely made it into the space. It was really a closet. But I didn't spend much time there anyway. I was usually in the gym working with the kids. I've told so many people about that unusual football field. It was barely squeezed into the footprint of the property. One end of the field ended at the water. In fact, we had to have a manager ready to go into the water to retrieve the extra point kicks." Robinson recalled.

The tales of the odd football field have induced laughter for years. There was a time when the "ball retrieval manager" was not available for a game. His father came to school to tell Les that his son had a cold and would not be able to swim after the extra points that night.

That manager retrieved a lot of extra points. After the Robinsons' first year there, the football coach left for another opportunity. Robinson took over the program. He had never coached football. The six-man league was a way for smaller schools to have the football experience, but not the high expenses and coaching attention to line play. It was, essentially, all about scoring. If schemes could be devised to move the ball effectively on every play, the other team would have to keep up. Robinson was creative in his approach. He had some tough kids who had innate talent. He had ways to overload a side of the field, perform reverses and deceive the defenses. His young and inexperienced players enjoyed his enthusiasm. A school with only 23 boys enrolled went through an undefeated season, 10-0, to capture the Florida C League Championship. Robinson did it with the smallest high school in the state.Only the ball-retrieval manager felt the effects. He stayed wet all season.

"Those kids were as tough as any I've ever known. They worked hard. They all had daily chores and their parents, many of them commercial fishermen, knew what it took to be successful. I was lucky, too. Given the small numbers of available players, there were some solid athletes that liked to play sports. So, what I had to do was to gain their trust, motivate them and get them into game shape. Much of that could be accomplished simply by playing pick-up ball in the gym." Les reflected.

"I didn't know that Les knew how to coach football, but like everything else, once he assessed his talent and capability, he could compete with anyone," Barbara offered. "And even though I was quite busy with the young children, I always enjoyed the games and getting to meet the players and especially their parents."

"Barbara knows more about sports, especially basketball, than many of the male parents I've met. She is a student of the game. She would have been a great coach on her own," Les noted.

Barbara went to the games. She had watched Les play since they were high school sweethearts in St. Albans. She had no doubts about Les's insights and coaching abilities. He could take average players and beat better teams more times than not.

The Robinsons would have two children born during their two years at Cedar Key. Barbara arrived there nearly three months pregnant with Kelly (born in December of 1966) and followed with Barbara Ann (born in March of 1968). When Barbara Ann arrived, Greg, the oldest of the four, was not quite five years old.

"Our families thought we were trying to break a record." Barbara said. "They really did give us a hard time about having four kids in less than five years. I seemed to be continually pregnant to people who saw me sporadically during that time. I can remember when we went over to Bronson to see a Cedar Key football game in the fall of '66 and I was obviously about to deliver with Kelly. I met the Bronson people and their athletic staff. We came back over the next year to play basketball in late fall and I was pregnant again with Barbara Ann. One of their coaches, without thinking, asked, "You haven't delivered that baby yet?"

The Robinsons endeared themselves to the community. They became friends with the grocery store owner, the principal, the church pastor, the mayor, and the hotel owner, among others. The town was ripe for adventures.

Les did not expect the adventure of pastoring a church for a month.

The pastor, Reverend Bill McLemore, convinced Les that he would be a good reader on Sundays. Les took great pride in learning the scriptures and reciting the readings within the sequence of the Episcopal Mass. When McLemore had to leave for a mission trip to Trinidad and Tobago, there was no substitute cleric available for the services. So he asked Les to still officiate the services and perform the readings around the choir performances every Sunday until he returned.

"I had a 7:30 AM and 7:00 PM service every Sunday along with a Wednesday night service. That first Sunday I was very nervous. I was 24 years old. And though I had been an acolyte back in St. Albans, I had never led an entire congregation. I just had to read scriptures between choir songs. But that first Sunday, I panicked. I lost my place. I thought fast and asked the congregation to pause for silent prayer. I was thinking to myself that I'd better find where I was before the pause got too long. Sure enough, I found where the next reading was to be—a Psalm. Thank God I found my place.

"As the service ended and I greeted the congregation outside, this older lady came up to me and thanked me, saying, 'I liked the silent prayer. Father Bill never does that.' She had no idea how panicked I was!"

Les even became a volunteer fireman, but never volunteered for the job. He recalled the circumstance.

"There was only an old water-tanker truck with ladders and hoses. There was an established group on call for fires there, all locals. Good guys. They showed up at my house one day and asked me to join the fire department.I didn't know the first thing about fires and am not very good with equipment, so I thought that, for their benefit, I should turn them down. I didn't think it was any big deal.

"Well, sometime later on, the crew showed back up in front of my house with the truck. They started hooking up hoses, so I came outside to ask where the fire was. There wasn't a fire. They needed to empty the tank every once in a while and refill it with new water. They usually emptied the tank by spraying the house of anyone that declined to join the volunteer fire department. I got the message. I joined the Cedar Key VFD right then!

"I was only involved in two fires," Les continued. "The first was just an abandoned car someone set on fire that had been off the road for a while.

We went there and put it out. No problem. But the second was another story.

"It was the first day of deer hunting season in Florida near the beginning of October. All of the volunteer firemen had gone hunting. I was not a hunter, so I guess I was on call. Cedar Key hosted a number of Peace Corps volunteers every year to train for similar heat conditions in other countries. One of the Peace Corps volunteers found me to let me know there was a brush fire on the other side of town that was getting out of hand. We got some other Peace Corps volunteers to man the truck and went to the fire.

"There were no other volunteer firemen available, so I was in charge. I had no idea what I was doing, but they didn't know that. So, I directed them to hook the hoses, something even I didn't know how to do, and they did it. They kept looking for me for instructions and I kept acting like I knew what to do next. I'd say, 'open the valve,' 'put some more over this side' or 'wet down that area over there' and they'd respond as if I did know what I was doing. By some miracle, despite my inexperience, we got that fire out. By the time the real firemen came back from hunting, the word had spread that I took charge and saved the town from a great disaster. They were impressed because they thought I really knew what to do. What they didn't know was that I was just winging it by the seat of my britches. They all wanted to buy me a beer at the L&M that night."

Les spent two years coaching at this very special speckle of America. He also taught English, History, and Mathematics. The Peace Corps volunteered to teach courses, as well, as part of their training.

"Those Peace Corps folks knew how to teach. I suppose that their presence there left those kids with much more than I might have taught them," Les confided.

The gregariousness by which Les had become identified played well in Cedar Key. He and Barbara had no trouble finding friends and staying busy. Putting together a respectable basketball team from the smallest school with the least players available in the state would be a challenge.

Les knew basketball. He was confident of his abilities and happy to begin coaching his own program. He practiced sound fundamentals, scouted other teams well, and proved himself to be among the great game management coaches in the state. He had only a few players, but the players were solid and worked hard. Les made the sport fun. He always had an edge. The chance of winning a few games at Cedar Key was always there, but rarely realized given the circumstances.

"I felt I had the nucleus of a good team, not even knowing their likely competition from the bigger schools. The fishing community was famous for breeding responsible hard-nosed kids. I didn't have a large number from which to choose a small number. Rather, I had a really small number that couldn't get any smaller. It was the entire male population of the high school and they could potentially fill the full allotment of uniforms I had. Losing a kid to grades or discipline could wreck the chances of winning even a handful of games. So I got to know the players, their parents, and their teachers well enough to focus upon the academic and conduct functions of the program.

"I didn't stay in my small office to read sports reports. I played ball in the gym with all comers. I schooled the players in the arts. There was the art of a crisp bounce pass, the art of a block out and importantly, the art of the free throw. Given these instructions, my coaching could make a large difference if I used my small roster well. As it turned out, the kids responded well," Les remembers.

Les played the harder early games 'up' in his schedule. He would take on Class B League schools as well as some Class A schools down in the Tampa. He played a few more Class A teams over in Gainesville. He knew the boys would rise to the level by playing better teams. With the experience and some well-earned confidence, his first basketball squad won 18 games while only losing 7. They played at a racehorse pace, Les taking advantage of the outstanding physical conditioning he espoused for his players. The entire town came out to see the purple and gold Cedar Key HS Sharks play. There was a new enthusiasm in their locker room.

"Coach Rob was in every game to win it," recalled former player Don Campbell, a two-year starter who still lives in Cedar Key, "and he made us believe we could win every game. We pulled together and became a better team on a mission. We beat plenty of larger programs that we had no business even playing."

In that first season, the buzz about town was how well the team was playing. They won games consistently. More and more fans were starting to come and see these miracle players from the tiny school. They beat good teams that had a history of beating Cedar Key handily over the years. There was a new attitude amongst the marshy vistas and tidal creeks. They played with ingrained fundamentals, determination, and enthusiasm. Cedar Key High School became a David busy slaying many Goliaths.

"In coaching as he did, he became a mentor to all of us. He made me a better person. And I'd bet there were others that would say the same," Campbell reflected. "I can remember he scouted other teams for LSU's coach, Press Maravich, by driving over to Gainesville to see the University of Florida play. Some of the players would sometimes go with him. Though the speed limit was 65, Coach would drive about 45 and talk basketball all the way there and all the way back. We felt special."

The unexpected 18-win season from the smallest public high school in the state was lauded and gave the entire community tremendous pride. The enthusiasm carried over into the next football season where Les coached on the gridiron for the first time. Les stepped in after the football coach left and engineered a memorable undefeated season. The miracle of a 10-0 season had all of Cedar Key brimming with even more pride. They were the Florida C League Champions of 1967.

Former player Don Campbell also recalls that the Cedar Key of his era was really a basketball town.

"Cedar Key had some outdoor courts in driveways, but they were not paved. They were mostly oyster shells and sand spurs. So, getting into the gym was great. Coach would come on a moment's notice and let us in anytime. He'd suit up and play, too. In fact, even when we were in football season, he had a rule. If you won the football game on Saturday, there'd be a basketball workout on Monday instead of football. That was a motivator. The guys would much rather be playing basketball. Our undefeated football team was really an extension of our teamwork as basketball players," Campbell beamed. "We were winners and Coach Rob was the reason."

High expectations followed since Les had no senior class starter on the previous year's basketball team.

"I worked with the boys on some college moves over the summer. I realized I had enough solid players to go 'up tempo' even more. That was something no Cedar Key team of the past could likely utilize. I played evening pickup games with the boys; many worked daytime summer jobs. I wanted to make them better players, and they wanted to be better.

"Many of the football kids that went undefeated played basketball. That attitude carried over. They would not accept losing." Les remembered.

Cedar Key ran off 20 straight basketball victories to start the 1967-68 season. With football included, these same kids had won thirty in a row. In fact, Cedar Key High School made headlines in the *Tampa Times* and *St. Petersburg News* as one of two programs in the state undefeated in both football and basketball. They lost their first game after their "celebrity" was announced. They lost only one more, finishing the season at an astonishing 23-2. Les's hoopsters had won 41 games over his two years, only losing 9, a winning percentage of .820, the same as that of Kentucky's legendary coach Adolph Rupp. Yet, Les did it at the smallest public high school in Florida. Cedar Key had never had such success.

In recent seasons, that same high school won a total of only one basketball game over a four-year period. The fishing village without enough kids to fill out a JV team played a varsity schedule most years without prowess. It took a special coach to bring championships to Cedar Key.

"Coach Rob put as much emphasis on an assist or a rebound as he did on a made basket. We were truly an unselfish team. We really didn't care who scored. We only cared that we played the game well and scored more than the other team. As a result, during my senior season, all five starters averaged double figures in scoring. No player was taller than 6'3". Yet we felt we could beat the bigger teams, even the Class A schools. And we did!" Campbell proudly recalled. "Good coaching? Yes. But the fact that Coach Rob truly cared about us had everything to do with it."

Many in the town bought into the excitement and traveled to the away games, as well. The town of Cedar Key had some profound characters, none more recognizable and selfless than their 4'1" mayor, J. Quitman Hodges. Hodges, born in 1914, would go on to serve as mayor or city commissioner for 39 years. As one of the "little people," he never minded being called a "midget" or his given nickname, Shorty. The political correctness hadn't made it to this remote village, but people were still quite reverent, so much so, that Shorty Hodges was among Cedar Key's most admired and respected citizens. He died in 2005 at the age of 90. Hodges had quite an impact upon Les Robinson.

"We were friends. Shorty ran the hardware store next to the post office. He never missed a home basketball game when I was there. As mayor, he was an effective and admired leader. Because of his lack of height, Shorty couldn't sit on the first row at the gym. We only had six rows. Shorty would come in early and negotiate the height of the box-type stands one step at a time so that he could sit up top and see the action. He'd always come by after the game to shake my hand and tell me, 'Good game.' I appreciated that man for what he meant to all of us." Les recalled.

"Oh, and those fishermen would come by the hardware store when I was in there for something and make some wisecrack—usually corny. But Shorty had heard every midget joke there was. It really never bothered him. He was really cool. Conversely, it was his attitude that made him a great choice for mayor. People appreciated that he did not carry a chip on his shoulder and could hang in there with anybody on any subject, especially on things that could benefit Cedar Key."

Hodges was also a commercial fisherman. At one time he had the largest commercial fishing boat in Cedar Key. Hodges was always much bigger than his stature to the residents there. Don Campbell remembered a valuable lesson.

"I was 12. My dad was a great friend to Mayor Hodges. One day I bragged that because I had grown so much I could take the small man down in a match. My dad asked, 'Are you sure? I know he's a midget, but he's a fully developed grown man.' I said that there was no way that Shorty could take me. So, my dad took me to the hardware store and announced that I said I could 'wrastle him to the ground.' He looked directly to a seemingly surprised Shorty. Well, the challenge was on. Shorty Hodges took me out back and within seconds grabbed both of my arms and had me flat on the ground. He sat on top of me while laughing out loud. I had learned my lesson. I think my dad knew just how tough Shorty was and wanted me to have that lesson to remember for a lifetime."

Shorty Hodges liked Les and was enthused to see the high school winning games for a change. Hodges Marine and Supplies on Main Street remained an integral part of daily life in the remote community of Cedar Key. Mayor Shorty Hodges became one of Les's most ardent supporters.

The high school had many other selfless supporters. One couple, the Walruths, owned one of the two grocery stores in Cedar Key.

"Every year, Mrs. Walruth would have a steak cookout for the players, managers and cheerleaders to thank them for their efforts on the athletic fields," Campbell recalled. "There were not very many steak dinners in Cedar Key back then. So, to have a steak dinner was a big deal. The Walruths had become great friends with the Robinsons. Everybody liked the Robinsons. So, when they had to leave, there was nobody sadder than all of those players that had those two special years that have become the glory days of Cedar Key sports history."

The day would come when the Robinson family, now with four preschool children, would move on.

The decision to go for the Robinson's was clear. Les needed to complete his master's degree in Guidance Counseling that he had begun at NC State. He needed to get his foot in the door at the college-coaching level. They needed a place to live inexpensively with a full family of six. All of these options became available at the Robinson's next stop in western North Carolina.

Leaving was still emotional and not without reservations. They not only left a town and their new friends there, but also left a major chapter in their lives. Les Robinson likely remains the only football coach in Florida high school history to compile a career mark as undefeated.

The experience of Cedar Key has become a most entertaining story as the years have rolled forward. In this way, Les became perhaps the greatest non-paid public relations source in the town's next forty years.

Cedar Key. The Robinsons came in a hurricane. They grew the family by two more children in two short years. They went undefeated in Les's only football-coaching season ever while a wet manager retrieved extra points from beyond the bayside goalposts. They won 23 games and a basketball championship with a male student population in the entire high school of the same number, 23. Concurrently, Les earned mileage reimbursement and timely additional income as an aside for his role as a college basketball scout, courtesy of his mentor, Coach Press Maravich.

In his time there, Les had performed as a pastor for a month. He acted as an erstwhile fire chief during a conflagration that threatened the entire town. Propitiously, that fire was contained and extinguished. Les became identified as a miracle worker in a small community that liked miracles. Barbara, his muse, was there always. She was the mother of four who became the mother of anyone who played for Les. She was always there, at every game—and every event the town offered.

Over the years, the true stories of the Cedar Key experience were thought to have grown into legend by some. Les's career had placed him in front of much larger audiences. When NC State brought Les back to coach the Wolfpack in 1990, many of the university faithful had heard the incredible stories of this special place. One was former star point guard Monty Towe, a diminutive playmaker who, along with the great David Thompson and 7'4" Tom Burleson, brought an NCAA basketball championship to Raleigh in 1974.

Towe, along with Wolfpack assistant Eddie Biedenbach, was in Tampa to sign an elite player to NC State. Towe noticed that Cedar Key was close enough to satisfy his teeming curiosity about the haven Les had described. So, he and Biedenbach took the narrow state road there to see for themselves. Their report back to others, as well as to Les, was that everything Les had long reported was true. They added that, if anything, Cedar Key was even better than he described. Towe and Biedenbach posed for a photo with the former mayor, Shorty Hodges, to prove that the fascinating character existed.

Towe's experience there was years later but revealed that Cedar Key was still a place he found to be both quaint and unique. Les and Barbara Robinson's decision to pursue the goal to which they had both committed had taken them through a place that became an experience like no other.

The community with the little mayor had a big heart.

Les's résumé could now add a lifetime of other-than-basketball knowledge from that condensed volume of a two-year period. Cedar Key was a difficult place to leave. And they would need a much bigger U-Haul. But Les had a childhood dream to fulfill.

"It was near the end of our second year. Barbara and I were walking down the beach and talking about our long-term goals. We were only 26 with four children. We both knew that we were loving Cedar Key too much. It was too perfect. And it would have been the easiest thing to just stay. But I had put off finishing my master's degree and had the dream of becoming a college head coach. We had kept in touch with Coach Maravich and Coach Sloan, as well. When an opportunity came up for a graduate assistant's job at Western Carolina, we knew that this was our opportunity. Barbara had an uncle that lived near and we could get a place he owned to live for hardly anything. We packed the family up and said our goodbyes to a most perfect place, Cedar Key."

Coach Press Maravich took over the program for Everett Case.
Photo Courtesy NC State University.

CHAPTER 9

PRESS MARAVICH & THE PISTOL

Relationships matter. Press Maravich's trip from Aliquippa, Pennsylvania, to become the head basketball Coach at NC State arched through West Virginia, Ohio, and South Carolina. His previous position at NC State as the assistant basketball coach under Everett Case was meant to prepare him for another basketball school outside of the shadow of a legend. He had no idea that his friend, the legend, would fall to cancer.

In the "business," there are inspirational leaders, teachers of the game, relentless recruiters, game-time strategists, and even slick imposters. The imposters are found out soon enough. Of the four positive coaching characteristics, any two can get you through a career. Three qualities will put you in the Hall of Fame.

"Coach Case had every quality as a coach. He could recruit, teach, strategize and motivate," Les recalled. "To be fair, Press Maravich was never a great recruiter and not known as a great motivator. But he could teach basketball and coach in a game with the best of 'em."

Press Maravich was a young Serbian immigrant forged from the slag of the Pennsylvania iron ore district that courted other ethnic names like Unitas, Marino, Parilli, Blanda, Lujack and Namath. His hard-nosed abilities earned him a starring role on his Davis and Elkins College basketball team in 1937, graduating in 1941. After serving with the Naval Air Corps in World War II, Maravich played two years of professional basketball before beginning his coaching career. His first head-coaching job was at West Virginia Wesleyan College. He returned to coach his alma mater, Davis and Elkins, until 1956.It was then that he accepted a tough ACC head basketball coaching stint at Clemson University. After six very diffi-cult seasons, he moved to Raleigh to fill the assistant coaching role under Everett Case at NC State. His record at Clemson was 55-96.

Maravich made the move because he wanted to get to a top bas-ketball program and Everett Case provided an avenue where he would have better future opportunities. Press knew the benefit of learning from the best in the business. When Case became sick at the start of the 1964-65 season, Maravich capably led the Wolfpack to a 21-5 re-cord and to the championship of the Atlantic Coast Conference. They had been picked to finish seventh by the media. The next year he ex-celled yet again, though picked to finish at the bottom. A very difficult decision was prescient. A father's career path was contingent upon a son's acceptance to a major college. Contingencies have tendencies to become dependencies.

Les explains, "Pistol was not a good student. His scores were below what NC State could accept. Press wanted him to play at the top level, but there were no opportunities in the ACC. But opportunities presented themselves both at the University of West Virginia and at LSU. The LSU program had been awful for many years and they were elated to take Press as coach in view of his success at State. It became the best hire in the land if they could get Pistol Pete enrolled," Robinson recounted. "You just knew that they'd find a way.

"Coach Maravich was in a box. There was the issue with his wife's al-coholism that needed a new beginning. He couldn't stay at State and miss the opportunity to see his son play if Pistol went to West Virginia. He had a good team coming back at State with Eddie Biedenbach considered one of the best players in the country. But he had made up his mind that he had to go because Pistol could not qualify academically at State. He as much as told Pistol that *they* needed to take the LSU "package" or Pistol would not be welcome to come home! I had no idea how much that family decision would affect me at the time," Robinson remembered.

To further his career, Coach Maravich had to choose between the secure legacy built by Everett Case over the prior two decades at NC State and the option of the incredible opportunity of coaching the most electrifying, crowd-pleasing showman that game has ever known. Pistol Pete played every available day in Reynolds Coliseum against the NC State players, some of the best talent in the ACC. He had great hands, quickness, outstanting court vision, and the confidence of a a boa costrictor facing off against a field mouse. He was obsessed with the game and perfected even the most creative shots. There was no shot too tough and no defender up to the task to anticipate his every move. He had made a mockery of every high school defensive scheme in the central North Carolina area while playing at Edwards Military Institute in Salemburg, NC.

"I saw the Pistol doing things in Reynolds coliseum that I thought were impossible," Les recalled. "He had this one routine when he was ready to head home after many pick up games that he called 'going down.' It was a globetrotters-type shot. It was a deep hook from the far right corner. You would never shoot a hook shot from that far away. It's even crazy that Pistol practiced that shot. He'd wait until 'game point' against the other players and head down to the right corner. He'd yell out 'going down!' and swish the shot never missing a step while in a trot to the locker room down the player tunnel. It was both brazen and at the same time incredible.

"Being a high school kid who was that good and that confident did not always set well with the State players. Some wanted to kick his butt, but he was Press's boy. That would not go over well," Les recounted. "He got a few pushes and a few elbows in the rougher pick-up games. He didn't seem to care, as long as he won.

"Press had the best recruit in America playing in Reynolds Coliseum often enough to be an NCAA violation, but legal because it was his son. The Maravichs, coach and player, were either going to split up the following season or find a happy circumstance. The LSU deal was their only path. You couldn't blame them, looking back," Les stated.

"When I mention that Press Maravich had two strong suits, I should emphasize that he was brilliant in those two areas. He was a teacher who also had exceptional abilities on the sideline as a game coach. It's true that he never warmed up to the recruiting wars or implored anyone to 'win one for the Gipper.' Everett Case knew this. It was Case who convinced Maravich to leave a head-coaching job at Clemson, a football-oriented conference rival, to take a secondary role at State—a basketball school. To underscore the basketball emphasis, Maravich received a salary *increase* for this transition. He was unaware that Everett Case was picking his own successor," Les related.

Maravich won 38 games in his two seasons at NC State, losing ony 13. He was an innovative coach and game strategist. If he had any semblence of above average players, he could win big. As it was, their player personnel was average over those two years.

"Part of that condition was related to the point-shaving scandal of 1961. The year after I came to State, the conference really handcuffed recruiting."

Les tells when Coach Maravich came.

"I was still more focused on becoming a coach and let everyone know who asked about my goals. But I wanted to be a better player. When Coach Maravich first arrived, he was perceptive enough to see that I had much to offer as a role player, and more to add as a coaching project."

In the summer of 1962 Les first met Coach Pater "Press" Maravich, the man who would become his mentor, his confidant, and his lifetime friend. The nickname "Press" was ascribed to him back in his hometown of Aliquippa, Pennsylvania. It was a moniker for his early ability to get a "scoop" on information much like a clever newspaper reporter.

During the 1964-65 season the legendary Everett Case stepped down in mid-season deferring to Maravich to lead the Wolfpack through the remainder of the season. Later, Maravich offered the opportunity Les to coach the NC State freshmen, his first college coaching opportunity. Les did not hesitate.

"Coach Maravich and everyone who was around me knew my focus. I wanted to coach college basketball. I felt like my whole life was pointed to that one goal. Coach Maravich was not only the first to give me the opportunity, but took the time to mentor me. If there's one man in my life that was like a father to me, hands-down that man was Press Maravich," Les states.

The relationship began as a coach to a player. But it evolved to that of a friend, promoter, counselor, and defender. Seldom do they come along as true as Press Maravich. And the very private coach had no better friend than Les Robinson.

Over two decades, Coach Maravich took the time to handwrite multi-page letters to his star pupil, Les. These insightful dialogues bypass the usual layers of cordiality to capture moments that friends share with friends.

Les has saved the letters.

The letter of September 6, 1966, addressed the young coach at his new job as both Head Coach and Athletic Director of Cedar Key High School. Maravich knew it was in the proximity of Gainesville, Florida. But he had no idea that it was a remote community, away from everything. Maravich's letter from the LSU basketball office detailed his grasp of the subject of hurricanes. His wife, Helen, had a predisposition of great fear at their mere existence.

With Hurricane Faith on the loose, I guess you and the wife really sweated it out… I would advise you not to spend good money on furniture. Helen worries pretty much about hurricanes… Best always, Press

Hurricanes began off the coast of Africa. Helen Maravich could sense them, it seemed. Meanwhile, Press stayed in touch with his protégé.

He wrote to Les a week later. *I sure hope you have a fine season, Les. Don't expect miracles the first couple years. Just work the youngsters on fundamentals and defense.*

The Cedar Key basketball team did work well in both areas. Les coached them to a record of 17-9. The following year, Les had record of

23-2, beating archrival Bronson High School three times. The basketball life of the youthful coach was becoming clear. He could get the job done. His combined record of 40-11 over two seasons belied one very impressive statistic. Over the two years he only coached one senior player—and he was sequestered in a small fishing village with the smallest public school in Florida.

Conversely, Coach Maravich was fighting difficulties that hampered his daily life. His wife had been unable to beat alcoholism. Things were becoming difficult for the new LSU coach.

I've got a clinic in Penna (Pennsylvania) and that is all. I cancelled seven of them because of Helen's condition." Maravich wrote on September 23rd, 1966. *"When I mention Hurricanes to my wife, she goes all to pieces. I know that once a hurricane starts in the Gulf, I will have to do one of two things—take her north until the hurricane dies out or put her in the basketball office under the football stadium.*

The hurricane in Coach Maravich's life had a steep eye wall. Helen Maravich could not cope without alcohol or a series of alcohol treatment failures. One or the other was ongoing for the better part of his career. Helen had been previously married and had a young son, Ronnie. He adopted the Maravich name. Ronnie's transition from the church-going Maravich home into the military presented a challenge to Press and Helen. Ronnie had fathered a little girl, Diana, who was being put up for adoption. Despite Helen's ongoing condition, Press could not bear the brunt of the adoption's likely impact. He stepped forward, and with Helen, adopted baby Diana as their own. Diana was now Pistol Pete's sister—and step niece. Press immediately became the primary care giver. On January 17, 1967, Maravich penned these sentiments:

My wife has been pretty sick, Les. Geez, I'll get <u>drunk</u> when she gets <u>well</u>. Can't do anything with her being sick. Must do home chores, feed, clean, clothe the baby, do dishes, coach, etc. Even doing a poor coaching job because of the situation…we are 3 –11. Didn't expect to win 3. Have the dumbest *club in America. No one can come close...on the brighter side, the frosh club is undefeated. They are 10 – 0. Pete has broken every LSU frosh record. Now he's aiming for Bob Pettit's seasons average. Bob averaged 29.2 a game in his frosh year. For ten games, Pete is <u>38.5</u>. I have a weekly TV show and I feature Pete every week. He does it all. Best Always, Coach*

His club was indeed a poor assemblage of players. They suffered a schedule- ending embarrassment by allowing a Stokely Athletic Center record 50 points to Tennessee forward Ron Widby in their last away game. Widby later went to "the league." Not *that* league, but to the NFL as a punter for the Dallas Cowboys. Maravich was trying to hold on until the posse arrived. The posse was one young man on one white horse. His name was not written on his birth certificate as it was known all across Louisiana. Pistol Pete Maravich was already bringing in thunderous crowds for the Frosh Tigers. Most of them left before the varsity game.

His proud father penned another handwritten letter dated February 21, 1967. It related the misery of the wait.

We have found so many new ways to lose it isn't funny, Les. Last nite Mississippi State beat us 66-64. We had them 64-60 with 27 seconds to go. Both times our <u>damn</u> <u>stupid</u> <u>seniors</u> threw the ball from out of bounds to M. State. Just damn stupid, dumb bastards. I don't know why I get upset. I knew we would be 3-23 for the season...Pete has been bombing the hell out of the hoop. Last nite the governor came to see Pete play for the 8th time. He put on quite a show against Miss State. He hit for 53 points, got 6 rebs and 8 assists. Beautiful, beautiful playmaking. He upped his average to 44.2 pts. per game. He now owns every record in the book...they have Miss. Frosh and Tenn left away. The frosh are 16 – 0 so far...Best always + love to the family, Press

The Freshmen would go on to a 17-1 record, losing only at Tennessee. The turbulence on the court was over for the LSU team. Pistol Pete could bring respectability back to the Bayou. The kiln-fired steel reserve of Coach Press Maravich could only make things better. He would place a winner on the floor.

Back at NC State, Coach Norm Sloan took over and had his own staff. The freshmen coaching job would also be changed. Les depended on Maravich for input and direction.

"Knowing my situation, this is the first time Press mentioned The Citadel to me. He knew that the small military school would take a youthful assistant and that the program had some turnover. I applied right away and got a letter of recommendation from Coach Maravich. The return letter stated that they kept my information for the future. The assistant position under former NC State player and now Citadel Head Coach Mel Thompson had been filled." Les detailed.

He adds, "They looked like a perfect fit. They had a great run under Norm Sloan and had even played West Virginia and Jerry West in the 1959 Southern Conference Championship finals. With Thompson there at the time and an Athletic Director, Eddie Teague, who had his Master's Degree from NC State, I knew they would have to take a look at me. When they declined is when I took the job at Cedar Key High School."

The colorful years at Cedar Key High School were a crucible for the Robinsons. It was there that Les proved his worth as a coach and there that the last two of his four children were born. But his ambition to become a D-1 coach superceded his legendary success at the idyllic end-of-the-earth mangrove fishing village.

Press Maravich was amused by it all as he wrote in his letter of September 29, 1967:

It was sure nice listening to your voice and telling me about your football team. Here at LSU, we have 13 coaches excluding the head honcho. Anyway, about 8 of 'em were in my office drinking coffee when I started on your coaching career as a football coach. I had 'em laughing and holding their stomachs. I said, "Now there's a coach who's put the bounce in the football."

Les became a brother figure to Pistol Pete because of his close relatinship with the Maravich family.
Photo courtesy LSU Sports.

Les noted that the tenor of Maravich's letters were not about what gave him a laugh or two. There were other issues.

"And he 'scheduled up' with Pistol," Les relates. "He wanted the world to see his boy. It was his life now. With Helen's situation, it was all he could hold on to."

The September 29 letter went on:

As you know I played the 8th toughest schedule in the land last year. Hell, I just don't believe in set ups or patsies. This year we should move up a notch or two on the tough schedule sheet. We added Wisconsin, Marquette, Clemson, Texas and others. If you get beat, you might as well get beat by the best.

Maravich continued. He couldn't help relating the schedule to Norm Sloan's NC State team, the program he left to coach the Pistol.

Sloan really cut down on his schedule—Wm.+Mary, Indiana State, Atlantic Christian, East Carolina and others. The letter cited Maravich's observances. He followed the program that he left with interest.

Pete is looking good, Les. He is the best ball handler and playmaker in the land. My only problem is lack of depth and experience. Hell, all we need is about 7 players if we keep healthy. Good luck during the season in football. Seriously hope you go undefeated. Write when you have time. Your friend, Press

In a crystal ball, Maravich would never have guessed the clairvoyance of his letter to Les dated June 6, 1968:

I haven't given up on the East Tennessee State job. The real reason I haven't called you back is that trying to contact the basketball coach there has been difficult. In fact, I have another call to him this morning. I've called three times and left word for him to call back. I'll be leaving for Buies Creek, NC (Editor's note: home of famous Campbell College Basketball Camp), *on Saturday for two weeks. In the meantime, if East Tennessee State should call and tells me what is what, I'll let you know.*

The head basketball coach at ETSU was Madison Brooks. He never called back. Seventeen years later Les became the head basketball coach at ETSU.

"Coach Maravich knew a lot of people. I depended on some of these contacts, but moreover, I depended upon his timely advice," Les states. "He was honest, forthright, and he meant every word he said."

In fact, it was his honesty that may have made it most difficult to compete for top recruits. As he recounted in a note to Les:

It is my understanding that the big 7-2 Tennessean is favorable to Vandy, Kentucky, and then LSU. Although, Tennessee is out, you can never tell. We have the best set up for him. If anyone cheats even a little to nab him, we'll be out.

"It's been said that he illegally recruited the best player in the land, Pistol Pete." Les deadpanned. "He romanced his mother, bought the player his first car and even gave him a few bucks in unaccounted cash for dates! Outside of the Pistol, Press was not known as a big dog in the recruiting game. He would not be too interested in players whose last names didn't end in "ski" or "ich." And once he smelled that a player was expecting any kind of inducement, Press moved on."

Les remembers his first out-of-state recruiing assignment.

In fact, during the 1964-65 season Maravich sent Les, his freshman team coach all the way to Youngstown to see a couple of players Maravich had a line on. In a driving snowstorm, Les diligently went to see the players for an assessment. Perplexed after talking with their respective high school coaches, a hesitant Les called Maravich at 11:30 at night (Raleigh time) from an outdoor phone booth. It was cold in Ohio.

"Coach, I've checked on both players and you were right about them. They can both play at the top level. One is playing at Ohio State and the other is playing at Kent State," Les noted. "Your information was correct except it was one year off."

Not to be dissuaded in the least, the serious-toned Maravich countered, "Good, Les. I'm not sure they could have made it here anyway. Why don't you head on up to Aliquippa and check on those other two kids on my list."

Perhaps the most famous recruiting story of all happened when Maravich was still coaching at NC State. Les was asked to pick up a 6'8" all-state (Illinois) high school power forward at the Raleigh airport. As was legal at the time, the recruit could work out during visits. Coach Maravich directed Les to find a couple of players in the Reynolds Coliseum gym and see what the big man was capable of providing to the Wolfpack. Les grabbed a varsity player and a high school kid who was shooting in the gym that day. They played "Make it, take it." When the workout was over, the recruit did not receive a glowing endorsement.

"I dunno coach. Pete and me beat him and Eddie Beidenbach five straight. We should pass on this one," Les recalled. "I was thinking I'm washed up and Pete's weak."

Although Coach Maravich and Les both knew that Pistol Pete was pretty talented, they didn't envision that the skinny show-off could dominate a burly all-state player to the extent that had occurred.

That all-state blue chip player that they passed on went on to make All Big Ten at the University of Illinois. The Pistol's overwhelming performance skewered the player's worth. But Pistol Pete Maravich had that effect upon many top players from all over the country.

The association with Coach Press Maravich was a confirming influence of Les's career direction. Les had enjoyed his two years at Cedar Key, but when it was time to move on and complete his master's degree so that he could get to the first rung of the college-coaching ladder, he responded. He moved on to Western Carolina to complete the post-graduate degree.

The course was set in motion. After a year at Western Carolina coaching their freshman team and completing his master's degree in guidance counseling, Les did find a path at The Citadel. His five years as assistant coach led to his being named as head basketball coach on September 23, 1974, coincidently on Les's 32nd birthday. He used that same date to send out his first letter to the person he felt he owed heartfelt appreciation.

Today, following George Hill's resignation, I was named Head Basketball Coach here at The Citadel. I felt it only proper that the first person I should write be "The Coach" that has had greater influence on my career than any coach in the business. I want to take this opportunity to say thank you for the solid foundation that I feel you have given me and also for going to bat for me on so many occasions. I am forever indebted to you and hope I don't let you down...

George had some personal problems that he needed to get worked out and decided it best to quit caoching, at least for the time being. He may go back and complete work on his PhD.

Coach, thanks again for everything. I hope you did as good a job teaching me asi feel you did. Needless to say I don't think I could have found a better teacher anywhere in America. I really mean this!!

Please give my love to Mrs. Maravich and Diana. Say hello to Pistol for me. Les.

Maravich was in his second of three years at Appalchain State University in Boone, North Carolina. Pistol was a thrill-a-minute NBA highlight for the New Orleans Jazz. Helen and the 10-year-old Diana Maravich were seemingly happy in the confines of Boone, far from the reach of hurricanes. Unfortunately, Helen Maravich was never far from her other demons.

Barely two weeks after Les's appointment into the ranks of D-1 coaches, Press Maravich was out playing golf with ASU assitant coach Russ Bergmann. Tragedy struck. Helen committed suicide with a .22 caliber handgun.

"Of course, I went to Pennsylvania for the funeral out of my deep respect for Press, and regard for Pete, as well. Press was devastated. We talked. He remained devoted to taking care of Diana," Les detailed.

Helen Maravich's funeral in Aliquippa was conducted from the same Serbian parish church that transitioned the Maravich family into blue collar America. The life that Press Maravich knew for so many years had dissipated. He redoubled his devotion to Diana and reassessed his resposiblities and the way forward. He knew that he would again see Les on January 12th, the scheduled game with The Citadel at Boone, North Carolina. It was Les's first year as head coach and his first visit to coach against his mentor.

Neither program was in good order, vying for last place in the league. But Les's Bulldogs beat the Mountaineers in Boone that evening on a last-second shot.

"Coach Maravich had approached me before the game and asked that I come into his office afterwards, win or lose.

"Under the circumstances, I felt uneasy about going to see him while the team was celebrating a win and getting ready to ride back." Les recalled. "When I went in, it was somber and quiet. He asked me to take a seat. He congratulated me on the thrilling win and wished me well the rest of the way. And then he said, 'Les, I've been waiting for you to come here since Helen died. This is the last game I'll ever coach. I wanted you to be the first to know. I'm walking in tomorrow and resigning. I can't do it anymore.' He had tears in his eyes. It was the end of his career. He chose the date on the calendar and told no one.

"Of course, I was stunned," Les related. "But looking back, he had been reeling since Helen's suicide just three months earlier. I believe he truly loved her, despite the alcoholism and other problems. Now, he had to take care of Diana by himself. There was nobody there but him. And he knew he couldn't focus on recruiting or the other facets of basketball given his circumstances."

Maravich resigned the next day. Assistant Russ Bergmann, who had played for Press at LSU as a teammate of Pete's handled the rest of the 1974-75 season. Just two months later, ASU hired the former South Carolina standout point guard, Bobby Cremins.

The Press Maravich coaching chapter was now closed. Almost. Another opportunity developed.

Within the year, the New Orleans Jazz hired Maravich to scout potential draft talent all across college basketball. The Jazz management also felt that it would be a benefit to Pistol Pete to have his dad around from time to time. Pistol was the reason the fans came to games. He was the franchise's most protected property.

During the following season, 1975-76, Les had an opportunity to return a favor. He contacted Press Maravich with an idea to bring him into The Citadel as an assistant to finish his career out and to give Diana a great place to grow up. Les also felt that it was important to look after Press, especially given the mentorship that Press had rendered him since his playing days at NC State.

Les did not know that the timing of his offer coincided with Press's appointment with the Jazz. Press respectfully declined.

They're paying me a fortune to do what I would do for free—watch basketball games all over the country. This is a dream come true!" Press Maravich replied. *"Les, I can never thank you enough for the kindnessses you have extended to me from day one. You have always been there for me and I will never ever forget it.*

Press Maravich remained around the game, and in Les's purview, around Pete's career. Maravich was diagnosed with prostate cancer in the spring of 1985. His son Pete had become a household name across America.

Pistol Pete had a predisposition for holistic healing and the chance of herbal medication.Both Press and Pete had become "born again" Christians. Press Maravich's cancer had gotten much worse and the normal medical treatment was delayed. Late in the process, Press Maravich was admitted to the Sloan-Kettering Cancer Center in New York, but he changed his mind inexplicably and canceled the treatment. Instead, son Pete took him to an experimental research facility in Germany. It had little impact. Pete had accepted the responsibilty of taking care of both Press and Diana. Press returned to Lousiana to live out his condition with Pete and Diana by his side. The condition continued to decline and Press Maravich passed away on April 15, 1987.

The elder Maravich did enjoy that son Pete was selected as a member of the Naismith Memorial Basketball Hall of Fame. Pete Maravich's career was storybook. He owns the alltime NCAA scoring average and career points records (44.2 and 3,667), even though he only played three varsity years. Pete was a three-time first team All American, the Naismith Player of the Year in 1970, and a five-time NBA Allstar selectee. He was named as one of the top 50 NBA players of all time in 1997. Sadly, Pete's induction into the Basketball Hall of Fame came after Press's death.

Les recalls the funeral of his mentor.

"I went back to Aliquippa for Press's funeral in 1987. I was at East Tennessee then and our season was just over. Pistol came over to me after the service and hugged me with tears in his eyes. He said, 'Dad loved you. You were family. He always said his best team was that State team you were on that was picked to finish seventh. He said you were a big part of that.' It was such a sad time."

Les reflects on the relationship.

"I guess Press saw something in me that I didn't see in myself. He liked that I was from West Virginia because he liked the blue collar work ethic. He also knew that I would adapt to his coaching well; and I did. He put a greater value on defense and ball control than most coaches. And he knew—because I told him—I was going to coach. To that end, nobody helped me more in my young career than Press. He was the only person I ever called a 'second father.' I used so much of his basketball knowledge—things he taught me—to benefit the teams I coached throughout my career."

In an eerie circumstance Pete Maravich was quoted saying at his father's deathbed, "I'll see you soon." Pistol Pete Maravich died just nine months later from a heart defect. Pete's passing was a sad ending to the two-generation influence the Maravich family had upon every level of the sport of basketball.

"There will never be another like Coach Press Maravich," Les lamented. "And when you think about it, we'll never see another Pistol Pete.

They were both different than anyone else in so many regards. I felt I was a part of the Maravich family because of Press. He meant everything to me in my career."

*Les, Barbara, Greg, Robby, Kelly, and Barbara Ann rented another U-Haul to coach at
Western Carolina.
Les completed his master's degree and gained coaching experience there.
Photo courtesy of Robinson family archives.*

CHAPTER 10
THE CATAMOUNTS OF CULLOWHEE

Cullowhee, North Carolina, is not too far from Asheville in the eastern side of the Great Smoky Mountains.

"Barbara's family had relatives there who had a vacant house we could rent. We took the job without knowing this, so this benefit was not even considered until we got there," Les details. "A job coaching the junior varsity team came with an opportunity to obtain a master's degree in guidance counseling. Western Carolina was still an NAIA college then. There wasn't a lot of money in coaching the JV at an NAIA college, but it was enough to get me through the year. That area is really nice—Cullowhee and Silva are next to each other. The hills are gorgeous in the fall and we enjoyed a contrast of what we experienced in rural Florida."

Jim Gudger served as the head basketball coach at Western Carolina. Press Maravich had recommended Les to him.

"When I was offered the job, I didn't know that they had a rule that you can't be in the graduate program and a full-time coach. We got in touch with the commissioner, an NC State graduate, Dean Kirkland. He gave us special permission. It made a huge financial difference. With the Pell Grant, my income jumped from $6200 to $9500. With four children all under the age of five, the rule exception was a major help to us."

Les had some un-expected inside assistance, as well. In a few instances Les had class at the same time that he was to coach a game with the junior varsity. The professor knew about it but devised a workable solution.

"I had a great professor there who loved basketball. On the couple of occasions when I couldn't be at both places, he split the class in two for a project by having me intentionally absent as a test subject for the group. Since I couldn't know what they were going to ask, I couldn't be there. So, I coached the games during those scheduling conflicts because the professor looked out for me," Les detailed. "Sometimes it takes a lot of luck and unexpected help to make the timing work out."

"While I was living in Silva, I applied to The Citadel for the second time. I knew that I would have my master's degree in a few months from Western. Since I had not heard back from the application, I followed up a few weeks later by calling the college. The Sports Information Director, Bill Hallman, answered the phone. He told me that an assistant coach, Bill Foster, was leaving to start a program up at Charlotte. When I told Hallman that I was just completing my master's degree and had coached at NC State with Coach Maravich, he got word to The Citadel's head coach, Dick Campbell.

"Again, the timing was good for me. Dick Campbell called me back. He said he was going to contact some other candidates, as well. But after a short time, he got back in touch. I went down to Charleston and interviewed and got the job."

Les packed up the four Robinson kids, none old enough for the first grade yet, and he and Barbara got one more U-Haul trailer. It was headed one way to Charleston.

"I was on a lucky streak with the cost of housing," Les recounts. "The Citadel job came with free housing. I paid next to nothing—$75 a month—in Florida, and less yet for Barbara's family's rental in Silva. At The Citadel, I paid a fee for the water and electricity. That was it!"

Sometimes, good fortune intersects with providence.

Les arrived in Charleston in mid-May of 1969, master's degree in hand, and an entire college-coaching career just ahead.

Cadets at The Citadel enjoyed the contests and made sure the opponents knew it.
Photo courtesy The Post and Courier.

CHAPTER 11

MISSION IMPOSSIBLE: COACH GEORGE HILL

His rèsumè accurately listed the United States Coast Guard Academy, when George Hill convinced The Citadel Athletic Director Eddie Teague to let him elevate the Bulldog Basketball program in 1971. In retrospect, it would have been appropriate to have called the Coast Guard to report a sinking ship. It was another thing altogether to bring in a demolition expert.

The halcyon days of Citadel basketball belonged to Coach Norm Sloan whose "Blitz Kids" enjoyed a four-year record of 57-38. They emerged as a Southern Conference contender. The 1959 Southern Conference Championship game pitted them against eventual champion West Virginia and the great Jerry West. But the years between Norm Sloan and Les Robinson brought about difficult times—for the most part—among a succession of tumultous coaching choices.

Former NC State player Mel Thompson sported a 67-96 record at The Citadel. His record included a 3-20 record in 1963. He succeeded Sloan with the drudgery best enunciated in former player Pat Conroy's book *My Losing Season*. Conroy's journal takes an inside look at college coaching in the 1960's along with Conroy's personal emotions in dealing with his overbearing father. One pundit cited the book cynically as the longest suicide note ever written by a person who did not commit suicide.

After Thompson's departure in 1967, Former Carson Newman Basketball Coach Dick Campbell brought a new look to the program. It included the successive hiring of two fine assistants—Bill Foster, who went on to start the new UNC–Charlotte basketball program before finding other successes at Clemson, Miami, and Virginia Tech and Foster's replacement, Les Robinson.

"I had just gotten hired to replace Coach Foster and two seasons later, Coach Campbell decided to take a job at Xavier. Looking back, it was a great move for him. But I had been in Charleston for less than two years and just knew I would have to pack up and move again," Les recalled.

Campbell's record of 45-54 was anything but glitzy. Yet Xavier University liked his mastery of the clock. He'd had two winning seasons in his four at The Citadel. His ability to control tempo made his undersized team competitive. He won 15 and lost 37 with Xavier University before moving on to Belmont College in Nashville from 1974 through 1978. He left college coaching after a record of 48-68 with Belmont. Dick Campbell died in 2009 at the age of 81.

Upon Campbell's 1971 departure from The Citadel, Athletic Director Eddie Teague summoned an apprehensive Les Robinson to his office. Teague told the young 28-year-old assistant that he was the only basketball coach left on campus. He would have to hold the program together while a new coach was being considered.

"He told me, with no guarantees, that he would hire a new coach and put in a good word for me to stay if I would look after the players. It meant keeping our workout regimen and overseeing the player's class attendance and performance. I stayed very busy, even knowing there was a good chance I would not be retained. It is always the choice of the incoming coach to name his assistants, so I was really at the mercy of whomever Coach Teague chose to replace Dick Campbell," Les explains.

By May of 1971, George Hill was hired. True to his word, Teague lauded the work of the young assistant with four toddler children. Hill retained him strictly on the Athletic Director's recommendation. As Hill was making the physical move to Charleston, Teague called Les back into his office. He felt that he needed to do so because Les had been a candidate for the head-coaching job. Though Teague liked the young and energetic West Virginian, he felt that he was not experienced enough to be named as head coach.

"He started the conversation by saying, 'I gave Coach Hill the job and also gave him my recommendation of hiring you. Now you have something you can give back to Coach Hill—absolute loyalty. To make his job easier, you must always give him your attention, your loyal support, and especially your trust, no matter what,' Teague stated.

The reputation of athletic director Eddie Teague was impeccable. Les gave the insight.

"Teague was a stand-up guy, one who would follow rules and protect the institution constantly. He was ethically centered and would not tolerate even the least infraction. He gave particularly strict orders that each coach commit to memory the rules of the NCAA. He was, perhaps, the cleanest man in college sports."

Hill had taken over the job at The Citadel as a 39-year-old native of Chicago. Two years prior, he sported a record of 0-21 at the Coast Guard Academy. After going 11-13 the following season, he was named their conference's Coach-of-the-Year. Prior to that season, Hill was an assistant coach at Tennessee under Coach Ray Mears.

Les committed each of Eddie Teague's mentoring words as an indelible part of his commitment to be loyal to his new head coach. He would be dedicated to Coach George Hill's program and support him vehemently. Les had no idea that the advocacy advice of such an exemplary man as Teague would test Les's keen judgment over the next three years.

Coach George Hill was not the man Coach Teague apprised him to be in his job interview. He was sometimes devious, sometimes quirky, and at other times inexplicably absent. He stayed out of the way of Athletic Director Teague while doing some things that Les decided he could not witness. He avoided situations he felt could place him in a poor predicament.

Hill came to The Citadel with a bulldog face framed by an imposing crew cut that flattened his head and made him look more the role of a drill sergeant than a game strategist. He had a domineering posture.

In short order he hired another young assistant. The young assistant who had been with him at the Coast Guard Academy over the most recent season likely already knew the George Hill routines. Mike Montgomery wanted to learn the game and build a career. His longish locks were the standard of the era when surfing became popular and hippies were diffusing the worrisome activities halfway across the globe. The Vietnam War was ever-present. Montgomery hailed from Long Beach, California and brought his left coast charm with him. He and Les became fast friends. Les served as first assistant and was maneuvered by Hill to relay all orders. These orders were directed to the team, the managers, and even to Montgomery.

Les was entrusted with the team's recruiting oversight, scheduling, and travel. Montgomery was in charge of practice schedules and workout regimens. They both checked the player's grades and classroom attendance.

Les was given a free hand in practice and sometimes ran practice with Montgomery if the head coach was delayed in places unknown. It was not unusual for Coach Hill not to make practice. He even missed games on the road. He had a secret life that nobody, including the assistant coaches, knew about. Both Les and Mike Montgomery knew enough not to ask.

It was during Hill's first season, 1971-72, that The Citadel was scheduled to open up near Montgomery's Los Angeles area home. The team featured a 6'3" center, Air Force Veteran Student Oscar Scott, The Citadel's first minority basketball player. The leading scorer was junior Steve Fishel, a 5'11" guard. The Bulldogs would travel 2500 miles to become a basketball's buff's trivia answer. They were destined to open UCLA's next great era under Coach Johnny Wooden.

Pauley Pavilion in Westwood hosted a packed house of 12,819 on December 3, 1971. The game would mark the very first UCLA varsity

appearance of two consensus All-Americans, Keith Wilkes and the 6'11"
Bill Walton.

Les had left after The Citadel's disappointing opening game loss to
Campbell College to scout Rice University. Rice was playing the University
of North Carolina in Chapel Hill. The Citadel would play Rice in Houston
on the way back from the UCLA game. Les arrived a day later than the
team at the team shoot-around practice at Pauley Pavilion. Montgomery
approached Les.

"Les, you need to talk to George. I think he's lost it. He wants to start
the second team tonight. He won't listen to me. See if you can't stop him
from doing something stupid." Montgomery pleaded.

Since Montgomery was back in L.A. where he grew up, he did not want
to be embarrassed. He would have many of his friends and family at the
game to see the young coach. Losing the game was a given, but losing respect was not. Montgomery was hoping The Citadel would put up a good
showing against the team picked to be the best in the nation.

Les went to head coach George Hill to see what he was thinking.

"Coach Hill started out, 'They (UCLA) have no idea who we are. I can
start anybody. Anyway, we need to teach our starters something. They lost
at Campbell because they didn't play well enough to win. We need to pun-
ish them. They'll be hungry when I get them into the game.'

"When he told me that, I knew he had made up his mind. So I had
discounted that he was trying to fool the UCLA team. Regardless of who
we started, we were not going to beat them with a 6'3" center," Les recalled.
"I suppose, looking back, he was again doing something quirky to keep everyone guessing. You really could not read the man. You never knew what
he was thinking."

The second string started that Friday night in front of a packed house
at Pauley Pavilion. It was not only Bill Walton's first game but was the first
game of the defending National Champions.

That night, before a screaming torrent of basketball-savvy fans, Coach John Wooden's team awaited introduction while a blue-clad Citadel team sent out surprised sophomore starters Chuck Cordell and Greg Weber along with other stupefied back-ups to play the mighty UCLA Bruins. The Bruins were in the midst of a five-year run as NCAA National Champions. They would win 88 games in a row over the next three seasons. The strategy of Coach George Hill was one of 87 other strategies that did not work. In their record streak, The Citadel was not the only overmatched team they would encounter. The feisty military squad was the Bruins 16th victim in the sport's longest collegiate win streak. The mighty Bruins had won 15 straight the previous season.

"I felt like I would get a few minutes because of some strong practices," sophomore guard Cordell remembered, "but with the senior guards we had returning from the fine year we had the season before with Coach Campbell, I knew I was only going to have a few minutes each game. Me starting against Walton and Wilkes? I thought maybe our seniors had gotten into trouble. I had no idea what Coach Hill's coaching strategy would be. Heck, nobody understood him anyway!"

The UCLA Bruins had taken a 16-0 lead when Coach Hill was able to get a timeout and shock the Bruins with his starters. Though Steve Fishel and Arthur McGriff played as well as could be expected, the Bulldogs went down to the Bruins that evening, 105-49.

Bill Walton scored 19 points and collected 14 rebounds in limited play. Senior Henry Bibby scored 26 points, and 7'0" sophomore Swen Nater came off of the UCLA bench for 16 points. The slick Keith Wilkes scored 12. The George Hill strategy turned out to be a nightmare. But the Bruins would create many more nightmares over the next few years.

Les, remembering the loyalty speech given to him by Coach Teague, never let any conversation with Hill get outside of the locker room. At first, when told of the strategy by Montgomery, he thought the young left-coaster could be humoring him. But as Coach Hill elaborated, Les knew that the tone would be set and he would have to accept and adjust. Often, there is uncommon valor entrenched in a vow of loyalty.

Losing the game was not the most distasteful part of that UCLA trip.

Owing to his West Virginia roots and childhood friendship with the great Jerry West, Les was able to have 25 tickets reserved at the Los Angeles Lakers' Will Call window. The Lakers were playing on Saturday night. Les had gotten permission from Coach Hill to procure the donated tickets. The team would be watching what many considered the greatest team in NBA history. With West and other future Hall-of-Famers Elgin Baylor and Wilt Chamberlain, the Lakers were in the middle of their 33-game winning streak—still the best in major league sports history. West had arranged to provide the impossible-to-buy tickets to The Citadel after visiting Les at the team's summer camp a few months earlier. He was doing the young coach an enormous favor because the Lakers game tickets were among hottest purchases in sports.

"On the way to the next morning's workout, Coach Hill decided that he didn't want the team to enjoy the trip. He told me to call Jerry West back and cancel the tickets. I said, 'Coach, are you sure? Jerry went through a lot of trouble. It's a sellout.' But, again, this was George's quirky way. He had already decided. He did not care what a difficult thing this was for me to do—to call Jerry West and cancel. In fact, I think it was another test of my loyalty to him. I passed that test, but I wished that I had never met George Hill at that time. I was upset at his decision.

"His reasoning was suspect. He said, 'Les, we have to discipline these kids. They got embarrassed last night. We can't reward them by taking them to an NBA game. They'll have to stay at the hotel. Instead, we'll go scout the player I'm looking at from near here,' Coach Hill really had no idea how hard it was to get those Laker tickets. And I doubt that he cared."

The game tickets would be forfeited back to West. Les had to call him.

103

As first assistant, Les made the Basketball Summer Camp and exceptional experience.

Photo courtesy The Citadel.

"It was one of the hardest things I had to do in my whole life. I had to call Jerry and apologize. He asked me 'What's up?' But I had to keep it short and not get into the details—owing to the loyalty speech Coach Teague advocated earlier. I said, 'Coach thinks they need to be taught a lesson' and I left it at that," Les recalls. "Though inside, I knew that it would have been much better for team unity and to build a program had we gone to see the best team in NBA history play that night.

"But Jerry had been to our summer camp in Charleston a few months back as a favor to me personally. Instead of getting upset, Jerry simply said, 'Les, don't give it another thought. I met your coach. This is to be expected from a guy like him.' He made it easy to explain. But I was still very embarrassed by the whole thing.

"To make matters worse," Les tells the story, "we drove out about thirty miles to see this player that Hill thought would come to The Citadel. Even I knew while watching the player that The Citadel had no chance of getting this kid. But George insisted. Sure enough, that kid had no interest and it was eating me alive that night that I had to give those tickets back. The recruiting visit was a sham."

There was a silver lining, however. Les had the opportunity to meet Coach Johnny Wooden the next morning.

"The next morning, a Saturday, the team returned to Pauley Pavilion for a hard practice. Coach Wooden had let The Citadel use the facility in preparation for the Rice game set for Monday night in Houston. Coach Wooden also came by the practice and spoke with the team for fifteen minutes. He spoke about teamwork and attitude. The players were quite impressed," Les noted. "He didn't have to do that. We got that game because Press Maravich scheduled it as a favor to me through the former coach, Dick Campbell. Press was a great influence on basketball around the country. He and Wooden were great friends. I wanted to make sure that I thanked him after he spoke, because I knew that Press had done it to help me."

Afterward Wooden finished speaking, Les introduced himself to the living legend—or as the media called him, "The Wizard of Westwood."

"I approached him after the talk and said, 'Coach, I played and coached for your friend, Press Maravich. I'm Les Robinson. I know he'd want me to tell you hello,'

"Wooden had attended a national coach's clinic each year at Campbell College in Buies Creek, North Carolina. He and Press became friends and would room together each year.

"I knew about Coach Wooden through Coach Maravich. Press spoke reverently of Johnny Wooden. So, I would be remiss if I did not identify myself and connect the dots to why Coach Maravich assisted The Citadel in getting the game scheduled in Pauley Pavilion," Les explained.

"Coach Wooden's eyes lit up. He was genuinely glad to hear about Press. He told me that Coach Maravich was one of the finest game coaches he'd ever met. He spoke highly of his intelligence for the sport. He was impressed that I was one of 'Press's boys,' as he called me. Wooden continued by telling me about some coaching conversations they'd had over a number of years.

"He began to tell one story, but then he put two fingers of his right hand up to his mouth, covering his lips, and added 'But oh! What language he uses!' I knew that Coach Maravich used edgy words from a rough childhood in Aliquippa. Coach Wooden was evidently startled by his colorful language."

Les knew the "expletive story" from Press Maravich's viewpoint.

"Press Maravich never held back a few choice words here and there around anybody," Les retold. "It was part of his way from a hardened background in Pennsylvania and on into the military.

"Coach Wooden said that every time any coach said a curse word at the Buies Creek coach's clinic, the offender would have to throw a quarter in a jar. Coach Wooden told me that Press almost filled the entire quarter jar by himself."

Les's prize recruit in the sophomore class, Chuck Cordell, remembered the John Wooden visit to The Citadel team for other reasons.

"Coach Wooden spoke about fundamentals and work ethic, and then opened up for questions we might have. I thought that going to UCLA was for top players and wondered how many homes he actually visited to get players. I was stunned when he said he'd only been into five homes. He named the players and they included Lew Alcindor (Kareem Abdul Jabbar).

"Because I knew of Henry Bibby from Franklinton, NC, and had guarded him in the game the night before, I asked Coach Wooden how he got Bibby to come to UCLA. He told me that Bibby's aunt wrote a strong letter. He sent an assistant to see Bibby play and then signed him when the assistant recommended it. After our practice, Bibby came into the locker room and asked for me. We were both first team all-state players from North Carolina two years earlier. We had a chat and a few laughs.

"Coach Wooden was everything we read about years later. He was a soft-spoken gentleman who never even left his seat on the bench. Henry Bibby told me that he never raised his voice. We had the other end of the spectrum in Coach Hill."

After leaving Los Angeles and getting beat by Rice to start the season 0-3, Coach Hill intimated doom to Les.

"He said, 'this team will not likely win a game this year.' I was genuinely surprised at George's comment as I felt that the team could be pretty good. It wasn't the time to panic. We played two decent teams around the best team in America," Les stated. "We had some talent and there was a good chance we could improve. Playing those first three games—all on the road—helped us."

"Coach Dick Campbell left George a good club. Hill could have won 17 games with that team, but instead we lost several close contests. We won 12 and lost 13 that first year.Several close games were lost by a lack of game strategy in the closing minutes. Some were by a poor substitution pattern, others by holding the ball with a slim lead, and others by employing the wrong defense for the situation," Les explains.

There was a half-dozen games that might have had different outcomes had the team been coached, by any standard, just a little better. It was only when Les persisted in suggesting alternate end-of-game strategies that he found out how deeply strategic his coach really was.

"Coach Hill finally told me about his career philosophy. It was clear that he wanted to gain personal accolades at the expense of the team. He said, 'Les, this is our first year here. To be Coach-of-the-Year next year, you have to show improvement. If we win ten this year and maybe sixteen next year, there's a good chance I'll get the award. We have a free pass this year. Nobody really cares if we win or not. It's next year that counts.' It was then that I understood some of the poor decisions he made at the end of games."

George Hill did not register in the Coach-of-the-Year voting when The Citadel finished 11-15 the next season. When 1973-74 season ended with a 10-14 record coupled with several other internal problems that involved Hill, Athletic Director Eddie Teague decided to take action. But he did not do so until the following school year had started. George Hill was fired on September 23, 1974.

Les details the three-year experience. "I can't say that George did illegal things that I saw and didn't report or that anything he did was an NCAA violation. He was cagey and street-wise, but also secretive and strategic. He knew how to make extra income, as well. But I stayed away from that side scheme, knowing it was legal, but would not be looked upon favorably by Coach Teague."

Coaching The Citadel basketball seemed to be something George Hill did on the side. He had myriad other interests.

After one practice in the fall of his second year, Hill decided that he would send a few commands out through Les. One of his disjointed thoughts was that Mike Montgomery should look more like a cadet than a West Coast surfer. He told Les to carry the message to an unsuspecting Montgomery to get a haircut that day. He dutifully relayed the message, knowing Montgomery would not likely part with his trendy locks. Montgomery rightfully noted that his chosen hairstyle was not part of Hill's oversight. Hill then exercised his option. He fired Montgomery. The head coach who had two of the NCAA's future coaching icons on his staff, dismissed one on the basis of his hairstyle. He then hired a young man with a similar haircut, Butch Estes. He never asked Estes, a graduate of the University of North Carolina, to cut his hair.

"To be fair to Mike," Les detailed, "I knew that Coach Hill was not messing around. I cautioned him that from what I could see was that Hill was quirky, yes, but also inflexible. I suggested that he trim it, even if it's just enough to get by. But Mike might have momentarily thought Hill to be reasonable! He was far from it. That Jerry West ticket situation with the Lakers in LA told us both that Hill was not a reasonable person."

Mike Montgomery's hair went with him to other opportunities, eventually to Stanford University. He won 393 games with the Cardinal and earned post-season tournament appearances in sixteen of his eighteen seasons. After coaching in the NBA, he returned to the PAC 10 as head coach at the University of California.Montgomery had a career record of 676-318 including an astonishing record of 27 winning seasons in his 28 years as a head coach. Montgomery proved to be one of the elite coaches in America. In retrospect, Hill may have inadvertently masterminded the major turning point in Montgomery's career by the simple act of getting him away from the wackiness that was George Hill.

Conversely, The Citadel had never been to a post-season basketball tournament until its lone appearance in the 2009 CollegeInsider.com tournament. They remain one of the four original NCAA programs to have never played in the NCAA tournament.

Les's first game as a substitute head coach was part of another George Hill operation that he did not want to know the details. The Citadel traveled to Chattanooga, Tennessee, to play the previous year's NAIA National Champions. The Moccasin team had most of that roster back. Les flew with the team the day before into Chattanooga. Hill stayed back with new assistant Butch Estes.

"We were decent, but our undersized Bulldogs would not likely upset the Mocs. Hill said he had a back injury, telling me he would come with Estes the next day. When I picked up Estes at the airport, Hill was not with him," Les chronicled.

"Where's George?" Les asked Estes.

"Butch said something like, 'He told me to tell you that you got this one. He says his back is out. He will not be coming. But, I don't think he wants anyone to know that he's not here, and that you would understand what his instructions are.'

"I said, 'Butch, the radio will know. The postgame show will know. I guess he's hoping that someone doesn't listen to the broadcast.'"

The very athletic Chattanooga Moccasins crushed the Bulldogs that night, 95-72. In Chattanooga, the Moccasin basketball program is the major local sports story. They have a solid following. A postgame press conference was a courtesy and part of the coaching responsibility. Les obliged the media and gave praise to the Chattanooga coaches and their fine athletes while lamenting the poor shooting performance of the Bulldogs.

"One of the reporters at the postgame conference, not phrasing the question as he should have, asked me, 'Coach, where was the first team coach tonight?'

"I couldn't resist and answered, 'Why, he's back home in Charleston with the first team.' The room broke out in laughter."

The remark made it into *Sports Illustrated's* popular 'They Said It' section the following month.

"Maybe whoever George didn't want to know about the Chattanooga game absence did not get *Sports Illustrated*, either," Les said. "George never said anything to me about the post-game remarks."

Les was used to the George Hill routines. He had a sense of where he was, but never asked. Loyalty required him to be detached.

"You never really knew where George was unless it was Saturday night at 10:00. Then you knew he was watching *Mission Impossible*. Otherwise, the coaches, the Athletic Director, his family, the players never knew where he was."

Les detailed another example of Teague's rules and Hill's responses.

"Once, when the NCAA sent out a new memo that you could have no contact in the gym with players before October 15, Teague called the basketball staff into his office. Teague began by reading the memo and then looked at George. He said, 'that means that you cannot walk from the front of the gym to the basketball offices when players are out there working out on their own or shooting foul shots or studying for a test. You have to go out the front door and into the side door. Understood?'

"George had to test him. He asked, 'What if it's raining, Coach?'

"And Teague jumped all over him. 'Then use your damn umbrella.' From that point on, George stayed away from Teague and did everything he did as if he were a part of a slick spy network," Les recalled. "Teague was trusting a fox inside the chicken coup. I saw where it was going but was sworn to stay quiet. I did even better. I stayed focused on my job and out any other potential conflict."

Hill ended the 1973-1974 home schedule with an embarrassing loss to Division II Madison College—a team that did not give athletic scholarships. But because he had a year left on his contract, that embarrassing loss still wasn't enough to dismiss Hill. It took several non-basketball antics from Hill to merit that result.

"What I remember about that last game George coached at home was that—for a change—we had superior athletes. But because George read somewhere that this team liked to push it up and down, and because we were a control tempo club, George wanted to hold the ball," Les offered.

"It was his show. You couldn't argue with George because he had an ego about things. It's the same reason we couldn't talk him out of some of the ten-dozen crazy decisions he'd made over the three seasons he coached there. Now he wanted to get into a possession game with a team we could clearly overpower with talent. We were 30 points better when the ball went up."

Coach Hill got his way. The Citadel controlled the tempo against a decidedly inferior team. His Bulldogs lost the game slowly, 43-41.

"I remember thinking that we had three senior starters that had played as George ordered—Chuck Cordell, Greg Weber, and Arthur McGriff. All three were the types of young men you would want to have as a son. I felt terrible about how their careers ended. But George didn't seem to have any concern at all about the players. That was a sad side to his personal aspirations," Les concluded.

Chuck Cordell ended his career as the finest free throw percentage player in Citadel history. The locker room complex was named for him in 2011. Arthur McGriff was the first minority basketball player ever to start at The Citadel. An Air Force Veteran, McGriff passed away in 2011. Greg Weber built an admirable career as a minister and educator.

Cordell, who was enshrined into The Citadel Athletic Hall of Fame in 2010, recalls one of the incidents that decimated Hill's coaching career with both he and other players.

"Coach Hill wanted to be recognized for something within the statistics of the conference—so the only thing he could come up with was best defensive coach. That's why he had us hold the ball. We could be ten points down with five minutes left and we would still be holding the ball just to keep the other team from scoring more points. That was his strategy for the whole game—to slow everything down so the other team couldn't score a big number on us. That would have been an acceptable strategy if we had a team of poor shooters and limited offensive skills. It was a terrible plan given that we had enough talent and scorers on our team to beat many of these teams that liked to run. The one thing we had in our favor was that we were always in better shape than the other team no matter who they were. We ran hard at practice. But we just stood around and held the ball because of his strategy. Looking back, it was not a good choice for this team."

Cordell was also named as an All-Southeast Region baseball player and was named to the Honorable Mention category as an All American first baseman. He served as the basketball team captain.

"He blamed me for a last second loss to Tulane at home because I wasn't guarding the guy who was throwing the ball in from out-of-bounds closely enough," Cordell recalled. "I couldn't cross the inbounds line. He looked to blame the close loss on someone. He accosted me outside of the locker room in front of the whole team. Of course, I made mistakes in every game, but I did nothing that was on the order of what he was yelling about."

Cordell continued. "Subsequently, he introduced a "20 pushup rule" at the next practice. When he blew the whistle, the person who was last to get into the huddle— wherever he was standing on those three courts during practice—had to drop and give him the twenty military push-ups. That rule was because of my not guarding the out-of-bounds Tulane player close enough and he was teaching us a lesson.

"I felt it was my fault he was invoking this rule for the rest of the season. It is obvious the last guy in the huddle is whoever is farthest from the huddle at the time he blew the whistle. So, as team captain, I started just dropping down for twenty pushups wherever I was standing so that no one else would have to do those negative-reinforcement punishments. That really pissed him off.But at that point I had all I could take of him and he knew it. I still started every game and played hard for the school and for my teammates. Thank God we had Coach Rob there, and that kept us together.

But the activities outside of basketball would catch up with George Hill.

"Whatever information Coach Teague found out later on, it was going to spell doom for George. One day, it caught up. The school year had already started. But Coach Teague couldn't find him to fire him. George must've known what was happening," Les recalls.

"Even when Coach Teague was trying to call him at George's home on campus, George would only answer the phone as if the he was a tape recorder. He did so until he found out who was calling. He kept his floor whistle by the phone at his house. It was an ingenious way to screen calls; and he pulled it off. I called him there one day towards the end when he was hiding out. The phone was answered, 'This is Coach Hill. I am not available to answer your call, but please leave your number and a short message at the whistle.' Then he would blow the whistle live. He had no recording device. It was him—live and listening in. This was his way of screening calls.

"Once you started a message, he would interrupt if he wanted to talk to you. He'd say, 'Oh, Les, it's you. What's up?'"

He knew that I was loyal. Despite everything, I made up my mind to stay quiet and do my job," Les repeated.

As Eddie Teague began by finding one incident, others started coming into his review. When he finally fired Hill, the timing was well outside of the normal cycle for hires and fires. Though Les had ideas about why Hill was finally fired, he never asked or was told of the details.

Teague knew exactly what should happen next. He called in Les. It was on September 23, 1974, the same day as Les's 32nd birthday. Teague initially had the intention of grilling Les about Hill's activities. He wanted to know what Les knew.

"I remember sitting there wondering where this conversation was going to go. Was I going to be fired, too? Or maybe I was going to be an interim coach," Les remembers the day.

"He started very seriously. 'Les, did you know about the subscription mailings and the basketball scouting service' Coach Hill was running out of his office?' Teague showed a lot of frustration on his face" Les recalled.

"I said, 'Yeah, Coach, I knew about it, but I was not a part of it.'

"He followed up with 'Did you know about this situation, that one, etc.?'

"I thought for a moment before answering. I knew that I needed to avoid that situation entirely. So I was not around George for the things he did that made Coach Teague angry. It was a lot like when those seniors were point-shaving games my freshman year at NC State. I needed to distance myself. I knew that I needed to tell Coach Teague everything I knew that I could answer truthfully. Other than not coming forward to snitch on George, I had done nothing wrong," Les recounts.

"I answered, 'Coach I knew about this or that, but not a few others. I thought it was none of my business.'

"He hit me with the next questions about stuff he had discovered. 'Did you know about what he did in Chattanooga, the deal down in Florida, or the other stuff over at the infirmary?'

"I said, 'Coach, I may have known about half of the things that Coach Hill did, if that. I know less than you or anyone might think. He was very secretive. And I knew I shouldn't get involved for my own good.'

"This is when Coach Teague raised his voice in the realization that all of this was going on and he felt betrayed because he knew nothing. The whole George Hill situation went south and Teague was livid.

"He shot back, 'But Les, why the hell didn't you come to me and let me know of the stuff you did know. You knew it wasn't something he should've been doing, didn't you?'

"I knew this would come down to what I had to say to him one day. So, I answered, 'Yes coach. If you're asking me if I thought it was not right and not ethical or even not legal—I got as far away from it as I could. I didn't want to know, and I never asked because I was afraid of the answer. I had a sense that much of it was not right.

'But you remember when you hired him, and you called me into your office three years ago? You lectured to me about how important it was not to question his authority and to be loyal. I never forgot that. I gave him 100% of my loyalty because you told me that was the most important thing I could do to prove myself as a future head coach. Coach, I did nothing wrong throughout all of this and I did my best to be loyal while being careful to avoid all the stuff I thought would cause me not to be loyal.'

"My summary to Coach Teague caught him a little off guard," Les recalls.

"There was a pause. Teague stared away for a moment. It was as if he didn't know how to respond. His unequivocal integrity was an example to us all. But he was temporarily stunned by the sage advice he had given to me as it was now a liability to the program and to the reputation he built at The Citadel," Les reasoned.

"He broke the long pause by saying, 'Les, when I told you to be loyal I didn't expect that you to be that damn loyal! Now you're the new head coach. Straighten all this crap out and get our program back on track.'

"He followed those words with 'And this time, let me know if anything comes up that may not be right. You're in charge, dammit.'

"It was probably the most unique hiring of a new basketball coach imaginable. But that's how it happened. I was not congratulated but dismissed from his office. I walked back to Hill's office to move my stuff and to call Barbara because she was sitting on pins and needles. We hadn't talked about a contract or years or a press release or anything. But he did not say 'interim coach.' He said, 'head coach.' That was the best gift I could have received on my 32ⁿᵈ birthday, no matter how it came down."

Hill moved on to coach at the lower levels of the sport for the remainder of his career from 1974. He coached at Oklahoma Panhandle College and Rogers State College before retiring in 1999. He even wrote a pamphlet-sized book, *The Season,* which followed a fictitious season of a small college basketball team. True to form, the only picture in the book is the cover photo of Hill barking orders from the sideline, supposedly at this small college team. There is a small inconsistency. The photo shows Coach Hill in action on the sidelines at McAlister Fieldhouse. The players behind him on the bench are his last Citadel team. George Hill was a peculiar and eccentric character, unforgettable is so many ways, and quite forgettable in others. He died at the age of 78 in 2009.

It's the George Hill stories that Les did know about but was commanded to repress that became the basis for his many entertaining insights to the foibles of coaching college basketball.

Les attended Leon Hillard's funeral in Chicago.
Photo courtesy of Robinson family archives.

CHAPTER 12
HARLEM GLOBETROTTER LEON HILLARD

Basketball aficionados may remember the great Leon Hillard, the dribbling superstar who took over as player-coach for the Harlem Globetrotters in the late 1960's. Hillard was a performer who endeared himself to audiences across the world. He made his home in Chicago.

Les had met several of the Harlem Globetrotters during his basketball coaching career. He was invited to go to a high school-player-camp in Chicago by a Citadel alumnus. Howard Alton had convinced Les that there would be outstanding talent in Chicago—a city with great recruiting potential. Alton, from The Citadel Class of 1959, had informed Les that it was an inner-city basketball camp that would have plenty of talent.

"I remembered what the great Al McGuire had said about 'finding talent where there was no grass in the front yard.' I made the trip. The camp finale was to feature a Saturday session with the former Globetrotter, Leon Hillard. I did not know when I arrived at the camp that Hillard had been tragically shot and killed earlier in the week," Les reports. "It was a stunning news story."

Earlier, when Les reached the Chicago area he contacted Alton so that he could make introductions and they could attend the camp together. Not remembering which Globetrotter was featured at the camp, he was surprised to learn of the tragedy in the phone conversation with Alton.

"Howard Alton thought it was a good idea to attend the memorial service and funeral. I had never met Hillard and felt that it might be awkward or disingenuous to just show up at the services. But Howard persisted.

We went to the Pilgrim Street Baptist Church and then to the Burr Oak Cemetery. It was in the spring of 1977.

"He told me that, as a college coach, the family would be honored to have me attend and pay my respects," Les retold. "I was there to look at some of the players from the camp and had not planned on being asked to attend a funeral. I felt that, since I was in Chicago and was asked, it would be the right thing to do. I thought of what my mother would expect me to do. I put on my best coat and tie and we headed to the memorial service. Other members of the Harlem Globetrotters came to serve as his pallbearers. I had not anticipated seeing such an outpouring of sympathy and respect. I was very impressed by it all. Leon Hillard must have been universally loved."

Hillard was young, only 45. As a long-term Globetrotter, he had appeared before Queen Elizabeth II and Pope John XXIII as part of the Globetrotter's very entertaining basketball troupe.

His dribbling exhibition was usually done while threading through defenders. He kept the ball low to the ground and ended the exhibition with a deft no-look pass to a breaking teammate for an easy basket. The other star players especially loved Hillard. By what was considered a great honor, Hillard became the first man to coach the team after the legendary Abe Saperstein died. His was a name and face that rivaled the familiarity of the greatest Globetrotters of later years—Meadowlark Lemon, Goose Tatum, and Curly Neal. But his life was cut short.

Les described the experience. "I guess I didn't ask the question others would have asked before going to a visitation and funeral on short notice. I should have asked 'What happened?' I only knew the generality that he had been shot. Once we arrived, I was overly impressed by the show of affection and love for Hillard. The sincere emotions of the moment were quite evident. There were many in tears. I noted that the lady nearest to the casket was most visibly shaken. I assumed it was his wife. And it was."

Les felt compelled to work his way up in the line to the front and pay his personal respects to Mrs. Hillard. Accompanied by Howard Alton, he edged closer. As he got nearer, he noted the nearly uncontrollable agony of Hillard's wife. He turned to Alton, concerned that they would be out of place interrupting her.

"I thought she was so emotionally wrecked that we should not disturb her. I whispered to Alton, 'Boy, she is really broken up.'

"He immediately answered, 'Yeah, she should be. She shot him.'

"What Howard Alton didn't know was that I had no idea that this was a domestic case," Les stated, quite surprised by the untimely revelation. "Now, I had to think about it hopefully being accidental."

Les remembered his reasoning.

"Prior to the service, I had assumed Hillard had fallen victim to some sort of street violence. I had just found out that the person I was a few seconds away from paying my respects to had actually fired the weapon. This was a puzzling and uncomfortable turn of events—and at precisely the wrong timing. But I adjusted to the situation quickly.

"Now we were standing right in front of Hillard's wife. What do you say? I just found out that she was the one that pulled the trigger. I fumbled a few words.

"At funerals, you never quite know what to say. So I said something really stupid because I was there suddenly in front of his wife and just learned the facts. I said, 'He's in a better place.' She was so emotional that I don't think she heard me—and then we moved away," Les recalled.

"When I told Barbara what happened, she nearly fell down. She said, 'Les, that was the worst thing you could've said.' She was right. I spoke low, so she probably didn't know what a dummy I was."

The newspaper account of the story gave the details. Hillard had recently retired from the Globetrotters and had opened a small food business in Chicago. A week earlier Hillard had come to his home after he and his wife had visited an attorney with plans to separate and divorce. He called her at their home and came there later that day. She left their apartment abruptly to go downstairs in the building where her mother lived. Hillard came after her and kicked in the door. Mrs. Hillard shot him immediately. The police closed the case as justifiable homicide. Incredibly, Mrs. Hillard had been charged with aggravated battery the month prior for shooting another woman, reportedly Hillard's girlfriend. That trial was pending at the time of Hillard's death. Eventually, charges were dropped.

"I had no idea that this great entertainer and ambassador for basketball had been shot by his wife—and that I was accidentally at the funeral," Les related. "All in all, it was a tragedy for the basketball world and especially the Hillard family. Looking back, I had not fully understood the circumstances of the funeral and visitation. And, as it turned out, who's to say that Leon Hillard may have ended in a better place."

Jerry West has been a key contributor to Les's playing and coaching career.
West's personal mentorship was Les's inspiration to practice every aspect of the game.
Photo courtesy Robinson family archives.

CHAPTER 13

JERRY WEST, THE LOGO

The great Jerry West came to The Citadel in 1969 in the immediate aftermath of the NBA finals to make a pre-arranged appearance at Les's summer basketball camp. Les had served as an assistant coach in his first year of Division 1 basketball under the tutelage of Coach Dick Campbell. Getting West to come to Charleston, SC, was a coup for Les and enhanced the attendance at the summer camp swell. West came as a personal favor. He liked Les and thought highly of his father, Inky.

Never a drinker, West still agreed to meet Les at the Round Holiday Inn across the Ashley River from The Citadel campus to sip a beer. There, at the top floor bar and restaurant, West spoke about the disappointment of the 1969 basketball season, the first full season with Wilt Chamberlain at the center position. Chamberlain was a key piece to the Los Angeles Laker hopes.

West, Chamberlain, and Elgin Baylor had rolled into the championship by posting one of the best seasons in NBA history. Meanwhile, the aging Boston Celtics finished fourth in the NBA Eastern Division, but shocked both the New York Knicks and the Philadelphia 76ers to reach the finals. It was game on. And like they had done in every series final of the 1960's, the Celtics prevailed. They won in seven games. The deciding game was won as Chamberlain with painful knees sat on the sidelines over the final six minutes. With the behemoth 7'1" Chamberlain missing from the floor, West's first NBA title slipped away.It was down the stretch that West tried to carry the Lakers on his back. In doing so, West became the only player in history to be named NBA Finals MVP despite playing on the losing team. His competitive fire controlled his every emotion.

Les's meeting with West with the panorama of the Holy City as a backdrop was a result of the ease and comfort of their common West Virginia background. West's association with the Robinson family began at Inky Robinson's popular tournament in the spring of 1959. 'Zeke from Cabin Creek' stayed in touch with Les and found the time to visit on several occasions over his career. He came from L.A. to The Citadel because of the friendship. He met Les for a beer, but more importantly to exorcise a demon.

"He said, 'Les, that series took a lot out of me. My insides are still raw. I can't get over it. To lose with that team we had and that season we produced is unacceptable,' he started to say.

"I responded, 'You gave it 100% and you had an unlucky break with Wilt's knees at just the wrong time. There's nothing that you could have done more to change the outcome.'"

Les's remarks were anything but conciliatory. He knew the famed West mindset. West was the fiercest competitor he had ever known, and the sport of basketball breeds an abundance of that ilk. West was perched atop that list.

"He continued to tell me how he felt. 'Les. I've been here before. It takes me so much time to get over these things and move on,' He continued, not even hearing my compliment about his effort. He said, 'I just wish I could be dead for two weeks.'

"He was referring to the usual time it took him to get over things like that," Les implied. "And you know, he had a lot of those memories from those wars with Boston. That's what made him among the very best to ever play the game."

West had an abundance of NBA accolades. The NBA emblem *is* Jerry West. It's the silhouette on every jersey from the Minnesota Timberwolves to the Phoenix Suns. It is trademarked to clothing, headwear, and even shoes across the national and international culture of basketball. West's competitiveness did get a payday in 1972, when the Lakers won it all. West was the league MVP and he won the NBA All-star Game MVP that year, as well.

Later, West became General Manager of a Laker franchise that won seven more NBA championships. West was a 14-year NBA All-Star selection who retired with 25,192 points, the second most ever in the NBA at the time. That 1971-72 Laker team won an NBA record 33 straight games in route to 69 wins that season. The 69 wins remained the NBA record until Michael Jordan and the Chicago Bulls broke it in 1996.

An admitted perfectionist, West was not content with anything short of the championship trophy throughout his legendary career. His desire for that perfection and winning every time was described by Les as being the basis for everything else in his life.

"One story I knew had a tie in to Tubby Smith, one of the great NCAA coaches who won the 1998 NCAA championship at Kentucky," Les noted. "The coaches and players were at a charity golf event when Tubby was paired up with West. West has been lauded as a fine golfer who took the sport seriously, much as he did basketball. Tubby Smith, meanwhile, loved the enjoyment of the sport and the chance to play with legends like Jerry West. Over the first three holes, Tubby watched as Jerry hit fairways and approach shots with what Tubby felt were very good results. Tubby would tell Jerry 'nice shot' after nearly every swing. On the fourth hole, Jerry hit a shot onto the green and, as expected, Tubby blurted out 'good shot Jerry!'

"The part of intense competitiveness that Tubby likely did not know about Jerry was that he expected perfection in everything he did. What was good in Tubby's eyes was not to the level Jerry expected of himself. A shot on the green might not have been close enough to the hole by Jerry's self-imposed standards," Les explained.

"After the shot and Tubby's verbal admiration of Jerry's golf skill, Jerry turned to Tubby and replied, 'Can you just shut up about the good shots. I'm playing like a dog!'" Les retold.

"Well, that's Jerry's way. He cannot accept anything, even compliments from others without grading himself to an impossible scale. Tubby had no idea what made Jerry tick. It's perfection and winning. It wasn't a good shot unless it went in!"

"It seemed that everybody in Charleston, West Virginia, knew Jerry West. He might as well have been governor," Les explained. "He put the Mountaineer State on the map. He may be the most recognized celebrity that ever came out of the state."

Former Georgia and UCLA coach Jim Harrick recalls when Les, a kid just out of St. Albans High School, was indoctrinated. Harrick played his college ball at nearby Morris Harvey College.

"We were in the Charleston Tournament," Harrick recalled. "Teams included the great players of the day from top college seniors to established NBA stars. Les was a 'throw in' player on my team, but because of his youth, was not expected to play much. His Dad, Inky Robinson, kept everything simple by giving us single-digit jersey numbers from 1 to 8. Les was on his way to NC State on a basketball scholarship. As the game against Jerry West's team progressed into the second half, the other guard playing with us twisted his ankle. The game was stopped, and we got the guy from the floor to the bench. Les had to go in.I had been trying to cover Jerry West, but that was something nobody in the entire world of basketball knew how to do. When Les came in wide-eyed and asked me what number he should cover, I saw my chance. I quickly answered, 'You've got number 4.' Of course, #4 was the great Jerry West. Les has never quite forgiven me for pulling that switch on him. You can't imagine how overmatched any high school kid would have been back then.West had a field day and Les has a pretty funny memory."

Les remembered, too.

"The trouble was that all of my friends from school were there to see 'Zeke from Cabin Creek.' They sure weren't there to see me. I got torched over the next few minutes, and those friends of mine reminded me for years just how badly I played. But the truth is—there were no two people in the country that could stop Jerry West from scoring at will—even with a double-team."

Les spoke about Jerry West and the relationship he had with West Virginia's earlier basketball phenom, Rod Hundley.

"Hot Rod Hundley was taken as a first round draft choice by the Minneapolis Lakers. The Lakers moved to Los Angeles in 1960—Jerry West's first season in the pros. But when Hundley was a senior at West Virginia in 1957, there was a story about him walking up to the Mountaineer freshman Jerry West in the WVU Field House. West was young and introverted, but everyone there, including Hundley, knew that he was special. By contrast, Hundley was very outgoing and liked to show off in front of others. He walked up to Jerry West, put his arm around him, and said to him, 'Jerr, look around. See this place. I'm making the payments.' Now Hundley was a big star, and everyone knew that he was just bragging like he always did. But West took it to heart. He didn't say anything back.

"In the spring of 1960, three years after this exchange with Hundley and West, I'm sitting on the bench as a towel boy for the McJunkin Corporation team that Jerry West is playing on. It was during my dad's last tournament in St. Alban's before they moved it to the Charleston Civic Center. I looked at both Hundley and West as really big celebrities. They were very different people. Hundley was boisterous, and West was quiet.

"Pros could not play in the tournament then, but Hundley had called my dad to ask if he could come and do the PA from the scorer's desk. He was coming because Jerry West and Oscar Robertson were in the tournament.

"Something happened with Hundley's travel schedule and he showed up to the game just before halftime. But just when he got there, Jerry West saw him and walked over during a break to speak to him. I was right there listening.

"Jerry asked Hundley, 'You remember what you told me about making the payments on the WVU Field House a few years ago?' Hundley nods to him and says 'Yes.' And Jerry said, 'Yeah, well, it's now paid in full!'

"Others heard it but didn't know the background story. Jerry was saying, 'I did you one better.' And Jerry West did pay for that WVU Field House many times over.

"Of course, I knew Jerry West back then, and he had been my hero since he showed up at my back yard in 1959 to work with me on basketball moves. Seeing him 'one-up' Hot Rod Hundley was unlike his personality, but something I never forgot."

The West Virginia bond with Les's father made the great NBA star Les's life-long friend. Les stayed in touch throughout West's amazing basketball career.

Les relates. "I could never thank Jerry enough for reaching out to help a little bratty kid from St. Albans. He did more for me over my career than I can ever possibly repay."

Les became the first coach in the history of Citadel basketball to win twenty games in a season, finishing 20-7. Captain Rick Swing (R) was drafted by the Cleveland Cavaliers.

CHAPTER 14

THE CITADEL CHALLENGE

As would happen later in his career, Les consistently entered into a situation of duress to assuage a controversy, a calamity, or a collapse. He was a D-1 coach. The fifth-grade essay he wrote came to fruition.

Once Les took over, he re-assessed his team. He had one of the finest players ever to sign with The Citadel, Rodney McKeever, as a rising sophomore. He had a fundamentally sound center in rising junior Richard Johnson.He had a young group coming along that could be good. The recruiting was solid. An unknown bonus was that the team would be relieved that George Hill was no longer the head coach. Les knew that the team was resistive to Hill's strategies. Nobody understood him. Other players—Rick Barger, Mike Ange, Ricky Day, Don "Beaver" Server, and John Rodgers—were very young. There was a chance to build something.

Les had personally recruited McKeever the year before. McKeever was a lightning-quick point guard who could excite a crowd and bring the house down with deft passes and electric ball handling. He averaged 23 points a game the following season and was named the Southern Conference Player of the Year.

McKeever came to The Citadel under-the-radar from local Garrett High School. The reason he stayed undiscovered by the bigger colleges was simple. His name was Rodney Edwards his junior year in high school and Rodney McKeever during his senior season. With so much military in Charleston, the bigger colleges likely assumed that his parents were transferred out. It was just the opposite. Rodney's father got transferred in.

McKeever had divorced parents. His mother, Mrs. Edwards, had some setbacks and his father, an Air Force Master Sergeant, took Rodney in. Before he began his senior year at Garrett, the talented player took his father's name. His father lived on James Island, but Rodney wanted to finish high school at Garrett High where his circle of friends attended.

Les loved telling the McKeever story as his best recruiting tale.

"Coach Alan LeForce at the College of Charleston was recruiting Rodney. He knew what I knew about the name change. Coach LeForce and I were great friends and had gotten into the habit of meeting during the off-season every so often for a beer and a few laughs. We both had a sense of urgency in getting the McKeever signature on a grant-in-aid. We both realized that the big colleges like Clemson and Georgia were on this special player but had lost touch because of the surname and address change. To further complicate matters, his mother—Mrs. Edwards had moved away. Rodney, with the new name, had moved into his father's home on James Island. So, this program-changing guard was going to likely stay in Charleston—which his father preferred—and was going to play for one team or the other. I knew that his father liked the structure Rodney could get at The Citadel," Les retold. "I didn't have to sell him. But I had to sell Rodney."

Although their one-on-one competition to sign McKeever was fierce, the LeForce-Robinson friendship was not impaired. The friendship became legendary. It had to be in order to survive the stunt Les pulled during the spring recruiting season of 1973. George Hill was still at The Citadel and had left the bulk of the player recruiting up to Les. Les knew that McKeever could play at virtually any college in America, so he was careful in the process.

"Alan and I would meet regularly away from the peninsula for a beer and to talk about basketball. Sometimes we'd meet over in Mt. Pleasant, on one of the islands, in North Charleston, or over at James Island," Les recalled. "On this particular day I was in my office at The Citadel and had called Rodney to arrange a campus visit. He didn't have transportation, so I needed to pick him up. We had pre-arranged a time at 3:00. So, after confirming with Rodney, I called Alan LeForce," Les smiled.

"When I got LeForce by phone, I just said, 'Alan, do you know that bar at the corner of Camp Road and Folly Road?' He said yes and mentioned it by name. I said that I'd be there by 3:15 and that I wanted him to wait outside because I had a surprise. I asked him that if he got there early to be sure to wait outside. He confirmed that he'd see me there.

"So, I picked up Rodney from around the corner at about 3:00, checking my watch to make sure I timed getting back by the bar on Folly Road at 3:15. There was a stop light at the corner. I planned to drive at a speed that would have me catch the light. The timing was perfect. I caught the light as the very first car. I looked over and there was Coach LeForce standing at the front door of the bar. I blew my horn and waved vigorously at Alan. He waved back, looking puzzled. He saw Rodney in the passenger seat. As the light changed I took Rodney on down to The Citadel where I called back to the bar to tell Alan I couldn't make it today because I had Rodney."

"He understood, and said, 'Maybe next time,'" Les continued with a grin.

"What he didn't know was the story I told Rodney when I stopped and waved at that stoplight. I said to Rodney that 'Coach LeForce was really a great guy and that he was trying so hard to fight a demon. But it looks like he has taken a step back. It was a bad sign to see him going into a bar in the middle of the afternoon and that I hoped he could overcome his problem. I'm sure he was standing out there wrestling his conscience whether or not to go in. It's really sad. I feel for his family.'"

"I came clean and told Alan that story later—after I had signed Rodney at The Citadel," Les concluded. "That was maybe my greatest recruiting victory, all that much better because of how it even made my main competition laugh at the incident.

"Having Rodney McKeever made it possible to beat better competition on our good nights. He was an amazing talent for the Southern Conference.

In the McKeever case, with the surname change and McKeever's move to his father's home, Les became a mentor to the Garrett High School star. Averaging 23 points a game as a sophomore was even more impressive when that number came from a team with a motion offense and the predisposition to slow the tempo.But McKeever was that one special player rarely seen at a level like The Citadel's.

Richard Johnson was his teammate.

"My senior year we played up at Furman in the Greenville Memorial Auditorium. Rodney had a very hard class schedule and couldn't miss an important afternoon class that day as the bus was leaving.One of the assistant coaches stayed behind to wait for Rodney's class to end while the rest of us went up to have a walk-through and shoot-around. The assistant coach drove him up. They got into the gym a half hour before the game. Rodney went out and warmed up and came back into the locker room and asked if he could get something to eat. The game was about to start. As Les started to chastise Rodney, he quickly told him that they left in a rush and he didn't have time to stop and get something to eat. So, Les sent a manager out to get Rodney food—anything. Rodney forced down two chilidogs and a Pepsi just before we went out to play. All he did after that was torch Furman for forty points that night.

"After the game, Les changed his whole philosophy about team meals and carbon loading, eating pastas, or high protein. Rodney had two chilidogs minutes before the ball went up and was unstoppable."

Johnson further explained how the talent gap may have further hurt the lightning quick McKeever.

"We were a slow bunch of guys playing with an NBA prospect. When Rodney would penetrate the lane, he had this unique ability to hang in midair and make a play. He had a unbelievable vertical leap at 5'11." But once he got into the lane, we would be more likely turn to the basket for a rebound instead of looking for the last second dish off. Instead of Rodney getting credit for an easy assist, he'd end up with a turnover. He was so much better than the rest of us that it actually hurt his statistics."

Having Rodney for his first two years, Les felt that he could build a tremendous program. Every team in the conference wished they had such a player. But with Rodney's sudden departure, Les would need to rebuild a new team to try and reach the top. He had some unusual experiences at The Citadel related to the crucible of competition in that pursuit.

In Les's first few years, there were some tough games—some which would be wars with Furman, Richmond, and East Carolina. One game against Richmond stood out.

"Richmond had a very athletic team, but we had beaten them twice during the 1977 season—by a point in Richmond and by thirteen at home. The way the postseason worked back then, the four bottom seeds were to play the four top seeds at the home court of the top seeds. We finished fifth. Richmond finished fourth, even though they had not beaten us.

"We had them at our place late in the season. They had this one kid, a big forward, who was a pretty rough customer. He played dirty. When the game was out-of-reach, he elbowed one of our players in the face away from the refs, injuring our guy. I saw it. I raised hell with the refs and their coach, Carl Slone. Slone did not take him out.

"After a timeout, I emptied my bench since it was over, and we'd won. One of the guys I put into the game was a military veteran who never played much, Johnny Mathis. Not related to the singer. Mathis had not shown much in practice and I thought he might be a little timid. I was wrong. Not long after he got into the game, he decked the Richmond bully who had elbowed our player. I was shocked when I saw it. Of course, he got teed up and ejected. I guess Mathis saw what the Richmond player had done to a teammate and got even.

Les followed, "Now normally when you see something that dramatic, the benches will clear. Mathis had nailed their guy; knocked him to the floor. I wondered why the Richmond team did not respond. Later I guessed that they knew their player from other stuff he had done and were not interested in coming to his rescue. He was a bad customer, and most of the coaches in the league knew it. His teammates must've known it, too.

"Going forward, we had to go to play Richmond in the first round of the tournament. Since we were taking a bus up, the families and wives could not go with us. At that time, state law would not allow anyone on the bus not directly affiliated with the college. And I told Barbara that—based on our first two games with Richmond—it was likely to be a rough game. She should not go. But Barbara is unlike most people. She loved basketball, loved our team, and wouldn't miss a game for the world. She packed up our four kids and drove to Richmond.

"When the bus pulled up coming from the hotel, Barbara was behind us with the kids. We all went into the team door at Robins Center. We just happened to go into the same door as the Richmond team. A few of their players were right there, including the player that Johnny Mathis decked in Charleston.

"As soon as their big thuggish player saw me, he pointed at me and yelled out, 'Coach, you're going back to Charleston in a coffin.'

"I looked at him, and turned to Barbara instinctively and said, 'See, I told you it was going to be rough!'

"We went on in. But a security guard was right there when the threat was made, as were several of his teammates. I said nothing to anyone, not even to my players about the incident, but about ten minutes before we were set to go out there, Richmond's Coach Slone sent for me. I went to his office and he awkwardly asked me about the incident. I could tell this was about to explode into something. It was evident that the threat had gotten around through their team.

"Slone asked, 'Les, did my player threaten your life when you came in?'

"I replied, 'Well Coach, it's all according to how you define a life threat. He pointed at me and said he was going to send me home in a coffin. How would you read that, Coach?'"

The Richmond power forward was a strong 6'8" starter who averaged over 13 points and 6 rebounds per game. He left the Richmond program eight games into the following season. But in 1976, Coach Slone wanted to sweep the incident away, if possible.

"Slone started by decimating the incident," Les recounted. "He said, 'Les, you know how these kids are. They say things they don't mean. Now, we can keep him out of the game and he's going to have a lot of punishment, but I wouldn't want this thing to get overblown. It's not good for the university. What if I bring him in to apologize? Would you accept his sincere apology?'

"What do you do when you know the way the coach wants it to go? I felt as though I needed to save Coach Slone from the embarrassment. So I consented to the apology," Les recalled.

"So the big guy comes in a minute later, all 6'8" of him, and apologizes. I said to him that I wasn't the cause of the incident in Charleston. I told him that he brought it onto himself and that my player just reacted on his own. But had I been on the floor I would've done the same thing that my player did to protect my teammate. I told him that he should take the lesson from this that his temper and attitude was going to get him into a lot of trouble well outside of basketball if he couldn't control it. I pretty much lectured the kid right in front of his head coach," Les retold the exchange.

"He played and Richmond won the game. But the Southern Conference knew of the incident from the game officials who had been apprised by the Richmond athletic director. The conference had recommended a player suspension for their next game in the Greenville Municipal Center, pending an investigation. The Richmond report went in and our report did, as well. But the facts didn't match up. The Richmond report was still shielding the gravity of the incident—treating it with much less seriousness than it actually was.

"Because of this, the league office arranged a conference call. We confronted the facts so that the Richmond report was corrected. It was in my court whether their big starter should play or not in Greenville where they had their next game. It was the conference semi-final. I relented and told the league office that I did not care if he played or not. Our season was over. I just wanted the facts to be accurate.

"He played, and Richmond was able to advance to the conference finals after winning against William and Mary. They lost the next evening to the conference champions that year, VMI, led by the Keydets fine player, Ron Carter."

The thuggish player did not heed Les's advice about his attitude and temper. After leaving the Richmond program, he spent time in prison and died young. Les did not know that the player who had threatened his life that evening in Richmond was very capable of delivering the threat.

Les remained busy building a solid basketball program at a college that had never reached the NCAA tournament. It became a quiet goal. He would need to recruit even better than he coached.

Bringing in Rodney McKeever was definitely a step in the right direction. But Les needed even more to compete favorably.

The Citadel's McKeever was again named the conference's Player of the Year in 1976. But after his third season, McKeever got into trouble at The Citadel for missing classes. He did not return for his senior season.

"I've had some great players at three stops. All of the great ones had a solid work ethic and loads of untapped talent. Rodney was the first of these. He was a gym rat. He'd skip classes to work on moves or crossover dribbling or free throws. He was special. But at The Citadel, skipping classes is a very bad idea."

During the 1977 and 1978 seasons, Les struggled to compete in the conference, but had transitioned from poor performances and bad losses to tight games-many lost by just plain bad luck. That team lost seven games by twelve points. The work ethic, confidence, and motivation had returned with most of the same players for 1979. That following year, Les's 1978-1979 Bulldogs would register a 20-8 record, the highest win total in the military college's history.

After David Thompson shattered the backboard at The Citadel's summer basketball camp, Les gladly reimbursed the Athletic Department for its replacement. Photo courtesy The Citadel.

CHAPTER 15

DAVID THOMPSON, THE SKYWALKER

Inky Robinson taught Les a lifelong lesson about promotion. Indeed, Les Robinson learned from a master. It was just into his second year as a head coach at The Citadel that he brought in David Thompson, Tom Burleson, and Quinn Buckner for his version of his Dad's tournament. It was the summer of 1975.

Les routinely checked through his strong basketball ties to find star-caliber players to bring to Charleston once their eligibility expired.

He would call Norm Sloan, Dean Smith, Bobby Knight, and others to bring in the key NBA draft picks. He knew that these players were not likely doing anything but improving their skills in anticipation of the NBA draft. These camps could give them a little spending money before their NBA signings made them completely unavailable. The bonus was that they would be performing something they enjoyed—playing and teaching basketball.

David Thompson's trip to Charleston in the summer of 1975 excited the local sports media and made The Citadel Basketball Camp a major part of the Les Robinson impact upon the hopeful emergence of The Citadel's basketball fortunes. Les had invited Thompson's NC State teammates, the diminutive Monte Towe and 7'4" Tom Burleson, the year prior—when NC State had won the NCAA Men's Basketball National Championship.

He had brought top players in subsequent years. As is usually the case, there is a relationship that was created years before. In the David Thompson arrival, it was a story of what might have been. Les actually recruited David Thompson for The Citadel when he was a high school junior. It was an experience he never forgot.

"I stopped in Marion, North Carolina, on a recruiting trip just before Christmas in 1969. Barbara was anxious for me to get home. With our four young children, we liked to do a lot of decorating at Christmas. We always loved that time of the year.

"The Citadel head coach was Dick Campbell, and we were bringing in a fine shooting guard, Chuck Cordell. He was the first college player I ever signed. I had visited Cordell at Marion High School in the town of the same name up in North Carolina. After visiting his mom and getting Cordell to agree to play at The Citadel, I went to see Cordell's high school coach, Eddie Brackett. Coach Brackett mentioned to me that there was a pretty good minority player over at Shelby High School. Although I was planning to go home for Christmas from Marion, I did not want to impair the relationship I had with Coach Brackett, so I called Barbara to tell her I would be late. I headed to Shelby near the South Carolina border. Shelby was not too far out of the way.I was interested to take a look at the player Brackett thought might be good enough to play at The Citadel.

"In Shelby, I met the high school coach, Ed Peeler. I told him I was only going to stay for a half because I needed to get home. I watched the first half. By that time in my life, I thought I'd seen—in person—maybe five of the top ten players who had ever played the game. I'd seen Jerry West, Wilt Chamberlain, Bill Russell, Elgin Baylor, and Oscar Robertson. I'd seen Jerry Lucas and John Havlicek, Hal Greer, Billy Cunningham, and others who wouldn't make my personal top ten list but became hall-of-famers. My instincts told me that I was looking at another incredible talent on a level that could reach the top five—and he was only a high school junior.

"By halftime, I was excited that I'd found a player who would put The Citadel on the map. I changed my mind about going home. I called Barbara again from the pay phone. I told her that I had just seen a player that was so physically talented, that I knew that I had to change my plans. To make it more amazing, I was the only college coach at the Shelby gym. I couldn't believe what I saw. Usually, I saw other coaches everywhere I went. David

Thompson's coach confirmed to me after the game that I was in early on Thompson. It appeared that I had discovered a secret. The big boys hadn't scouted David Thompson. The Citadel was a real possibility, I thought.

"After seeing the second half and asking about Thompson to Coach Peeler, I asked permission to chat with Thompson. I saw him and arranged breakfast the next morning, explaining to him that I wanted to talk to him about a special place—The Citadel. He was a quiet and respectful young man. He was exceptionally likable. I told him where The Citadel was located and that it was military.

"I went by his home to meet his family. He was one of eleven children. I drove him to the Holiday Inn where I was staying, to have breakfast. After breakfast, I took him to the room to show him the film about The Citadel— an old 16mm reel we used called *The Whole Man*. The film was well out-of-date, but it was the best we had. It was the first time I had seen it since I was new to the coaching staff. Though The Citadel was integrated, being all male and military—it was still a tough sale. What made it tougher was that the only minority seen on the film was rowing a boat for a white couple. It's the last time I ever showed that film."

Les continued to describe the unlikely process.

"Thompson liked what he saw, despite the dated film. He showed sincere interest. He was an under-aged junior. The Shelby High School schedule took him to places where the fans were treated to a show. That slow fan murmur had turned to a buzz. The local newspapers caught on. The explosion of other sports media followed. Competition was on the way. But just halfway through the season, incredibly, there were not many coaches that knew of this small-town *phenom*. I should have figured that it wasn't going to stay that way.

"The others found him eventually. In a month or so, the party was over. However, I wasn't sure he had ruled us out yet. He was so personable and respectful that I sensed that he still might come. As a practice, we would mail things to recruits periodically—a calendar, a brochure, a postcard, a poster, and our schedule. Under Coach Campbell's system, we would check off each item as we sent them. I made sure David Thompson heard from us regularly. We were simply the first in. We weren't going to have the showcase he would encounter in the ACC. I realized that. In a few weeks' time, the big one got away!

"Every top basketball college recruited him. In the end, my Wolfpack teammate, Eddie Biedenbach at NC State, signed him. All he did after that is to go undefeated one year, win an NCAA National Championship the next, and then he changed the structure of the National Basketball Association.

"Years later, because of my relationship with Eddie Biedenbach, Coach Sloan, and others at State, I was able to get David Thompson to come to our Citadel Basketball Camp in Charleston. I had become the head coach. I took Thompson down to the campus on a beautiful day and parked near the front of the First Battalion, where the campers were staying. The assistant coaches were there waiting. They all knew that I had tried to recruit Thompson at The Citadel.

"David gets out of the car, takes a look around and yells over to me, 'this place is even more beautiful than the film.' He really busted me! It made it worse that the assistant coaches heard it because they knew the backstory.

"I also had Quinn Buckner and Tom Burleson at the camp. At 7'4", Burleson was part of the 1974 championship team with Thompson. Buckner was considered the best defensive player in the nation at the college level. My best player at The Citadel, and maybe the most talented player I ever coached among my three Division 1 programs, Rodney McKeever, also worked the camp. All four of them dazzled the campers.

"Mid-week, I had lunch with David Thompson when Rodney McKeever's name came up. He told me that he was scoring on Quinn Buckner at will in their pick-up games.McKeever was flashy and dedicated—a gym rat. Rodney McKeever signed to play in Europe before the NBA draft. I believe he underestimated his own ability. He played basketball in Europe for nearly 20 years. Without a doubt, he could have played in the NBA.

David Thompson was quite impressed with McKeever because he frustrated Quinn Buckner.

Les switched gears to talk about how Thompson changed professional basketball.

"During the week that David stayed with us out at the beach house, he was weighing whether to play for the NBA Atlanta Hawks, who had drafted him at #1, or the ABA Denver Nuggets, who took him #1 in their separate draft. I heard him talking to several people from our kitchen wall phone. It sounded like he was about to make a decision, but I did not want to pry," Les intimates.

There was a major undercurrent of professional basketball league positioning before Thompson made his apocryphal choice. The NBA had hoped to lure Thompson in a bid to dismantle the upstart ABA. The Thompson signing would be critical to the future of both leagues. The two leagues were in their biggest duel and their sabers rattled fiercely.

"We waited down by the cars while David made another important conference call at 6:00. When David came out later on, I asked Quinn Buckner if he would mind riding to the game with Tommy Burleson. Burleson had a van because he had trouble fitting into regular cars. I thought I'd take Thompson on my own in case there was something he needed to talk about privately. I'm not sure I could advise him, but I knew I could listen well.

"I asked David which way he was leaning as we drove from my Sullivan's Island home into the campus. As I was a former NC State Wolfpack player and coach, he felt comfortable talking about the choice with me. He was rather quiet otherwise. I think he was tired of the media sticking a microphone in front of him every time he showed up somewhere," Les divulges.

"Thompson had already told me about his visits to both cities, so I was intrigued." Les recalls.

The Denver Nuggets had traded three players to the ABA Virginia Cavaliers for the rights to David Thompson earlier. The Nuggets went "all in" on Thompson. Les explained the thought process during their drive conversation.

"That last call from my kitchen wall phone altered the future of professional basketball," Les contends.

"As a sounding board, I asked about his reasoning and the experiences of visiting the two cities. He said that 'both offers were similar, but the impression he got from their two front offices was worlds apart.' He said he 'went to Atlanta and the Hawks management took him to a fast food place, showed him around the offices and the arena, but seemed to be unenthused about him signing to play for them. They assumed that he was coming to the Hawks without courting him for his services.

"He said, 'it was as if, because they were the NBA, I would not waste my career on going to play for Denver.' Then he talked about the impression he got from Denver. He said, 'They met me at the airport, showed genuine excitement for me being there, took me to the best places in Denver, the best restaurants; and generally, stopped everything they were doing to make sure I was treated like a king!' It was obvious to me that he was disappointed with the Hawks experience and inspired by the Nuggets," Les established.

The Denver Nuggets offered Thompson a slightly lesser contract than the Hawks, $1.35 million over three years with deferred compensatation. But they impressed Thompson with their commitment enough to persuade him. Thompson's agreement with the Nuggets forced the merger of the two leagues the very next year. The Shelby, N.C., native was the most electrifying player ever to be signed up to that time—and the NBA lost out. The only way they could get over it was to bring David Thompson and his purported 44-inch vertical leap back into primetime television by merger.

"Looking back, the Nuggets and the ABA owe me a percentage. I think—after the contract was agreed upon—the few bucks I gave Thompson to come to my camp was pretty much inconsequential," Les added. "His career was as advertised. After injuries and some personal struggles, he rose up to become one of the finest role models and player counselors that league has ever known."

"Knowing I had Thompson there for camp and an exhibition game of all-stars, we advertised selling tickets for $5 in the paper. Earlier in the week, we did a dunk contest for the campers. The highlight came when David shattered a backboard on a whirling power-dunk. The whole gym went crazy at witnessing the spectacle. It was something that was rare to see in person—even with the best players in professional basketball. It was a jaw-dropping moment.

"Coach Teague charged me $500 to replace the backboard. But I knew I would at least make that money back in the all-star exhibition. Once the word got out about the shattered backboard, the crowd would swell. I was certain of it," Les recalls.

Richard Johnson, a 6'8" Citadel post player who was also in the camp, was a witness. He became head coach at Wofford College before moving into the athletic director's role.

Johnson recalled, "Thompson started from the right side and looked like he cuffed the ball. When he started going up, you really didn't know when he'd reached full elevation because he continued rising for so long. I was sitting with camp kids near the goal. I was in awe myself. As he got way above the rim and came down with the ball, there was an explosion I can best describe as a bomb going off. The backboard just disintegrated. Thompson came down in a rain of glass. Much of it came down on him, but he didn't have a scratch. He just brushed it off as the crowd roared. He was okay and he just smiled sheepishly like he was embarrassed that he broke the backboard.

"I helped sweep up the glass but kept a big chunk. I still have it. I love to show it people so they ask me about something I'll never forget. We had to get a dozen guys to move the broken basket and put another one in its place. Needless to say, the 'Skywalker' won the dunk contest that night," Johnson concluded.

Richard Johnson became Les's assistant coach after his senior season at The Citadel. It introduced him to a new world that led to a magnificent career at Wofford.

"From a fans viewpoint, the best player in college basketball, David Thompson, was playing in an exhibition game in Charleston. Every General Manager on every NBA team wanted him. He was lauded as the most thrilling player to come along since Oscar Robertson and Jerry West. I had no idea of the size of the crowd that would show to see that evening exhibition, but I knew it would reach into the thousands."

Les made the schedule and tells the sequence. "That dunk contest was on Tuesday night and the all-star exhibition game was on a Thursday night. The newspaper advertising had worked. The campus traffic personnel did not expect the volume of vehicles that lined up all the way off of The Citadel campus that evening.

"As David and I rode onto the campus, the traffic was at a snail's pace. David asked me what was going on. I told him that there was something going on at the Daniel Library that night—and there was. They probably had thirty people there. Meanwhile, we ran out of parking for McAlister Field House. We pulled up in back. That huge throng—thousands of basketball fans—were all there to see the great David Thompson.

"Because of the traffic jam, we got in a little late. David asked me, 'Coach, what time will the game start?' I quickly answered him, 'whenever you feel you're warmed up enough. The rest of that crowd can wait until then.' He laughed. But I was dead serious," Les retells.

"The summer all-star game of 1975 included Quinn Buckner as the NCAA National Defensive Player of the Year with David Thompson, the NCAA National Player of the Year. Rodney McKeever was the Southern Conference Player of the Year, also participated—as was allowed by NCAA rules at their home team camps. Tom Burleson, at 7'4", was his own spectacle," Les recounts. "Most people might go a lifetime and never see anyone that tall. And he was a legitimate force as a college and NBA player."

"As I mentioned, McKeever made an impact with the defensive-minded Buckner. David had a subtle sense of humor. And he gave Buckner a hard time about not being able to stop McKeever. He would name great players in the NBA and tell Buckner that he would be laughed at if he couldn't stop that little guy from the Southern Conference."

Even Buckner had to question about McKeever, who was not quite six feet and weighed about 170. Les recalled the conversation.

"Buckner started, 'Coach, I've seen some great guards over my four years at Indiana, but I've never seen anyone like Rodney McKeever. Where'd he come from?'

"I smiled as he was asking. It told me I scored a victory for the little colleges everywhere by bringing McKeever to The Citadel," Les relates.

Buckner was in awe of the little guard from local Garrett High School.

"Why have I never heard of him?" Buckner pressed. "He is unstoppable. I've never seen anyone that quick and that good?"

"Thompson nodded as Buckner said it as to say, 'Hey Coach, this guy McKeever is something special,' Les beamed. "They had played ball with him for a few days and couldn't stop talking about how good he was. When Quinn Buckner, considered the best defender of his generation in college and in the pros over the next decade says that someone is unstoppable, that is an opinion you have to take seriously."

"Rodney had drawn raves from Thompson, too," Les confirms.

"Thompson was the best player in college—maybe with Bill Walton. But the 6'11" Walton couldn't get a crowd excited like David Thompson could. He had the full package of a superhuman. He could defy gravity, hit the buzzer-beater, and challenge seven footers trying to shoot over him. We may never see that dynamic package ever again in one player."

McKeever got a chance to play in the camp and in the all-star game. He was there when Thompson made everyone in the gym gasp just two nights earlier with the dunk that shattered the backboard. McKeever was not the only one impressed.

"It was fair to say that Thompson won the dunk contest because his last dunk destroyed the backboard, and thus closed it out. Now he was destroying the high-end competition in the all-star game. I think it was because he had just decided on playing in Denver and the decision wasn't hanging over him anymore," Les assumes. "What he told me in the car on the way down to McAlister Field House loosened him up."

The basketball showcase that the fans saw on the last night of the camp was a small footnote to what was going on in the highest level of basketball that week. Behind the scenes, David Thompson was changing the landscape of professional basketball. He was a thrilling player—so much so that ten years later Michael Jordan credited Thompson with being his childhood inspiration.

The NBA that Michael Jordan enjoyed was directly because of David Thompson. Thompson was Jordan's hero growing up. Jordan asked Thompson to give his introductory speech to the Basketball Hall of Fame. Thompson consented.

Les Robinson and the player nicknamed "the skywalker" for because of his gravity-defying leaping ability had traveled full circle.

Five years earlier, when NC State signed him out of Shelby, N.C., the intensity of that recruiting war exploded. The teams that thought they had Thompson were, understandably, upset. NC State was investigated. They were charged with a variety of minor violations. The action taken by the NCAA could be said to have been both too stringent and too lax.

The NCAA violations that led to the team's ineligibility for postseason play stemmed from a few nights Thompson stayed for free in the dorm of some friends working a basketball camp. Another charge was for playing in a pick-up game in which assistant coach Eddie Biedenbach played. Thompson said the NCAA treated it like he had been given a tryout. Only a fool would think that a tryout was necessary.

"They considered that a tryout, which I think is really stupid. I'd already signed with the school," Thompson said. "Why would they have to try me out? I was one of the best players in the country. It was just little nit-picky stuff."

In fact, NC State went undefeated in the 1972-1973 season with a record of 27-0. They sat home while the NCAA tournament was being played.

They became the only undefeated team in NCAA Basketball History to not win the National Championship.

Once the probation was lifted, they won it all the next year.

ESPN Color analyst Len Elmore played against Thompson. Elmore's son, Stephen, was playing at The Citadel when Elmore recalled the pain of losing to NC State in a game tabbed 'the game of the century.'

During the 1973-74 season, the University of Maryland likely had the second-best team in America. Elmore and Maryland didn't qualify for the NCAA tournament. Only conference champions and high independents qualified back then.

Elmore elaborated. "David Thompson was the greatest player I ever played against and I still maintain that he was the best player the college game had ever known. My reasoning is that there was no other player before him or since that brought in both the physical spectacle and predictable results. For those two years, NC State only lost one game and 'DT Skywalker' was the greatest show on earth."

"I still say that the best college game ever played was Maryland vs. NC State in the ACC Tournament Final of 1974," Elmore stated. "State was 26-1; we were 23-4. Winner take all. Loser go home. We were determined to knock them off and have them sit home for the second year in a row."

Elmore and two of his teammates took three of the ten All-American places as the top players in college basketball during that 1974 season. Elmore, Tom McMillan and John Lucas all went on to NBA careers. With Mo Howard and Owen Brown, they were likely the finest starting five in America. Maryland had a banner year. They just happened to be in a league that had Thompson with a solid supporting cast of Monte Towe, Tom Burleson, Mo Rivers, and Tim Stoddard.

The ACC Championship final that year could be considered as the finest basketball game in NCAA history. The #1 ranked NC State Wolfpack won in overtime, 103-100. The #5 ranked Maryland Terrapins went home. Three of their five losses were to NC State.

Lefty Driesell stepped onto the NC State team bus in Greensboro to congratulate the victorious Wolfpack team, exhorting them not to let their effort go to waste. He implored them to win it all and become champions. Driesell had never gone to congratulate an opponent in his career. But this game was different.

Elmore elaborated. "It was the most exhausting game I ever played. John Lucas and I played all 45 minutes. Our team shot 62% for the game and lost. We left it all out on the floor that day. It was, in my opinion, the very best college basketball game ever played—especially given all that was on the line. I can honestly say that NC State won against a team that was not only equal in talent, but had given them their very best."

Maryland won 73 games in three seasons from 1972 to 1974. They won the National Invitation Tournament in 1972 and they made it to the NCAA East Regional Final the previous year (1973) when NC State was ineligible. Over the previous two years, five of Maryland's losses came were administered by NC State. In 1974, their losses were at UCLA (by 1), at North Carolina, and three losses to NC State. They were the best team in the East that was not NC State. They may have been the best 'other team' in America, to include UCLA and Marquette.

Norm Sloan concurred.

"We played UCLA two overtimes in the national semifinals, but the Maryland game was tougher," Sloan said. "It was as draining and exhilarating an experience as I've ever had. I still remember turning around on the bench at one point and just saying out loud, 'My goodness, this is a hell of a game.'"

Burleson and Thompson combined for 65 points that day. The country saw David Thompson as a spectacular athlete that was, in the end, a player with a special will to win.

"That year," Les opined, "you could have made a case that the most complete team in America went home to watch everybody else play it out. Lefty Driesell's Maryland team was likely the reason that the NCAA Men's

Basketball Tournament expanded the very next year. Fans were cheated out of seeing McMillan, Elmore, and Lucas see how far they could go. Of course they may have faced David Thompson a fourth time!"

Those that swooned at seeing the near-mythical Thompson cut the nets for the NCAA Championship were trying to find parking places outside of a packed McAlister Field House. The all-star game had Thompason and top talent beyond. They were coming to see a once-in-a-lifetime player.

"We were fortunate to have a good gate that night. I wasn't too worried about the price of a new backboard that Thompson shattered anymore. The place was packed," Les remembers. "There may have been a good crowd to see Buckner or Burleson, but the guy they were lining up to see in person was *the Skywalker.*"

"So, the night that he made a major decision that would impact professional basketball and the value of franchises across America, I was taking him in to a meaningless contest that had tremendous upside for me and The Citadel. He was there because he proved to be both humble and unassuming. He built that crowd when word got out that he demolished one of our glass backboards with a thunderous dunk two nights before. Somehow, I think he upped his game that night, just knowing the decision was no longer going to be haunting him every day. He had a scintillating all-star game that was worth a whole lot more than $5 to enjoy. He was incredible that night. I could have charged $20 and had the same crowd."

"After paying all of the players—all was legal—we profited on the all-star game well more than the proceeds of the weeklong camp. And I may have paid David Thompson his smallest check ever as a 'pro.' If anything, that week confirmed that I was truly my daddy's son," Les reminisced.

CHAPTER 16

AN EYE FOR TALENT

Symphonies are segmented so that they become one. The sound comes from each section. So it is with college basketball teams. In an orchestra, one would locate percussions, woodwinds, brass, and string families broken into instruments like oboes, flutes, and violins. Basketball teams have a similar composition. To recognize the stronger trumpet and the weaker tuba, a conductor has to have an impeccable discernment of sound. Basketball coaches are conductors, but their mastery of performance only has one final bow to the audience: firing or retirement.

Les always had the ability of discernment in his back pocket. He could determine a weak free throw shooter or a strong defender from a keen sense that few enjoyed. The one quality he championed above all others was basketball smarts. Those players were in a section that he preferred to have on the floor at the end of a game. They could bring the basketball symphony to a standing ovation.

Locating that one key quality—a player who could step forward and change an outcome—had routinely advanced his coaching career. Talent was a premium, size was a bonus, but basketball smarts was a commodity often overlooked.

It was in the mid-cycle of his first contract as an NCAA basketball head coach that Les spotted a scrappy undersized point guard in a gym down in Florida.

"I was down at Stetson University to look at another player while watching a game between camp all-stars. I was sitting up high and speaking with Auburn's head basketball coach, Sonny Smith. He actually pointed this player out to me, knowing that he was way too small for the Southeastern Conference. He had been watching a short skinny kid take control. As I watched, I noticed that he was both aggressive and made wise decisions."

Randy Nesbit did not look like a basketball player. A freshman point guard at Gulf Coast Community College, Nesbit was passed over by every Division-1 college in America. Nesbit was short at 5'8", scrawny at 145 pounds, and unorthodox. His one-handed free throw was like nothing Les had ever seen, but it was consistently successful. When not on the floor, Nesbit wore glasses. He looked like the guy that would become a top accountant or a CFO—but not like a college basketball player.

Les, though, detected something. Nesbit was fiery, determined; and hustled for every loose ball. Les knew that Nesbit's lack of size would create match-up problems against every opponent on The Citadel's schedule. Besides, The Citadel had rarely taken junior college transfers simply because the indoctrination process into the Corps of Cadets was so stringent. Knob Year was a filter. Some could do it; some couldn't.

Without a clear performer to sign, Les was likely to leave the summer camp with nothing but trivial hotel and gas receipts. The player he came to see was not going to pan out. But Nesbit had caught his eye. He had decided to talk to the diminutive player after the game. He saw that Nesbit was a crafty ball handler with court vision and a penchant for getting the ball inside. And he was tough. Les's unorthodox player evaluation gave extra points for toughness.

"There was one play in a scramble that Nesbit came out with a bloody face," Les recounted. "I thought the officials would stop the game, but Nesbit took the ball and headed the other way, blood all down his shirt. He paid no attention to his injury. In fact, it was if he used his bloody face to throw off the defense. He showed high end court savvy. It was basketball smarts that made me think he could play higher up."

Les continues. "When I spoke to him after the game, I asked if he had ever heard of The Citadel. He had not. But he was interested to find out more. When I told him it was military, he mentioned that he had a friend at West Point. He indicated that being in a military college would pose no barrier to him. At that point, it was just a matter of me being comfortable with offering a basketball grant-in-aid to someone so small."

Nesbit was a kid that arrived in Florida from places unknown. He just wanted someone to give him a chance.

"I repeated that he would have to undergo a rigorous knob year," Les recalls, "but he didn't seem the least bit phased. I got all of his information and gave him my spiel. He didn't have to think about it. He said he'd show up. I hadn't even asked him about his grades or where he was from. All I knew is that this kid that looked nothing like a college athlete could become a major impact player in The Citadel's program. What I saw on the floor was what I liked."

As it turned out, Randy Nesbit came to Gulf Coast Community College from the Pittsburgh area because the small junior college would give him a chance to play basketball. He was an excellent student.

Nesbit became a three-year starting point guard. He was a fiery catalyst for The Citadel's 1978-1979 team that won twenty games—a first for the military college. He was voted as captain of the 1979-1980 team. He made *All Southern Conference* 2nd team both years. He led the team in his first season with a 54.0 field goal percentage, quite unusual for a backcourt player. His one-handed foul shot became his trademark as he sank 92.5% of his free throws in 1979-1980, the second-best percentage in the entire NCAA. Nesbit was a winner in every phase, including the classroom.

"He was a coach on the floor," Les stated. "His instincts were as good as any player I ever coached or coached against. As small as he was, he was large on the floor. He controlled tempo, and he dared you to foul him. That toughness I saw one day in Florida was just a sample. Randy

Nesbit was going to give 100% one hundred percent of the time. And he adapted that attitude to the military, as well. He emerged as a top student—accumulating a grade-point ratio near 3.6 on a 4.0 scale. Many of my players adapted quite well to the military, some even signing contracts for military service. Others did not. Randy could have done either. As an overview, Randy Nesbit could have been whatever he wanted to be—a general, a CEO, or what he eventually became, a great husband, parent, teacher, athletic director, and head basketball coach. Whatever he pursued, he was going to succeed.

"There's more to his story. After he didn't start the first few games, he asked me if he could speak to me a moment outside of the locker room," Les recounted. "I was thinking that he had a complaint about the military commitment or that he might even leave. But that was not it. He was quite respectful and simply said in a controlled low voice, 'Coach, I just want you to know that if you put me in the game I will not let you down.' And he was so sincere, that right then and there I thought 'I really do need to see what he can do at our level.' I made the decision to get him on the floor. And Randy made the decision to never leave the floor."

The Citadel already had two established guards, both with skill and size—Rob Hoak, an NC State transfer, and Rick Swing, a 6'4" shooting guard. Swing became a first team All-Southern Conference player and was drafted by the Cleveland Cavaliers as the fourth player in the fourth round of the 1979 NBA draft. Hoak had an outstanding career—and his career after The Citadel flourished, as he became the state president of a large regional bank.

"That team was loaded with top quality people that also played basketball. And they played basketball well," Les realized. "I had to find a way to get the right mix with a solid substitution pattern."

"We were down ten the next game and I looked down the bench just to shake things up. This kid kept looking up as if to say, 'now would be a good time, coach.' So I made the move." Les recalled the game's momentum changing.

"He did not let me down. He was the game-changer I had forecasted, and the game turned to our favor. This kid had raw nerve and amazing confidence. The very next practice I pulled the coaches over and told them that Randy Nesbit was going to play. From that game on, we went with a three-guard offense."

Indeed, the Pennsylvania native established The Citadel's record of 120 assists in a single season. He also set the school's record for most career assists (324). And Nesbit played only three years having lost a year of eligibility playing in Florida. After graduation, he served as an assistant coach for the Bulldogs until Les departed campus to assume coaching duties at East Tennessee State.Nesbit became the Bulldogs new head coach. During his tenure as The Citadel's head coach, his teams won 75 games, to include an improbable 88-87 upset win over a very strong University of South Carolina team in February of 1989. The Gamecocks recorded an 18-11 season and were selected to compete in the NCAA Tournament. The loss to The Citadel was their only blemish over their last eight regular season games. Nesbit had coached a magical victory in front of a hostile Gamecock crowd. The team played with confidence because their young undersized coach knew no other way.

As an aside, the starting point guard on that 1988-89 Citadel team was Ed Conroy. Conroy went on to become head basketball coach at The Citadel and Tulane. His 2008-2009 team won twenty games for only the second time in program history.

Nesbit's coaching career was also impressive. He completed his 23rd year (2018) at Roane State College, extending their record for career wins with 376.With his 75 wins at The Citadel, he is a sure bet to win 500 or more games before his retirement.

Keith "Mister" Jennings was only offered one NCAA scholarship.
Les saw the talent, leadership and determination. Jennings later played in the NBA.
Photo courtesy East Tennessee State University.

Les had other surprises that came because of his attention to "smart over big." It was his way of paying attention to the individual sounds that make great music. With graduations and injuries, there was a place in the 'orchestra' that often needed to be filled for basketball smarts.

"Keith 'Mister' Jennings would have to be in any conversation about floor leadership and basketball smarts," Les smiles. "Like Randy Nesbit, there were no takers when he finished his career at Culpeper High School in Virginia. At 5'7", nobody was willing to take a chance. But I thrived with smaller guards while coaching at The Citadel. In addition to Nesbit, I had Eddie Paone, Greer Huguley, Ed Cornwell, Richie Sawyer, and a few others. I never hesitated to take a player based on size. The old saying that 'the court is longer than it is high' fit my attitude about small point guards who were smart and feisty. Mister Jennings was all that and more."

Jennings led ETSU to three consecutive Southern Conference Championships and to a top 10 national ranking in 1991. He finished his NCAA career as the #4 leader in assists all-time with 983. Jennings matured under Les Robinson to become a 13-year professional in both the NBA and Europe.

"Mister was much like every other gym rat that has ever been written off as too small. It just makes them that much more determined," Les continued. "All of the ACC and SEC schools passed on Mister, yet he was better than just about every point guard in both of those leagues. I had a predisposition for small guards who are smart and show great leadership. Mister was a no-brainer for me to sign at East Tennessee. He made me look like a genius when I was just doing what my training had prepared me to do—sign players who could fit and contribute regardless of their physical stature."

There were also players Les saw that were not immediately ready. For them to become great players would take patience. Regan Truesdale was one from that section of the orchestra.

"Regan (*pronounced as 'Region'*) was recruited to play football out of Andrew Jackson High School by most SEC and ACC institutions in the South. He was strong and had size. At 6'4" and 220 pounds, he looked the role of an all-conference linebacker. That's exactly where the football experts had him slotted during his senior football season. But the recruiters that came to Heath Springs, South Carolina, missed one critical detail. Regan wanted to play college basketball," Les retells. "I knew that. My first assistant, Richard Johnson also knew that. We stayed on Regan all along. We just kept quiet while all of the big schools were salivating about where he could fit into their football programs. When we signed him to play basketball, those football schools were all caught off guard."

Richard Johnson told the sequence.

"When I scouted him, everybody told me that he was going to play football at a high level. But Regan didn't tell me that. So, I knew the basketball adage about recruiting as an assistant. The main goal is to sell the boss. Once I could get him in to see Les and Les to meet his family, I knew there was an excellent chance we'd have Regan in school at The Citadel. Les has a gift like no one else. He could go in and talk to a mother or dad about the structure, the importance of a degree, our nationally ranked graduation rates, and the proven success of our past players. He was the best closer I ever knew. Selling a military college basketball program is difficult enough. But Les made it look easy," Johnson notes.

Truesdale was soft-spoken, courteous, and quite impressionable. He was not a basketball star his freshman year. He was barely a factor. Unassuming, Les knew that to maximize Truesdale's talent, he would have to be methodical and work with him at a pace.Meanwhile, the under-sized power forward lifted weights and perfected his skills. From a small town and being quite introverted, Truesdale was not quite ready for college basketball as a freshman. He had to grow into it.

Truesdale came in from the bench during his first season, only averaging two points per game. He had flashes of excellence, yet moments of concern. But the basic talent was evident. Halfway through his sophomore season at The Citadel, he began to play as a starter, then emerged late in the year as a terrific player. He ended the season averaging 13.1 points per game. His confidence had been elevated, and his coach had learned to handle his amazing humility. Truesdale had displayed reticence at taking too many shots in practice and was so reserved in the locker room that Les felt he needed to devise a plan to change his role.

"In truth, Truesdale had no idea just how good a player he was," Les states.

Les recalled the method that he used to install Regan Truesdale as a star player. It was by deception.

"I knew Regan was too humble to ask for the ball more. So, I had a plan that I felt would force the issue. I sent Regan to the locker room on an errand that would take a few moments in the middle of practice. Once he was gone, I called the team together and began speaking in a low voice. I told them that he was too humble and selfless to hear what I had to say. They knew that. He was a great teammate. They loved the guy. And what

I told the team was that his offensive efficiency rating was off the charts. I reminded them that our goal was to do whatever it took to win. I scolded them for not getting the ball to him at every possible opportunity. He was at the top of the conference in every good statistic, especially offensive rebounding, field goal percentage, scoring, and free throws," Les explained. "I simply said, 'If you want to win, it's simple. Get Regan the ball!' If you want to sit, you can do that too by not getting the ball to Regan.' Once Regan came back out, we ran our offense and every time he got the ball in scoring position, I told him, 'Regan, you are hurting this team when you do not take that shot.' That practice changed everything. He had amazing tools and great instincts. We just needed to turn him loose."

He was on to something. Truesdale averaged 22 points a game over the next two seasons. He had 130 steals and 315 offensive rebounds—a startling number for a player at 6'4". He made nearly 80% of his free throws. He had nearly 700 career rebounds. He set the all-time scoring record—surpassing Art Musselman—exceeding every player who ever stepped onto the basketball court at The Citadel. He was twice named as the Southern Conference Player of the Year.

The crowning point of his career came against the University of North Carolina in 1984. UNC Coach Dean Smith tried every defensive scheme he knew to stop Truesdale in a game that went down to the wire with the feisty cadets from Charleston. He switched from the future all-NBA defensive player of the year Michael Jordan to 6'11" defensive specialist Joe Wolf. The net result was that Regan Truesdale torched the #1 ranked Tar Heels for 26 points. He made it look easy. The undefeated Tar Heels pulled away from a four-point lead to win by sixteen on deft free throw shooting over the last four minutes when The Citadel had to chance the unlikely upset. Truesdale received a standing ovation from the Tar Heel faithful at the end of the February 4th game in the Charlotte Arena.

Truesdale recalled the thrill. "My best memory of that game was playing against Michael Jordan and Sam Perkins in what turned out to be a close game until they made the free throws at the end. They were ranked first in the country then and I believe they left the floor with much more respect for Coach Rob and our team. I knew that they were trying everything to stop me, but I was determined to score. My teammates trusted me and I did not want to betray that trust."

The Citadel recorded a season record of 18-11 the following year, much to the credit of Regan Truesdale—and the patience of his coach. Along the way, Marshall University coach Rick Huckabay decided to clamp down on Truesdale with defensive switches and double-teams. Truesdale responded with 41 points including 22 made free throws. The Cadets upended the eventual conference champions, 84-76. The Citadel's home record during Truesdale's junior and senior seasons was 26-1. They won twenty-three games in a row at McAlister Field House. The streak created the atmosphere Les enjoyed on his home floor. The "Animal House" themed cadet crowd tormented the visiting teams.

Two-time SoCon Player-of-the-Year Regan Truesdale.
Photo courtesy The Citadel.

"Regan gave me a great send-off. He dominated our opponents during my last season as head coach at The Citadel. In a way, my road to the ACC and coaching my alma mater had a lot to do with Regan Truesdale's coming out of his shell and believing in himself as he did. He was a project recruit that turned out very well," Les details.

As a power forward, Truesdale was deemed too small in the NBA. He was drafted by the Phoenix Suns and evaluated as a small forward and #2 guard. His lack of ball-handling skills did not suit at the NBA level, though Truesdale played in other professional leagues for four years. Les helped to build his confidence while elevating his impact on a very good team.

Les summed up his attitude about selecting high school talent. "The best players are not always the prep stars. Sometimes, they are the kid that stole the ball or made the key pass but ended the game with six points. I learned to look past physical attributes. Teams have signed plenty of 6'10" players that could not play dead! Height is not an indicator, it is just a measurement."

Les explained his player theory.

"Sometimes when you're trying to build a team, it is important to not overlook players who may not be the perfect size for their position. I loved taking players that might have been overlooked by others. It may have given them determination and usually gave me a player on a mission. If that player had a work ethic and the basketball smarts I sensed, he could turn a bad team to a good one and a good team to a great one."

"Using the full roster personnel sometimes gets overlooked. I had several walk-on players that gained roles that helped us to win. These were important.

"Because of the sanctions imposed at NC State, we played several games that tested this resource. There were a number of times that the only scholarship player I had on the bench when the ball went up was Migjen Bakalli. He did a magnificent job filling in where there was a need at several positions and performed his role well.

"But my best story about using a roster was back at The Citadel where I coached from 1974 through 1985. We had a walk-on player, Richey Sawyer, who had a special skill. He could make foul shots. I saw in practice that this small guard was well schooled as a free throw shooter. He would sometimes shoot ten in a row without ever drawing iron. And the more important the shot was, the more likely he was to swish it. Pressure didn't matter.

"We had an outstanding point guard, Jimmy Tharpe, playing ahead of him. But if we got into an end-of-the-game situation, I didn't hesitate to take one of the big guys out and put in Richey Sawyer, the walk-on. He went almost two years without missing a free throw in a game.

"His senior year bore this out when we hosted Chattanooga. Chattanooga had a great team, but we were ahead late and their coach, Murray Arnold, had to start fouling to get possessions and milk the clock. Murray's wife kept statistics for the team and sat at the scorer's table. I switched out a player and put Richie Sawyer in, who had not been in the game at Chattanooga or played in this one either. Normally, a coach would see a cold player coming from the bench in these situations and he'd instruct his players to foul the new guy on the inbounds. You could see this on the film later, but Coach Arnold pointed to Richie to get his guys to foul him. Meanwhile his wife sees the 100% statistic for Sawyer on free throws. She frantically tries to get his attention to call off the plan, but he doesn't catch her protesting in time. They foul Richey, and he makes both. We go on to the upset win.

"I knew I had made the right move because when Richey got fouled, he smiled. Even he knew he was automatic," Les notes.

When Les got to NC State, it was no longer a matter of finding hidden talent. He knew that Raleigh could be a fine place to recruit five-star players, but he would need to coach well enough to beat the best teams in America. There was ready talent on his first Wolfpack roster—enough to qualify for an NCAA bid his first year and to reach the round of sixteen.But maintaining an ACC level of talent with the harsh restrictions that were to follow made Les realize that he would need to find high capacity students that could play in the NCAA's best league. Through no fault of his making, this would prove to be nearly impossible.

Fate is a sultry friend. Circumstances related to the previous coaching group forced Les to rely heavily on floor coaching skills that he had learned at The Citadel and East Tennessee State. His knack for finding special players was delayed because of the sanctions he did not cause but would have to experience. With scholarships taken away, he would be forced to compete without the recruiting latitude that other coaches enjoyed.

"The institutions get punished. The incoming players get punished. And the persons that caused the mess—coaches or assistants—have moved on to another program. It made it even more important for me to evaluate abilities across our roster and use what I had wisely," Les laments.

He was back to getting the most out of the limited talent that the situation produced. His teams would enter most games as underdogs, even to many teams outside of the Atlantic Coast Conference. Les's abilities as a floor coach would again be tested, as would his ability to assess and sign major talent again. He knew how to evaluate and to recruit. He would need to exhibit extraordinary patience.

Nonetheless, his formula had worked in the past. He knew how to conduct an orchestra, even if the percussion section didn't show up.

Les and College of Charleston Head Coach John Kresse make their case to the head official. Photo courtesy The Citadel.

CHAPTER 17
DON'T BLAME THE REFS

By design, the neutral human element in basketball is the referees. Some coaches go to great lengths to assure their neutrality. Others let that part of the game proceed as it should—trusting both that neutrality and the acumen of the game officials. Les spent his career as the latter.

The players may be bigger or faster—or more fundamentally sound; but the game officials are simply monitors of the rules who exert their impact by trying not to imbalance the contest of abilities.

"Two times I was confronted about a purported favoritism with referees and both times the charge backfired. In fact, both refs involved were related—the Owens brothers, Chandler and James," Les noted.

"The first time was at the Southern Conference meetings. The Davidson coach, Bobby Hussey, spoke up while we were on the subject of the officiating. He was very direct and brazen. He said to the conference commissioner, 'I'm tired of going down to Charleston and seeing Chandler Owens in The Citadel's gym every time. Owens lives right outside The Citadel's front gate. That's got to be changed.' He was looking right at me as if waiting for his statement to be challenged," Les recalls.

"So, I spoke right up. I immediately countered with a rebuttal. 'That's an outright lie,' I said. 'You can't believe what Coach Hussey says or where he gets his information. I know for a fact that Chandler Owens lives twelve miles from our campus. The reason I know is because my daughter dates his son. We checked the mileage on the car's odometer one time and it was right at twelve miles. If I were Coach Hussey, I'd get all of the facts before I spoke up.'

"Well, the roomful of coaches broke out laughing. Needless to say, we didn't see much of Chandler Owens at McAlister Fieldhouse anymore! Coach Hussey never challenged my integrity in a meeting again."

Chandler Owens, who died young of cancer, was considered among the finest officials of both the Southern Conference and the ACC. He was beyond reproach, and yet he was most cordial and gentlemanly to all of the coaches. Other officials could have learned much from Chandler Owens.

His younger brother, James Owens, may have been even more accomplished. James Owens was not only a top basketball official, but a major professional tennis official as well. Owens officiated the final matches of the U.S. Open Tennis Championship in Flushing Meadows, New York. In doing so, he was accosted verbally by John McEnroe.

"There was not much a basketball coach could say to me that could ever approach the outbursts I heard from John McEnroe," Owens remarked. "After seeing guys like McEnroe, Ilie Nastase, and Jimmy Connors get bent out of shape, it was easier to tolerate a coach on the sidelines pleading for a walking call or a charge."

James Owens, like his brother Chandler, became a highly regarded game official. He showed no partiality, but the association of his Charleston residency would sometimes incite a dilemma to the league office.

Les detailed another incident that became a classic opponent's strategy that backfired.

"The second time was even better. We were up at Marshall in Huntington. It was Marshall's second year in the league, 1978, and their coach, Stu Aberdeen, had a well-known paranoia about game officials. He researched who they were and where they lived and what college they attended. When we went to play them in Huntington, James Owens was one of the scheduled officials. James, like his brother Chandler, was widely considered one of the best officials around, no matter where he lived or which airport he used to get to the game. When this happened, Owens was likely the most respected official in the league. But Aberdeen saw that he was from Charleston, South Carolina, and called the commissioner the day before the game. As a result, the league office—to appease Aberdeen—replaced James Owens.

"Another Southern Conference official would call our game. Ironically, this official came from West Virginia, where Marshall University already had one of the best home records in the league. I had no problem with it, whatsoever. There was a good reason that I did not protest. Marshall's Coach Aberdeen would not have guessed my reason.

"Because the Marshall coach liked to use our basket in warm-ups so that the crowd would boo us when we protested, I had pre-arranged and took our team to the St. Albans High School gym twenty minutes away. So, to Marshall and their home fans it appeared that we had just gotten to the arena without warm-ups and that we were in complete disarray. They assumed we had gotten stuck in traffic.

"We had gotten off the bus and went right to our bench. As the teams stood for the National Anthem, the replacement official came over. He knew why he was in Huntington because of the league office switch. He seemed to know that Coach Aberdeen forced the change, as well. The replacement official was Ron Ferris. I broke out laughing about the irony of the league replacing James Owens with Ron Ferris right when Ferris came over. I had hoped that Coach Aberdeen saw me making a big deal about it.

"Ron Ferris is a guy from my hometown, St. Albans, who started kindergarten and finished high school with me. Aberdeen's craziness had backfired. It was epic! Ferris asked me about Barbara and the kids. The three of us were in the same class all of the way through high school. His mother was my seventh-grade teacher! In fact, he told me that his Mom had driven over to the game to see me and wanted me to stay after the game so that she could say hello. We were both trying not to break out laughing as the music from the Star-Spangled Banner began. Coach Aberdeen had out-strategized himself."

Les theorized the impact of the result that would have been better left as scheduled. He enjoyed the benefit.

"Sometimes it seems best to just let the coaches throw their weight around so that there is no overwhelming advantage allowed on either side. I may have gotten a few of the close calls that night because the other coach wanted to show off," Les recalled. "It was great to see Mrs. Ferris, my seventh-grade teacher, after the game that night. It was a happier time because we pulled off the upset and beat Marshall in front of their home crowd. And I should've thanked Stu Aberdeen for reuniting people that truly cared about one another. I couldn't wait to get back and tell the dismissed official, James Owens, that story!"

Marshall had a fine basketball team during the 1977-78 season. They went to the championship game of the Southern Conference tournament that year, losing to Furman University. But on the night that their coach insisted upon changing out a game official on their home floor, they lost to The Citadel, 74-57. Marshall had just been beaten by nationally ranked Louisville the game prior, but not by as many points as they lost to The Citadel that night.

"I never really had trouble with the officials, though I did get kicked out of a game once. Even that was a freak thing," Les recalled.

"We were coaching at East Tennessee and playing Appalachian State. We had a rabbit-eared first-year ref that my assistant Dave Hanners said something to after a call. Unexpectedly, he tee'd Hanners up. The ref should've known better, but he was new. The rule is that any call against the bench goes against the head coach, so I had to be careful. Later in the game an App State player slammed the ball down in frustration and it bounced up high over his head nearly reaching the scoreboard. That's an automatic technical foul for conduct, but this same official saw it and inexplicably didn't call it. I simply suggested to him the unfairness of the circumstance by saying, 'Hey, you're a technical caller, so call it by the rules.' The veteran officials turned away. The good ones know how to handle these tense situations. But this guy was new, and he overreacted. It's crazy but he responded by calling a technical on me.

"By virtue of Hanners' earlier technical, I had to leave the bench as an ejected coach. On those rare occasions the league office will get a written report and the film, if available. There'll be a conference call on the matter because the conference certainly does not want coaches leaving the floor. After my report and conference call, the league office called the young official. He got the worst end of that deal."

The story came full circle.

"Years later, when I was on the NCAA Men's Basketball Selection Committee I was the featured speaker at an officials' conference in Asheville, North Carolina. The same official that threw me out for the only time in my career was in attendance. After I spoke, another official that I knew for years came up with the official that kicked me out. He introduced him as if we didn't know each other. The ref was a little embarrassed. He sheepishly interrupted the guy introducing him saying, 'Oh, I know Coach Robinson already. Coach taught me a valuable lesson when I was a young ref several years back. Believe me, I learned a lot from it.' I figured that the league got on him about that ejection and he was really embarrassed.

"Some coaches spend more time trying to get calls and grinding out games than coaching the sidelines. I always had the attitude that they were going to get some calls wrong every game. It was human nature. There could be no perfectly officiated game. I did not want to get involved in the personalities and checking where the official graduated, or lived, or worked. I just wanted them to call it as best they could and not to determine the outcome with a badly blown call. That's all. Having said that, I can only remember one bad call that likely cost me a game—and that was the block-charge call on Mister Jennings when we could have beaten the overall number one Oklahoma with a sixteenth seed. That one gave me nightmares!" Les concluded.

*Coach Jim Calhoun of the University of Connecticut and Les
became great friends. Calhoun won three NCAA Championships
and 877 games in his sterling career.
Photo courtesy University of Connecticut.*

CHAPTER 18

THE HOT TUB GAME AND OTHER RUSES

With all of the adversity of NCAA sanctions caused by previous coaches, Les's chances of winning while reprising the affected programs was certainly diminished. It seems to be an aberration in his career that his coaching record on the University of Connecticut's home court is 2-0.

Les reset the circumstances. He traveled to Storrs, Connecticut, in his first season after the Valvano departure. It was a game Jimmy V had scheduled. Connecticut was a juggernaut program with a great coach, Jim Calhoun. Les arrived with a fine team roster full of players the endearing Valvano had recruited. But he was not favored to beat UConn.

Les tells the story with a cunning smile.

"I had been to Storrs in 1991 with a pretty good NC State team up against the University of Connecticut in their gym. The Huskies had not lost to a non-conference opponent in over 17 years. I had overheard people constantly talking about their consistent success at the hotel and then again around the arena when we had the shoot-around. They all seemed to have such an earned pride in the fact that the Connecticut Huskies rarely lose in Storrs. We were supposed to be the next guinea pig. They had definitely taken a win over us for granted," Les details.

"Everywhere you went there was someone who was overly confident that the game was over when it was scheduled for the Storrs Arena. They just never lost at home. It was a given. I used that fact to motivate my team in my pre-game remarks. I challenged them to stay focused and to be the aggressors."

The story would not have happened had Les not been an accomplished salesman— in the mold of Inky. The bloodline was irrefutable.

"That game in Storrs would have been different had I not put every ounce of effort I had into keeping Corchiani and Monroe. When it was announced that Jim Valvano was stepping down and I was to be the next head coach at State, I felt that my first job would be to re-recruit the players that were already on the team, especially these special two senior guards, Chris Corchiani and Rodney Monroe. It might be a hundred years before State gets a pair like that again. Thank you, Jim Valvano! I was able to accomplish the re-recruiting, despite a Raleigh media that had projected doom across the entire program," Les relates.

"I had to transition the program from a coach I knew was held up as a legend in all of sports for his amazing 1983 NCAA Championship run. And I really admired Jimmy Valvano, so I knew there was heartfelt rejection headed my way. No matter who I was, I was not Jimmy!"

There was no mistake that the personable and often humorous Jim Valvano enchanted the media, his players, the fans, and even the administration at State. He was insightful, loved, and well respected all at once. The National Championship run of 1983 is lauded as the best "Cinderella Story" in the annals of NCAA Basketball. It remains among the greatest sports stories ever—tucked between the 1980 Winter Olympics "Miracle on Ice" at Lake Placid and Jack Nicklaus' 1986 Masters golf win at the age of 46. The Wolfpack went into the first round of the ACC Tournament that year at 17-10, hoping for a bid to the lower level National Invitation Tournament in New York City. They had a very slim chance of making it past North Carolina with Michael Jordan and Sam Perkins—or Virginia with Ralph Sampson—to reach the NCAA Tournament.

ESPN writer Wayne Drehs summed it up.

In seven of the team's last nine victories, they trailed in the last minute. The Wolfpack needed to win the ACC tournament to even qualify for the NCAAs. And they barely did that, beating Wake Forest 71-70, North Carolina 91-84 in overtime, and Virginia 81-78. In the postseason, NC State managed to beat Ralph Sampson-led Virginia (again), which it had lost to twice during the regular season. In one regular-season stretch, the Wolfpack lost six of eight, including back-to-back 18-point losses to unranked teams. In the team's opening-round tournament game against Pepperdine, the Wolfpack rallied from a six-point deficit with 24 seconds left to win in overtime. No team had ever won the NCAA championship with 10 losses.

After defeating Georgia in the national semi-finals, the "Cardiac Pack" would register as a heavy underdog against Coach Guy Lewis's Houston Cougars in the championship. After all, Houston had Hakeem Olajuwon and Clyde Drexler—both named to the 2015 list of the NBA's greatest 50 players ever. Houston was ranked as the #1 college basketball team in America. The upset came when the Wolfpack's Lorenzo Charles dunked in a short desperation shot at the buzzer.

Jimmy Valvano could inspire. He could recruit. He could motivate. And he could coach. The NC State faithful and the players felt he would be impossible to replace.

"I came to State under dire circumstances and followed one of the most well-liked coaches ever. It was natural for the players to reject change. It happens all the time. Players transfer out. They cannot adjust often enough—and sometimes it's a rejection statement to the Athletic Director or to some authority that they are in vehement disagreement with the change," Les detailed. "I was the next guy in. I was unproven, and I was likely to be the option that players would not readily accept. I knew that. And I knew I had to gain their trust before we had our first practice."

The quick understanding of the relationship that Chris Corchiani had with Rodney Monroe as the team of "Fire and Ice" was essential. Les's explanation about gaining value in the NBA draft by learning to be a much better defender made sense. Les had gained both Corchiani's and Monroe's trust. He had arrived to play the University of Connecticut with players Valvano recruited and Les was barely able to keep. The UConn game would provide Les had a baptism into the national television spotlight of major college basketball. The transitioned Wolfpack had come to play the mighty Huskies. The arena at Storrs was sold out.

"In an unbelievable tough defensive game, our spunky senior guards, Chris Corchiani and Rodney Monroe, won it for us down the stretch. We slipped past them by one, 60-59. Both teams shot poorly. But the intense defense was the reason for that. We made twelve of sixteen free throws and that was really the difference. They also had sixteen free throws, but only made eight. Rodney Monroe had 24 points that night. The loss was a bit of a shock to those following UConn basketball," Les noted. "They have a great facility, great fans, and one of the finest coaches in the history of the sport, Jim Calhoun. I was elated that we were able to escape Storrs with a W. Winning there in 1991 was so much the exception that it took me a while to come back to earth."

Les came back to the ground thanks to an unusual circumstance of mistaken identity. Les recounted the re-entry into reality.

"After the game, Barbara and I went to the hotel bar to wait on Todd Turner, our new AD at State. Todd had been at UConn the year before and was extremely familiar with the area. We had planned to meet at the hotel bar before going out to a late dinner, win or lose.But Todd had seen a few old friends after the game and told us he'd be a few minutes late meeting up.

"As Barbara and I started to order a beer waiting on Todd, we noticed that a few people in the lobby were staring at us. At first, we just thought they had recognized me from the game and were upset that UConn had unexpectedly lost that night. But they did not have that look of a sporting-event disappointment. They looked much too serious.

"After a while a few of the men and a woman came over and told us that they had called the police and that they recognized me as the person who had extorted businesses in the Hartford area for $20,000 sometime before. I had no idea what they were talking about except that I put together that I looked like somebody else. I told them that I just spent my first night in the state of Connecticut *ever* the night before. They didn't buy it. I realized that I couldn't dissuade them from their purpose. So, I consciously decided to withhold my occupation since I didn't want a mistaken identity to be in the newspapers and raise any doubts about my character to our NC State fans. I thought about how it might play out in the newspapers in Raleigh assuming that I could actually be locked up. They seemed sure that I was a fugitive criminal. When the police arrived, they asked for an ID. I smiled and reached for my wallet, but only then did I realize that I had given my driver's license to a 19-year-old NC State equipment manager in order to rent my coach's vehicle. The manager still had my license!

"Now things got a little more intense as Barbara and I tried to explain that we were there visiting from North Carolina. Barbara was shuffling for her license.

"I was just about to be arrested for the worst case of mistaken identity I could have ever imagined. Barbara was protesting while looking through her pocketbook. But I had told her not to tell them who I am for the reason I gave. Even a mistaken identity can make a few of your home fans become paranoid. Besides, we had just beaten UConn an hour and a half earlier and I was certain I would not find a friendly face anywhere in Hartford or Storrs. At a minimum, the police were determined to take me in to be certain I was not the criminal they sought. Just then, Todd Turner walked up. He saw the policeman and the others there and asked what the problem was.

"The manager of the hotel bar knew Turner from his previous years at UConn. After hearing what they were accusing me of, he laughed and told them, 'I doubt Les has ever been in this state before. He's our head basketball coach at NC State.' They apologized all over themselves and wanted to comp our evening meal. I insisted that it was okay, even though the incident may have taken a year off of my life. Turner did take them up on free desserts. But the whole matter had me concerned after we had pulled off a great win over Jim Calhoun. I was probably not welcome in Storrs, and there may have been others that could have mistaken me for that criminal look-alike outside of the hotel area, as well. I stayed close, as a result. I also managed to get my license back—just in case!"

Les left Storrs with an unexpected win in the basketball world. Nobody told Les or his confident "Fire and Ice" guard tandem that they were supposed to write an "L" on the schedule before the game was played. The road win did even more for the NC State fans—the "Redcoats." The players who were ready to transfer to places other than Raleigh a few months earlier were now convinced that the street-wise Les Robinson was the real deal. He was not the charismatic Jim Valvano, but he exhibited his own endearing personality. They saw that he could make the right moves at the right time.

"And I left Connecticut with another side story nobody expected," Les added.

"When Jim Calhoun heard the story, he told me years later, he wished they would have locked me up for the charge of 'stealing a win in Storrs.' I never found out whether they ever caught that guy that looked like me."

Jim Calhoun went on to win three national championships at UConn over his forty-year coaching career. His .697 winning percentage and 877 wins are among the best in NCAA basketball history.

Les had to come back to the Hartford area the next year after the big win, but he was missing the all-time leading scorer at NC State in Rodney Monroe and the NCAA's all-time assist leader in Chris Corchiani. Both were playing in the next league up, the National Basketball Association.

He would return to Connecticut the next season.

After walking his team through practice and the pre-game shoot around the night before the 1992 ACC-Big East Challenge, Les headed into the adjoining hotel fitness center for his daily workout. The next night's contest was part of an early-season basketball doubleheader scheduled by ESPN for the Hartford Civic Center. He would be facing Pitt, a team that would gain an NCAA tournament spot at the end of the 1992 season.

"I had a habit of working out everywhere I went. Often, I would find a hot tub or a steam sauna after my workout just to relax. I worked out after our walk-through team practice at the Hartford Civic Center.

"I was looking for the hotel hot tub. Once located, I grabbed the last available towel and took a relaxing dip into the tub. There, while working the game plan through in my mind I considered the key points of a near-perfect execution it would take to beat a heavily favored Pitt team on national television the next evening," he explained.

"One unexpected break was about to materialize. As if scheduled by luck, four sturdy athletes meandered into the pool area and headed for the hot tub. They asked if they could join me. I knew right away that these were four of the basketball players my team would face the next night and that they were likely breaking the Pitt team curfew.

"Immediately I knew they did not know that I was the coach of the NC State team they would see the next night. They started talking basketball. They had 'Pitt' insignia clothing. They seemed pretty happy to be away from the confines of their hotel room," Les retold. "They never asked my name and likely presumed that I was a businessman traveling through the area. After a few minutes of chat, a young lady came over to bring some extra towels for them. One of the Pitt players asked her if she knew of a great place for entertainment, specifically asking if they had an all-night bar or lounge near. That raised my attention. After a few minutes of banter, I told them 'thanks for the conversation' and that I wished them well in the game they were chatting about. I casually dried off and headed to the lady attendant with the towels.

"I told her that she should find them a good place to go since they were from out of town. I was effusive in my praise of what fine gentlemen they were and how they deserved to have the best time while they stayed in Hartford, reasoning that she should help the community put its best foot forward. I told her that her hospitality would go a long way towards persuading those very nice four young men to come back or even to possibly settle in the Hartford area. She promised she would direct them to a top all-night lounge so that they would enjoy her hometown.

"I hung around long enough to see them bite on the information. They headed out to change. This was just too good to believe," Les grinned.

Les finally got to reveal his true occupation on the sidelines the next evening as the Pittsburgh team was going through layups.

Les recounts, "They looked quite surprised as they tapped each other on the shoulder during the warm-ups to point me out on the sidelines. Now they were concerned that I was going to rat on them to their coach, Paul Evans. I wanted them to worry about that. But I knew we had another advantage. They had been out all night. It was likely that they couldn't jump or sprint quite as well. I didn't want Coach Evans to know that. They had a very good team and I needed every advantage. Pitt was heavily favored, and I was playing two freshmen in key positions including point guard. The four players being out all night might be worth fifteen or twenty points to us when they began to get tired in the second half.

"They had just beaten Kentucky at Rupp Arena in Lexington. They had a couple of top NBA prospects in Sean Miller and Darren Morningstar. They had a much more experienced team than ours. The game was up and down and the more they ran the better my chances were that they would run out of gas. It was a tough and physical game, and they did run empty late. Sure enough, we pulled off the upset, 78-77."

"I guess Coach Evans never knew the real reason some of his players were a little flat that night. I have seen Paul Evans since, but I've never told him that story. One of those players became an assistant coach and has seen me since and always gives me that knowing grin that says that I knew how to recognize and exploit any small advantage.

"So, I went 2 and 0 in the state of Connecticut by a total winning margin of two points over two nationally ranked teams. Each of those teams entered the game as heavy favorites. Paul Evans never knew the reason. Of course, I have stayed in touch with Jim Calhoun. He and I became great friends," Les beamed. "We try to catch up every year at the Final Four. Oh, and I was almost jailed there, too."

Some ruses were planned; some were spontaneous. Yet there remains another category—the accidental.

The "Hot Tub Game" against Pitt holds nothing to the advantage Les had much earlier in his career when he was coaching a team that needed every possible edge. It was 1981 and his Citadel Bulldogs were rarely favored over anyone on the road—if ever. The game against the College of the Holy Cross Crusaders was no exception. Holy Cross, one of the great American Jesuit colleges, is located in Worcester, Massachusetts. They have an impressive basketball history. Holy Cross had boasted former NBA greats Bob Cousy and Tommy Heinsohn. Future NBA standout Kevin Stacom was the star of their 1981-82 team. Even their coach, George Blaney, had been a star at Holy Cross and played for the New York Knicks. Beating them, even at the neutral site of the Charlotte Coliseum, would take a miracle.

"No sane person would pick us to beat Holy Cross with their incredible player Kevin Stacom as an impossible match-up for us. I'm not sure that the game plan I had would work back then, but it didn't matter. Something changed enough to have me put together an emergency game plan that I knew would work," Les recalled.

"The Citadel was scheduled to play Holy Cross as a part of a college invitational doubleheader hosted by Davidson College," Les recalls. "Coach Teague took the game just before the season began when another team canceled, and a higher-than-normal payout was guaranteed. The Citadel needed the money. Coach Teague had figured that The Citadel had lost to worse teams at places much further away for a whole lot less money," Les recalls. "I agreed."

It was an early December game that had been booked even though the players were still finishing midterm exams. Les had to find a way to compete and try to knock off Holy Cross. The way to win that game echoed through the walls at that old Charlotte Coliseum—literally.

Les explained that a common-walled restroom and shower facility separated the player locker rooms. The Citadel fielded a smart and feisty basketball program under Les's guidance; but as was normally the case, the team lacked the athleticism to compete with many other schools, especially those from the basketball-rich Northeast. A win against Holy Cross was unlikely. The Crusaders had beaten UMass and UConn that season and lost to Duke University by only 6.

The Citadel's thin 6'5" center, John Sterling, needed a quick bathroom break before Les's pregame talk. It was while at a urinal that Sterling noticed the coach at Holy Cross was bellowing pre-game instructions that could be heard clearly through those old cinder-block walls and thin ceiling tiles.

"Sterling came back to get me quick. I went in to see what he was listening to. The instructions were being given as if I were actually in the room with his players. This information was so valuable that I worried about it being a reverse set-up. Maybe they knew the sound traveled well and Coach Blaney was trying to set *me* up. One instruction heard clearly was that they were going to open with a full court zone press without the worry that we would take it to the basket," Les recalled. "He said 'don't worry about taking chances and going for the steal since they will simply try to break the press and hold the ball. They will not take any advantage in numbers to get to the basket. The Citadel will want to run the clock.'

"I thought to myself, 'Oh yeah, Coach! We'll see about that! Coach Blaney also divulged their offensive strategy and the type of zone they would go to from the press. He spoke about our previous tendency to throw weak cross-court passes against a zone. I had everything I needed if I could counteract it with a good enough plan and good enough play," Les stated. "And I had the type of players who could execute a strategy. This team listened well. I told my informant-player Sterling to keep the information to himself—to tell absolutely no one. Then, I returned to the team locker room. Of course, I told my team *our* game plan in a much lower voice.

"I huddled my players up," Les continued. "I told them to expect a full court zone press, how to hit the middle and break it, and how to take that advantage all the way to the rim. I told them 'three on two, two on one, whatever numbers advantage we get, we are to force the issue by going straight to the basket. I emphasized that we were not to pull the ball out and set up if we had numbers. I said, 'Absolutely no passes across the top of a zone.' I told them exactly what they were going to run on their offensive end and how to counteract it. We didn't have great athletic talent, but I had a roster full of pretty smart players. We were in a defense that would counteract their first offensive option on the inside. By breaking the press, we jumped out to a nice lead. We completely crossed up their coach's scouting report. The team did much as I said early on and we went into the locker room at the half with a double-digit lead. The second half brought the game a little closer, but in the end, we kicked Holy Cross's butt that night, 89-80. Nobody figured on that win, except me and our team.

"Only my player, John Sterling, and I knew where we picked up the advantage," Les added. "I had asked him to keep that information close to the vest for a reason. If we lost that game, knowing our opponent's every move, it would only have been embarrassing to just John Sterling and me. Winning it made others take note that we could succeed in a hostile environment against the odds. It also gave my players some game confidence and, importantly, the impression that I knew what I was doing. What they didn't know was that I also knew exactly what Holy Cross was doing!"

There was a side story to that game.

"Our chaplain then was a Catholic Priest, Father Sam Migliarese. 'Father Sam' as we called him, was a huge basketball fan and would go with us whenever he could on the road. He made this trip to Charlotte. But Holy Cross had the Jesuit Priests, and as I have always understood, the Jesuits are the 'Marine Corps of the priesthood.' When their team came out, three Jesuit Priests sat on the end of their bench. So, I immediately summoned Father Sam out of the stands and asked him if he could sit on our bench. I knew it was long odds—one against three, but they had no idea how much Father Sam prayed for us to win. Those Jesuits were probably only praying for nobody to get hurt. Father Sam simply wanted to win. So, I have always referred to that game as 'the game Father Sam beat the three Jesuits,'" Les laughs. "And I never told Father Sam about spying on Coach Blaney's game plan because I wanted him to have his miracle moment. In fact, I've never told Coach Blaney."

Sometimes other fates played a role in devising a way to win. Though basketball is an indoor game, Les knows at least one time when weather earned him a victory.

"It was towards the end of the season, and the Bulldogs were not playing well. The Citadel was to play the Richmond Spiders on regional television at 1:00 on Saturday. A severe snowstorm had gripped the Northeast and Midwest. Several top regional games with much more impressive basketball programs than The Citadel and Richmond had been canceled because of the power outages and travel hazards. So, I got word just before I went into the locker room for the pregame talk that we were going to be the only game televised at that time slot east of the Mississippi. The television producer told me about the timeout rules and then told me that our game would be seen by more than four million people," Les recalled.

"So, I took a regular stat sheet into the team locker room before the game.I began by saying that 'The good Lord has blessed us today in ways beyond our dreams.' I read out some bogus numbers. I told them that 2,011 saw us play VMI; 1,890 saw us play Furman. I went down the sheet mumbling numbers and ended with a total of 27,562. I made it all up.

"Fellas, we've coached like crap and you've played like crap. And we know—up until now—that 27,562 people have an opinion that we are a crap team. But the Lord is good. Because of the snow—severe weather elsewhere, we are the only game on TV today and more than 4 million people who have never seen us play can form their own opinion. All is forgiven. We have a fresh start. We can be a winner—a team that they like to watch, or we can be the crap team we've been up until now. We're not going to draw Xs and Os because you don't listen anyway. Now let's go out there and establish for four million viewers what they should think in about two hours about your hustle, your effort, your team pride, and your poise. Will they see a team of winners or a crap team? It's your choice."

The motivational ability of a coach can inspire teams to perform extraordinary feats. The Citadel beat a stunned Richmond team that day by double digits.

A beat writer, James Beck of the *Charleston News & Courier,* wrote an editorial at the end of The Citadel's 1977-1978 basketball season calling for the firing of head basketball coach Les Robinson. The team was competitive but had lost seven games by a total of twelve points. They did not win any close game during that season.

Les had every reason to look elsewhere for other opportunities. He was well known in basketball circles. He could recruit. He could coach on the sidelines as well as anyone. He also could endear himself to a fan base. But writer Beck saw the lack of wins as a reason to call for the coach's head. The vehement support from The Citadel's longtime basketball fans became a backlash against the newspaper. Subscriptions were canceled. The editorial backfired, not just publicly, but in the locker room as well.

With the three-guard offense returning—Randy Nesbit, Wade Moore and Rick Swing—the Bulldogs served notice by winning each close game early. Combined with Tom Slawson and Dale French, the fivesome started together in all but one game that season. Four of the five starters were back from the year before. They had learned how to win. They completed the season with 20 wins and 8 losses. Sharp-shooting sub Chris Davis along with board horses Mark Cartwright and Wells Holland gave the Bulldog coach ample quality bench support. The sportswriter was sent to the city desk.

The 1984-85 season was another banner season for the amicable coach. The team went 18-11 with star forward Regan Truesdale leading the way. Remarkably, the Bulldogs picked up where they left off the season before and rolled up 23 consecutive wins at McAlister Field House. That home-winning-streak record still stands as the Bulldogs longest in program history.

Success at a military college is the exception—not the rule. Yet Les found the right combinations often enough to win 132 games as the Bulldog mentor, the most in their history by a coach up to that time. At the end of the 1985 season, Athletic Director Eddie Teague had announced his retirement. School President Major General James A. Grimsley offered Les the position of Athletic Director, but he would have to leave coaching. It was a tempting offer, but Les was only 42 years of age and wanted to continue coaching.

Les had received several inquiries from other programs to coach basketball and finally settled on a larger school with a basketball tradition in place—East Tennessee State University. Much like when Les left Cedar Key High School, he and Barbara had to make a very difficult decision. He saw ETSU as a path to coach with a wider array of recruiting talent. If he didn't take the opportunity then, he knew that he never would. He had to see how far he could go in the career he had selected in the 5th Grade. He and Barbara packed for Johnson City, Tennessee.

Les celebratees with Barbara as the ETSU Buccaneers win the Southern Conference Basketball Cahmpionship. It was a long road back from the probation status Les inherited. Photo courtesy ETSU Sports.

CHAPTER 19

THE BUCS REBUILD

The transition to East Tennessee State in Johnson City was not a given. It really happened by accident. Though there were offers, Les was not looking for another head coaching job. The job was looking for him.

"I was at the Final Four in Lexington, Kentucky, when I was approached in the lobby of the hotel next to Rupp Arena by a coaching friend, Sonny Smith. Smith was the coach at Auburn University but was told he would be replaced at the end of the season. The year before he had both Charles Barkley and Chuck Person—and they won twenty games. But during the following season they were struggling, and Auburn University officials had made a pre-mature decision. At the time, Sonny Smith would have a diffi-cult time securing a winning season. As a result, he was set to take over the program at East Tennessee State the next season from Coach Barry Dowd, who had been released.

"However, Sonny's Auburn team went on a winning streak after he had been asked to step down. They won the last few games of the regular sea-son before shocking the SEC tournament with four tournament wins. They qualified for the NCAA's as the SEC Champion. Auburn continued win-ning all the way into the Sweet Sixteen. They had 22 wins by then. Sonny no longer had Charles Barkley, so the winning streak was a complete sur-prise. Sonny had coached his way back into the job he lost because they thought he couldn't coach!

"Sonny saw me in the lobby and made a bee-line towards me. He hur-riedly brought up that he was recommending me for the job he was previ-ously supposed to take at ETSU. He told me that I would be getting a call from the ETSU president that very day. Sure enough, I did get the call. I agreed to talk with him after he had cleared it with Coach Eddie Teague at The Citadel. The ETSU president peaked my interest enough that I wanted to visit in a few days up at Johnson City. I did so, and in a few more days, I signed on to be their new head basketball coach."

Some things had changed at The Citadel. Les had completed an exciting 18-11 season with the conference's Player of the Year, Regan Truesdale. The Athletic Director, Coach Teague, was stepping down in June. When others had begun talking with Les about stepping up to that position and out of coaching, it did not feel like the time to do so. Les knew that he wanted to continue his coaching career.

"Barbara and I had our youngest, Barbara Ann, at home getting ready to go off to college within a year. Our situation had changed. We had looked at other opportunities over the years and came to the family conclusion that we should remain where we were. We had so many good friends that leaving would be difficult. But I was always open to options. I had not coached a varsity program at a college yet without the somewhat restrictive recruiting guideline imposed by the aspect of a military institution. I started coaching at The Citadel when the Vietnam War was still on the nightly news. I was always able to get great kids—dedicated and focused. But I could not go after junior college players like my opponents could to reload their programs. I couldn't go after borderline academic students or kids that had an aversion to authority. In a way, that was a blessing. It taught me how to coach up and to take a sometimes-lesser athletic team to a higher level."

The Citadel experience also set a system of other successes in motion. Les had graduated all twenty-six of the final twenty-six players he had recruited. The Citadel's players stayed focused upon the completion of their academic requirements for graduation in four years. The college was among the best in America at achieving four-year degrees. It was a culture that thrived. Many went on to other professions well outside of the gym—several becoming doctors, engineers, ministers, small business owners, and lawyers. His player alumni roster was its own recruiting tool to parents' wishing the best for their sons.

"When that lobby conversation with the Sonny Smith moved into action quickly, I had to make a tough choice. In short order, I met with their college president. The package was much more than The Citadel could afford. But it really wasn't about money. In the end I made the decision to see what I could do under the same rules as my competition. I had a series of difficult situations since my first game as a coach. Coach Maravich took me in as a freshman coach when an assistant left suddenly. I coached the smallest public high school in Florida. I coached the junior varsity at then-NAIA Western Carolina; then I coached as an assistant under a very weird head coach in George Hill, followed by eleven years as head coach at that same military college. I was only 42—with my children mostly grown. I came back to the thought about an opportunity to see what I could do playing with the same rules as everyone else. If I didn't make the move then, I would probably never know what I could do. I would never be able to validate what I had dreamed of becoming since the fifth grade," Les recounted. "So, I took it."

The ETSU student population was at 11,000, several times the population at The Citadel, then less than 2000. Their gym was a mini-dome seating 12,000 in the same building where the football games were played. It was an unusual facility for the Southern Conference.

Les again came to a university where the cupboard was bare. They had finished dead last in the Southern Conference. Coach Dowd had no recruits in the mill that made sense for the program. It may have been propitious that they had no significant player returning. Les took the job based on what he knew. He could deal with rebuilding. But there were things he was never told during the hiring process.

Sometimes the appeal of a new coach motivates players to perform. Les took that twelfth-place team up to 5th the next season while recruiting to bring in a winner. But his plans were interrupted. Things that had happened before he had arrived were discovered. Les was never quite sure whether the administration had already known this before he was offered the position. The number of basketball scholarships awarded was reduced. Some players became ineligible. The ETSU probation terms took away the specter of postseason play.

Les never had to be concerned with such issues while at The Citadel under the oversight of Coach Eddie Teague as Athletic Director. But reality was that he would lose a few key signees and that his team would likely have the worst talent in the league in 1986. They did. They only won 7 games in the 1986-87 season.

Once eligibility for postseason play returned and the full slate of thirteen scholarships were restored, Les began to recruit the finest team in ETSU history. They doubled their win total in 1987-88 with 14 wins.

"I had Greg Dennis and Mister Jennings playing right away as freshmen," Les recalled the times. "With Major Geer and Alvin West coming along, I knew we could be good the next year. Chad Keller transferred in. I brought in Calvin Talford, an exceptional athlete, the next season. I also brought in Marty Story. We were young, but we had the key roles filled. All five of my starters averaged double figures—much like the high school team I had in Cedar Key that owed much of its success to unselfish play and scoring balance. That team was fun to coach. I had realized my ambition when I left The Citadel. Recruiting under different circumstances for two years, I had pieced together a very fine basketball team. It validated what I felt I could do as a coach."

Youth had its moments.

"We had a good club at East Tennessee, but we were really young. I had a great 5'7" point guard, Mister Jennings from Culpeper, Virginia. I had gotten 6'11" Greg Dennis out of Charleston, West Virginia, and Alvin West from Jacksonville, North Carolina. The next year, we had another freshman starter from Castlewood, Virginia, Calvin Talford. He was an unbelievable athlete still learning some of the finer points of the game. He was Michael Jordan in the rough. In fact, he won the NCAA dunk contest as a senior before being drafted by the NBA's Chicago Bulls (1992).

"In spite of us winning the Southern Conference tournament by 23 points over Marshall University in the finals, the committee placed us in as the #16 seed to play the overall #1 team in America at season's end, Oklahoma. We started three freshmen and two sophomores, and our record was only 20-9. That might have been a factor in their decision.

"Our opponents had Mookie Blaylock and Stacy King, both top picks in the NBA draft. They were loaded with talent," Les remarked. "It was easy to see that the NCAA committee had little respect for us. I saw that as a motivational advantage.

"When we arrived at Vanderbilt's Memorial Coliseum, I noticed that we had a lot more fans there than we expected. It was another mistake that the NCAA made in placing a #16 seed in their home state. I also noticed that the gym had scoreboards at every angle. I counted them. There were seventeen!"

Les continued. "I used those scoreboards in my pregame motivational talk. After we warmed up, I went in and told my young starters that they had more scoreboards than any arena in America there, seventeen. I added that we would be playing a game against the team that writers, media, and coaches all felt was the best team in the country. Then I paused. I said that when we got down by 36 to 9, not only would millions of people in New York, Chicago, and Las Vegas switch channels, but that our little team would not be shown in places like Culpeper, Castlewood, and Jacksonville, NC. The network would switch to another game, too. So, the only ones that would see us getting our ass handed to us would be those people outside—and they'd see it on seventeen scoreboards all across the gym."

Les added, "But we can keep that from happening. We can share the ball, play D, block out, fill the lanes, and make solid decisions. That team out there is soft. They think they've already won this game because no number 16 seed had ever beaten a number one seed ever. So, they are looking to see who they'll play in the next round.

"Then I finished the talk. 'If we play our asses off, every small town in America will know us. Every newspaper writer, every basketball fan, and every school teacher you ever had growing up will have a new opinion about you—and this team that will never quit. Everybody will know East Tennessee State as that little team that would never give up. All we need to do is get them in a game early and let them know that we are not quitting. When we get it to the end, the weight of the world will be on them, not us. And we can pull off the biggest upset in the history of the NCAA tournament. This tournament has been around for fifty years. The lowest seed has never beaten the highest seed. We can change that today."

The pumped-up youth who Les had went out in the first half and built a lead. Nobody was switching channels. The 5'7" Keith 'Mister' Jennings became the face of ETSU determination. His stature was their stature— and little 'Mister' Jennings was not backing down. ETSU raced out to a ten-point lead, never losing their focus. A Stacey King basket at the halftime buzzer made the score East Tennessee 39, Oklahoma 31. The Bucs raced out to a 48-33 lead out of the break. But when the diminutive point guard Jennings got into foul trouble, the Sooners chipped away at the lead. Jennings hit free throws to put the Buccaneers up by one with ninety seconds left but fouled out on the next exchange. The Sooners went up 72-71 and avoided a buzzer-beater for the upset as time ran out. The game remained as the closest that a #16 seed ever came to beat a #1 seed until March 16, 2018 when The University of Maryland Baltimore County shocked #1 seed Virginia, 74-54.

Les was again named Southern Conference Coach of the Year and also garnered the Coach of the Year award for the State of Tennessee.

"There were a few close calls that could have gone one way or another," Les remembered. "That's how close it was. My club played like champions. Greg Dennis, Calvin Talford, Mister Jennings—they all gave it 100%. We lost that game, but I knew we had something. The next season we continued our progress. We won 7 my first year, 14 my second. That '89 team won 20. The next year we broke through and won 27. We were ranked 16th team in America. They were just as fun to coach as they were for our fans to watch."

The ETSU Buccaneers swept through the 1989-90 Southern Conference tournament. Even their losses were impressive—to Maryland, Wake Forest, and UCLA. They beat the University of Tennessee and Les's alma mater, North Carolina State University. By December, they made it into the Top 25 polls for the first time in school history. They made it all the way up to #9 nationally by February.

The ETSU team with Les's key recruits Calvin Talford and Marty Story as seniors and a redshirted Greg Dennis playing tough, did pull a huge upset in the NCAA tournament in 1992. The 14th seeded ETSU Bucs upended the #3 seeded University of Arizona in the first round.

"Bigger than life" stories occur at every stage and stop in sports, but perhaps the saddest that Les remembers happened at Johnson City.

"I remember that in my last year at The Citadel we brought in a tough young football player with a major pedigree. Marc Buoniconti was the son of NFL great Nick Buoniconti. Then the next year, The Citadel comes up to play in Johnson City. It was the first contest between the school I left and the school I had joined. So, it was a bit awkward seeing so many of my friends from Charleston at the game."

Marc Buoniconti had been recently named the Southern Conference Defensive Player-of-the-Week for his stellar performance against VMI. His famous father was in attendance at Lexington, Virginia, for that game. The elder Buoniconti was the middle linebacker for the 1972 and 1973 World Champion Miami Dolphins. He was from the Boston area and played at the University of Notre Dame. Retired from football by 1976, Buoniconti became a lawyer and a familiar television analyst for professional football telecasts. He had sons playing football at both The Citadel (Marc) and Duke University (Nick, Jr.). He was not at the game in Johnson City, deferring to see Nick, Jr., play at Duke.

On October 26, 1985, The Citadel traveled to East Tennessee State University for a game in the mini-dome. On a third down play in the first quarter, ETSU running back Herman Jacobs was tackled by Citadel teammates Joel Thompson and Marc Buoniconti. All seemed routine. Except Marc Buoniconti did not get up. He remained on the ground limp and motionless. He had broken his neck.

"I was there watching the game and I knew right away that the tough young kid I met the year before at The Citadel was seriously injured. It was a sickening feeling to find out he was paralyzed and fighting for his life," Les recalled.

"I was down on the field," Les continued. "Our trainers were there, EMS, and Citadel Head Trainer Andy Clawson, who was and is among the most experienced in the business.Everything stopped. The silence in the dome was noticeable. People were saying prayers. Citadel players were down on their knees with their heads in their hands bewildered by the reports. Buoniconti was tended to carefully. He was taken to the Johnson City Medical Center. Along with so many others, I went there. Without the proper facilities for spinal injuries, Buoniconti was flown out to Miami the next day where there was a trauma facility."

Marc Buoniconti's journey would be both arduous and extensive. He would require around-the-clock care after those critical early hours and days. In seven months, he was able to breath on his own again. Joel Thompson, his tackling partner on that play, became both a dedicated friend and motivator. After some vitriol associated with lawsuits related to Buoniconti's suitability for contact at the ETSU game, time sorted out the realities. The Citadel embraced the brave young man, now focused upon a mission to help others. The Buoniconti Fund of the Miami Project (a $200 million project whose goal is to end spinal cord paralysis) is hosted each year at a Citadel home football game. Marc Buoniconti meets classmates and teammates there each year. He credits the discipline he learned at The Citadel for getting him through his most difficult times.

The Citadel did something that was never done before or since. Marc Buoniconti, The Citadel Class of 1988, was awarded his class ring on September 28, 2006. The Citadel awards rings only to members of a graduating class at the beginning of their senior year. The tradition is especially honored because of the physical, military, and academic rigors required of each student. It is not The Citadel Diploma that is fervently displayed as an achievement by 175 years of proud graduates. It is all about the ring.

Buoniconti spoke to the 2006 team, who kneeled all around his wheelchair.

"Let me tell you something. Not a day goes by, not a moment, that I don't think about what I'd give to be back on that football field," Buoniconti said. "I would do it all over again. I want you guys to know how lucky and fortunate you are to be in the position that you're in, to play football for The Citadel, to have teammates around you. I want you to know how much each of you can rely on your teammates. Because I'll tell you right now, I would not be here if not for the teammates behind me."

Les had been Director of Athletics at both institutions. As The Citadel's AD, he had come full circle yet again. He was on the field in Johnson City moments after the tragic injury and was back at The Citadel in 2006. It was Les who guided the halftime festivities and enthusiastically supported the added surprise of the jersey retirement Les recalled the special day. Buoniconti had worn #59.

"Seeing that awful injury in person, then seeing 21 years later, this tough young man come back around in a spirit of friendship and family was an emotional day, and one I will never forget," Les emphasizes. "There was a time when nobody figured he would survive. There were a lot of tears in Johnson City, and then again in Charleston."

Les had a handful of years in Johnson City and an overload of issues and concerns within the program. But none of the struggles in Johnson City meant anything after seeing 19-year-old Marc Buoniconti lying on the ground unable to move.

"There is so much in life that supersedes sports," Les expresses. "Sometimes we get too caught up in the small things when the big things are what really matter."

After he arrived in Johnson City, Les knew it would be beneficial to go out into the community to meet supporters and help sell season tickets for the basketball team. Although the administration likely knew that there could be reprisals due from the NCAA, they never divulged the issues associated with Coach Dowd's firing. They never let Les know that he could be stepping into a fiasco. Gregarious and energetic, Les visited the car dealerships, the mortuaries, the dry cleaners, and the hoteliers. He sold the blue and yellow pride across the Tri-City market (Bristol, Kingsport and Johnson City). He spoke at the Rotarians, the Exchangeites, and the Civitans. He gave away hats and tee shirts. He played tennis at the country club with the donors. He answered questions on the drive-home radio talk shows. Les knew how to do the grunt work it took to build a fan base. He immersed himself in the culture to promote building a winner.

When ETSU president Ronald Beller hired Les, he had no idea of his willingness and ability to appeal to supporters in the community. They were 9-19 during the 1983 season after making it into the NIT in 1982 with a record of 22-9. They lost 18 games in the 1984-85 season. There were a lot of unknowns in the circumstances that had ETSU and President Beller buy out Dowd's contract. Les was not in Johnson City to follow the past but rather to embrace the future.

After the dire circumstances and the NCAA sanctions, Les was able to compile an 81-70 record over five seasons. He took ETSU to two consecutive Southern Conference championships and left his good friend and assistant coach Alan LeForce with the firepower to earn invitations to the NCAAs the next two seasons, as well.

"We had built something and the kids that came in were impressed with our commitment to win," Les recalled. "We could compete across conferences and beat the ACC, SEC, and Big 10 schools," Les related. "And not many of those were happy about scheduling us when we were down as we got better each year."

Les took on the role as Athletic Director simultaneously with his duties as basketball coach before his first year was complete. The university was able to grow the brand and build a strategy for excellence under his tutelage. He left East Tennessee State in much better condition, athletically and financially, than what he inherited in 1985.

Les's tenure at East Tennessee State ended poetically. He was summoned home by NC State to right the foundering ship for the Wolfpack. This time he knew in advance that there were problems. His final Buc game was a gut-wrenching loss to his best friend in coaching, Bobby Cremins. The Georgia Tech Yellow Jackets and "Lethal Weapon 3" defeated Les's upstart team in the first round of the NCAA's in 1990. Georgia Tech made it to the Final Four that season with Kenny Anderson, Brian Oliver, and Dennis Scott. All three players averaged over 20 points per game against formidable ACC competition. They lost in the National Semifinals to eventual NCAA Champions and #1 seed UNLV and their controversial coach, Jerry Tarkanian.

Les's five years in Johnson City produced the best teams that ETSU had experienced back-to-back in their basketball history. He was able to turn the program over to Alan LeForce. LeForce and Les had remained close friends. LeForce had earned the role of head coach. When Les came to ETSU, he still owed LeForce for the humorous incident that helped him to land Rodney McKeever while LeForce was coaching Les's crosstown rival at the College of Charleston. Turnabout is fair play! LeForce had a great team to coach.

"I knew the NC State coaching position would likely come open because it seemed that there was a lot of information flying around about the situation over there. But, as coaches, we don't sit around wondering what might happen somewhere else. We have to take care of business in our own back yard," Les warns.

"We did go over to NC State that year and won against Jimmy's team. But to be honest, I liked Jimmy and appreciated what he had done at State and the great run he had in 1983. It made me proud to see my college win it all like it did back in 1974. You always want your college to succeed. I wanted State to win, but not against the team I was coaching. Winning in Reynolds Coliseum that year, as it turns out, brought my stock up with the NC State fans. But I didn't want to win at the expense of another coach's firing. As it turned out, these things were not in my control, anyway."

As the season threaded into early March, Les's ETSU team was rewarded with another NCAA bid. Meanwhile, the rumors in Raleigh were getting louder. The two programs were going in opposite directions. Valvano's enthusiasm for coaching had waned amid the turbulence. He would negotiate his last year's contract buyout and step down. But the finalization of the agreement took months. In Raleigh, these negotiations spurned even more rumors and left the program in a state of turmoil.

If the Wolfpack athletic director wanted to contact the ETSU basketball coach, the protocol required that they contacted the ETSU athletic director first. Les, holding both job titles, could not be advised. NC State would have to move up the administration to the college president. But Dr. Ronald Beller was away in Europe. Timing was skewered. NC State needed a way to facilitate an inquiry to their first choice—Les Robinson.

"Clemson's AD Bobby Robinson called, and I just knew it had to be a prank. It sounded like something that Bobby Cremins might do or one of my friends back in Charleston. So, not knowing Bobby Robinson's voice, I quickly asked if I could call him right back. So I called the number he gave me back within five minutes. Sure enough it routed into the Clemson Athletic Department. Cliff Ellis was the coach at Clemson. He was doing well, and I knew he was not being fired. I thought maybe he had taken another job. All of this was running through my mind when I called Clemson's Bobby Robinson back. I had no idea what he was calling about."

Clemson AD Bobby Robinson was calling Les to inquire if he would take the NC State head basketball coaching position if it were offered. It was an unusual conversation with a third party who was just relaying questions and answers.

"I was confused at first. But then the Clemson AD told me he was re-turning a favor for NC State from a situation that cropped up a few years back," Les retold.

Les detailed the payback circumstance. "When Danny Ford was being hired by Clemson years back, it seems that there was a similar situation. As a result, NC State's Director of Athletics called Danny Ford to ask him if he would take the Clemson job if it were offered. He did take the job—and they later won the NCAA Football Championship under Ford. For all these years, Clemson felt like it owed NC State a return favor. I suppose some of these third-party conversations go on more than we know so that a college can avoid the media getting advance information on an important story. It might also save embarrassment if a coach is not interested," Les explained.

Les gave Bobby Robinson an affirmative answer.

"I told him, in effect, that if the situation presented itself and we could come to a contract agreement that I would accept the position. But, I told him that, if anything were agreed upon, I would have to wait to accept when Dr. Ronald Beller got back from Europe in a few days. I owed him that," Les qualified.

Dr. Beller was the president of East Tennessee State University.

Within the week Les Robinson became the 17th head basketball coach at NC State on April 23, 1990. He was the first NC State alumnus and for-mer ACC player to become the Wolfpack head coach. Barbara and Les were on their way to Raleigh. In basketball, things seem to happen in April.

Two key mentors would have been justly proud. Both Everett Case and Press Maravich exerted a nurturing influence upon Les's career. They both died in the month of April—Case in 1966, Maravich in 1987. Tragically, Jim Valvano would die just three years later, in April 1993.

Les and Jim Valvano discuss the program at NC State. Valvano suggested that Les should replace him as coach the following year. His suggestion came to fruition. Photo courtesy NC State University.

CHAPTER 20

JIMMY V

"How could someone not enjoy being around Jimmy Valvano? The man was such a large personality and he always smiled, even when the refs screwed up," Les remembers. "So, it was troubling to me, as a State grad and a fan of Jimmy's, when the glory of that 1983 season was fading into the problems of the program that came out in the late 1980's," Les details.

Jim Valvano, an endearing personality with a distinctive New York brogue, came to NC State from Iona College in 1980. He had it all—charm, wit, and basketball savvy. He won twice as many as he lost at Iona (94-47) over his five years there. He took the 1983 Wolfpack, a 17-10 team, to the NCAA tournament by virtue of winning the ACC's season-ending tournament. It was the only way he could get in.

"Jim earned the respect of every coach in the business," Les stated. "It was because he got his players to buy in and to believe in themselves."

The 1983 ACC tournament was a gauntlet. The Pack eked out a one-point win over a tough Wake Forest club in the opening round, 71-70. Valvano knew that, as the fifth place ACC team, he'd have to win the ACC tournament to go to the 'Big Dance.' He wasn't even sure he'd be invited to the NIT if he had lost. His semi-final opponent was heavily favored—the defending National Champion Tar Heels of North Carolina. Their roster included Michael Jordan, Sam Perkins, Matt Doherty, Brad Daugherty, Jimmy Braddock and Buzz Peterson. They were loaded with talent. But NC State took them to overtime and pulled away at the end. It was the harbinger of what was to come.

Perhaps the best team that the University of Virginia ever put on the court was up next. The three-time College Player-of-the-Year, Ralph

Sampson, would dominate the lane. They also had the speedy Othell Wilson, Ricky Stokes, and sharpshooter Rick Carlisle. The Wolfpack and Valvano were decided underdogs yet again. In a precursor of things to come, the Wolfpack earned their NCAA bid by downing Virginia, 81-78.

Their next six games were much of the same—always the underdog in a close game that the Pack won at the end. They beat Pepperdine and UNLV in the first two rounds by a combined three points. They matched up with Ralph Sampson's Virginia again in the West Regional final, and won again, this time by 63-62. The all-red-jersey Final Four featured NC State against the University of Georgia and Louisville against Houston. The final against Houston sealed the fate of the most unlikely of NCAA Champions.

Valvano's 'Cinderella season' ended in the visual of trying to find a player to hug as the Pack won six straight NCAA tournament games, including that last-second classic over the heavy favorite, Houston. The *Phi Slamma Jamma* Cougars had won 26 straight games until that amazing Lorenzo Charles catch and dunk of Dereck Whittenburg's short shot in Albuquerque. Valvano became one of the most recognized coaches in the land.

But things changed.

"When the problems surfaced a few seasons later, some were ready to fire him without getting all of the facts right," Les stated. "There were some tough choices. Jim would have benefitted by having a drill sergeant-like assistant coach. When he traveled to speak out of town is when the players got into trouble. But he got 100% of the blame," Les said. "They just never understood what he did for some of the other players that would never have that opportunity if it wasn't for Jim."

The Valvano years at State had two sides. On the one side, the Wolfpack nation, 'the Redcoats,' got a great show. 'Jimmy V' could recruit at a level with Duke and North Carolina. He could coach. He was able to endear the fans and the press with an overflow of charisma. His record of 209-110 brought back the glee of the golden years mindful of Everett Case and Norm Sloan. On the other hand, the problems all seemed to come in a matter of months.

Valvano seemed to know that the run at NC State was nearly over.

"Jimmy called me in late August of 1989, wanting a game over in Raleigh. I had a pretty good team. He had an opening just before the Christmas holidays for a game to be played on December 19. But our team and fans were flying out on December 20 to Hawaii for a tournament there. To play in Raleigh, we'd have to ride a bus all night back to Johnson City to make the morning plane ride.

Les proposed a solution that Valvano quickly rejected.

"I knew I had a good club. I knew Jimmy had a fine team, as well. But I thought it would be great to use the situation to schedule a home game with State in our mini-dome. Les continued. "But Valvano knew that could be a snakepit place to play. He declined to swap a home-and-home contract but thanked me for the time."

"Just two weeks later, he called me back. Evidently, he'd had no luck filling in a game for December 19th. He took the home-and-home deal where we'd go there, and he'd come play us here. So, we set up what I thought would be a major benefit to my team. I figured we could sell out our gym in 1991, and we did. Only, I wasn't the ETSU coach in 1991.

"I was so happy with making that deal with Valvano that I told my coaches about it, smiling like I had won the lottery. I had no idea by the following year, what a bad deal Valvano had made.

"My last team at ETSU went to Raleigh that year (1990) and pulled the upset in Reynolds Coliseum. Before the game, Jimmy and I had both spoken at a tape session for my Sunday video show I did for ETSU. After the taping we met for a few minutes. Jimmy Valvano tells me in a low voice, 'This might be a good blankety blank place for you to coach next year. My ass is outta here at the end of the season.'"

"He already knew before Christmas that he was leaving," Les recalled. "I had not expected his assessment of the situation and felt bad about the revelation.

"By the following season I had replaced him as coach. The team I built at ETSU was ranked #20 in America and my assistant, Alan LeForce, was now coaching them. They beat us in Johnson City that year just as I had predicted. I would have never scheduled ETSU in Johnson City had I been the NC State coach the year before. As it turned out, I forced Valvano into a bad deal that came back to bite me.

Valvano had been fighting the media battle for a year. In early 1989, author Peter Golenbock's *Personal Fouls* was released to bookstores. The book directed scathing charges of NCAA violations at North Carolina State under Valvano's leadership.Much was targeted to one of NC State's early recruits, Chris Washburn. Though a previous NCAA investigation cleared Coach Valvano, the university was penalized. The program was cited for players selling personal items like practice sneakers, practice jerseys, and game tickets. As part of the response from the university, Valvano was forced to step down as athletic director in the fall of 1989. It was the first sign of things to come.

Under additional pressure from the administration and the new chancellor, "Coach Jimmy V" stepped down as basketball coach following the 1989-1990 season. It was the plan he had told to Les privately. Since no egregious violations were uncovered throughout six separate investigations, his only stark failure seemed to indicate that he took too many at-risk players as academic exceptions. It was the academic under-performance of the players that became the basis of the demise of this well-loved coach.

The rest became the butt of poor jokes.

Philadelphia 76ers General Manager Pat Williams even chimed in. "I hear [Valvano] had a big scandal at NC State. Three of his players were found in the library."

To be sure, much of what happened was true, but not illegal. The findings that were illegal were of a minor nature, but the constant investigations—all six of them—were well publicized and disruptive to the program. The coaching change was imminent.

"Being at NC State when the allegations were the daily buzz around the program was difficult, especially for recruiting. Though I again realized that I was moving into a program that would be impacted, I was hoping the sanctions that were sure to come would be light. I also had a friendship with Jim that I felt good about. I didn't want anything to take away from his legacy. You couldn't help but like him."

After several allegations, the most egregious that prompted six separate investigations was the admittance by former NC State player Charles Shackleford that he received money while playing at NC State. The program received a 2-year probation beginning in 1992. The Wolfpack were not allowed to compete in any postseason tournament, though they could participate in the ACC tournament. The college was also ordered to pay back $365,180 from their most recent NCAA appearance shares. The NCAA had effectively set the course for Les to repair dire issues again. It was *Round Three* of Les's penchant for taking over a program to fix problems. He had done so in the wake of the George Hill fiasco at The Citadel and again after finding out about violations at East Tennessee State under Barry Dowd. Les had become the emergency repairman of college basketball.

"I read a story that a professor from Duke stood up at the annual convention of the Phi Beta Kappa honor society in San Francisco. It is considered the most prestigious of all of the college honor societies. Duke, North Carolina, and Wake Forest already had a chapter. NC State had applied for membership. The Duke professor stood to denounce the application based on the embarrassing situation with Wolfpack basketball. Looking back, it was an absurd reason that punished the rest of the university unfairly. But the denouncement gained support. Valvano was the head coach and the administration made a concerted effort to fire him. That denouncement from two thousand miles away became the focus. In fact, after Valvano, the restrictions that were placed upon the basketball program had a major impact on my ability to recruit against Duke and North Carolina. The administration didn't care as much about winning basketball games. They wanted the best students. Nearly every administration in America would have that attitude and that's fair. The college experience is first and foremost about education.

"By 1994, NC State had the #1 basketball team academics in the ACC. I had the top GPA team in the league and our players had the highest average SAT scores. We were ahead of them all—Virginia, Duke, Wake, UNC, Georgia Tech—all of them. The administration was happy. We reapplied for Phi Beta Kappa and were awarded the chapter.

"Meanwhile, I had to figure out how to win with the NCAA sanctions, the loss of scholarships, and the high standards of acceptance for my recruits. In essence, I needed to find top students first. On the other side were the "Redcoats." These were the fans that had seen the 1974 and 1983 national championships and expected me to bring that kind of magic back to campus. My task was to win with many players I had to take that I likely would not have recruited back at East Tennessee. It was a predicament. I needed to work miracles. They saw Jim Valvano do it on emotion. But I would need to do it with different kids than were going to the schools I would play. I knew the challenge, but I was not getting on that train of complainers who blamed Jim Valvano."

Les related to the magical personality of his predecessor.

"After coaching, Jimmy took to the airways and became a terrific color commentary voice on NCAA basketball broadcasts. He was knowledgeable, well prepared—and most importantly—entertaining. We remained great friends and went out of each other's way to support one another in our new roles. Valvano had a charmed sense of endearment to the press with his casual and warm personality. With the exception of a few who wanted to get headlines for their investigative journalism, the media loved Jim."

Les, with his Hot Rod Hundley, Jerry West, Pistol Pete Maravich, and David Thompson portfolio of anecdotes, became one of the classic storytellers in all of college basketball circles. It made sense that he and Valvano were destined to become great friends.

A constant source of lighthearted banter was Valvano. He still lived in the Raleigh area and would have occasions to encourage Les not to let them divert him from his goal to bring the program back to the top. It was an irony that Les found oddly endearing.

Jim Valvano's world changed dramatically when he began experiencing back pain at a Final Four telecast in Minneapolis. He eventually had an MRI [Magnetic Resonance Imaging] that revealed an abnormality. The result was told to him in two words he had never seen nor heard in his 46 years—metastatic adenocarcinoma. This aggressive cancer had a mortal grasp on the gregarious ex-coach. He had been apprised of the dire outcome. He was, in many ways, the most exemplary cancer patient ever preened from the sports world.

From his spirited fight, he initiated the Jimmy V Fund for cancer research. There are hundreds or even thousands of cancer survivors who owe their life to the Jimmy V Fund. It had raised nearly $150,000,000 by 2015. It all flowed out of Jim Valvano's sense of giving back. He was to leave a legacy. Les was there for him and visited often.

"Jim was a wonderful friend and ally. He knew all of the personalities in the university that I was dealing with at the time, so he would wink and tell me to 'hang in,'" Les stated. "And at the same time, I was praying that he would hang in. His fight was much more important than mine."

Les gave an insightful overview of the basketball situation as it related to Valvano.

"I never blamed Jim for anything. He was a great coach and even a better motivator. He could recruit with Dean [Smith] and Mike [Krzyzewski]. He could win close games—and that's the norm in the ACC—there are not many blowouts. They say they forced him out because he lost 'institutional control.' I never quite got that. Yes, he had players that were borderline students. But college basketball has built a tremendous reputation for taking young men who have little chance to succeed and presenting them with an education—and an opportunity to excel. There are amazing stories of how the sport changed lives for the better. I have never known one player whose life was not better because they had that opportunity. Jim may have taken too many borderline kids too often. But I'd argue that those borderline kids he took had Jim Valvano as a mentor.

"Then there were the other outliers. A few kids sold items like shoes and tickets. As a coach you scream at kids about the rules and accountability. But some of these kids have nothing. They're tempted. It probably happens more now than it did back then, and it is still wrong. But Jim got all the blame. You know he had nothing to do with it. I came into NC State as a player when they were busted for fixing games—NC State, North Carolina, Iowa, St. Joseph's, and others. That's worse than anything in the basketball world. It may have been the reason that Everett Case went downhill. That was way worse than anything the administration blamed on Valvano."

During Les's first season on the freshman team at NC State, 37 players from 22 schools were implicated for a national college point shaving scandal. It was the worst period of corruption the sport had ever known. The bombshell FBI investigation of February 2018, had high impact, but it was about illegal payments to buy prep players. One could make a case that the widespread point-shaving scandal was more egregious.

"The biggest issue Jim had, looking back, was the Charles Shackleford situation. Again, Jim was not a party to anything there. But he was the coach and the press can be malicious. The events insinuated that Shackleford was in a point-shaving scheme. A federal grand jury found no evidence of that. What Shackleford did was to take money from an agent, a strict no-no. I'm sure Shackleford knew he was trashing NCAA rules. But did Valvano know that? Hardly. Kids get caught up in these things, but coaches are the last ones to find out. Usually the coach gets the information from a reporter. All of the above spelled doom for the Wolfpack program as the NCAA took back tournament money and restricted the number of scholarships we could award. And because the NCAA penalties were nothing in comparison with the harsh oversight of the NC State administration, an impossible situation developed. And again, I had to deal with the circumstances, but I never held Jim Valvano up for blame. We were both victims. He lost the job he cherished, and I ended up coaching my dream job with a pile of restrictions that were nothing short of ridiculous."

Valvano reflected on the loss of his fairytale-coaching job in his autobiography, *Valvano: They Gave Me a Lifetime Contract, and Then They Declared Me Dead.*

Basketball had come a long way through multiple scandals and transgressions since the late 1940s. There were winners and losers. In retrospect, the outcome was the same for Jim Valvano and Les Robinson.

"I like to think that Jimmy and I had a lot in common. We both liked being around people and we both enjoyed telling old stories. We both came out on the wrong side of the NC State head-coaching job. He lost his job and I was brought in to do something impossible—clean it all up and win in the face of the reprisals.

"You never saw Jimmy without a smile. No matter where people stand on his career, I remain convinced he was a fine coach and a really good guy. I never thought he got a fair shake. He was my friend and I respected him."

"Many people wanted to blame Jim Valvano for the tough years we had after he was forced out. But I'd like to turn that around. Jimmy was a great coach and motivator. It was—and remains—unfair to blame him. He took some chances on some kids that nobody else would take. He had given those borderline kids an opportunity to get a college degree from a top-notch institution. Some of those kids let him down. But looking back, the university administration over-reacted with their set of restrictions. My contract with N. C. State was not about wins and losses. It was about bringing academic respectability back to the basketball program. We did that. When I felt that my job was done and that I needed a new challenge, I resigned under my own terms," Les chronicles.

When Les was called back to coach at his alma mater in 1990, it was to improvise the impossible with the improbable. He may have been the only coach in America that had been vigorously trained in that discipline.

Les takes the Wolfpack to the NCAAs in 1990. His six-year tenure resolved deep academic issues. Photo courtesy NC State University.

CHAPTER 21
BACK TO THE PACK

Les took over the NC State program that had been under scrutiny for nearly two years.

The officials at NC State had difficulty reaching Les because he was both coach and athletic director at ETSU. Under those circumstances, protocol is that the pursuing college communicate everything through the other college's president. But the ETSU president was traveling in Europe at the time. So NC State officials used another means to reach Les. They called the Clemson AD, Bobby Robinson. Bobby Robinson and Les Robinson are not related. Clemson's Bobby Robinson was asked to simply inquire if Les would take the job if offered and a suitable contract was agreed upon.

"I received the call from Bobby Robinson at Clemson, but I thought it might be a joke. So I took down the number he gave me and called him right back. I started wondering why Clemson was looking for a coach. Their coach, Cliff Ellis was recently named Coach of the Year in the ACC. But Bobby Robinson was returning a favor to NC State, he explained, from something State had done for Clemson years earlier in the hiring of Danny Ford as football coach.

"I was simply asked the question that 'if the Wolfpack job became available to me tomorrow, would I take it?' Being a 1965 grad, I answered that I would accept the job should the contract be amenable."

Les's appointment came 16 days after Jim Valvano was forced out. NC State agreed to pay Valvano a $500,000 buyout settlement. The Les Robinson era was set to begin.

In the primer of coaching in the ACC, the best league in America, no rookie coach was supposed to emerge as a threat to the status quo. Les didn't read the manual.

In his first season at the helm, he beat that year's national champion, Duke, by 8 points in his first-ever showdown with Coach Mike Krzyzewski. The Bobby Hurley, Christian Laettner and Grant Hill team that thrilled America was beaten by a rookie tactician who knew how to keep his team loose.

"Our guys were not intimidated. We had excellent senior leadership and played good defense when we needed a stop," Les intimates. "Often the tone is set when you get after them early and win the loose ball wars. We tried to do that all season long."

The "Fire & Ice" led Wolfpack would log twenty wins, making Les the first coach in the history of the league to win twenty games in his first season. The Pack even performed the impossible in an amazing comeback that got everyone's attention. Unranked, they came from twenty points down in the second half to beat Jeff Jones's 18th-ranked Virginia Cavaliers in regulation. They won by seven [83-76]. Les never gave up and the team followed suit.

The Wolfpack won six games against ranked teams that year. Les had repaid his friend Bobby Cremins, as well. Cremins had beaten him the year before in the NCAA's, ending ETSU's season. The rookie coach's strategies worked well as NC State beat the nationally-ranked Yellow Jackets three times—twice in the regular season and again in the ACC tournament. Les and Bobby's head-to-head basketball games became a running commentary for each other's bragging rights many years hence. Their strong friendship overcame the constant needling they gave each other over a career of mixed results.

"Yeah, he beat me pretty good his first year," Cremins recalls. "But I got him back. I hated coaching against Les because I liked him and I knew how ridiculous the university was to him back then. I wanted him to succeed despite the lack of support he got from State. He was as good at coaching at that level as anyone—Dean, Gary, or Mike—but he couldn't compete consistently if they wouldn't let him recruit against the best. Regardless, I hated playing Les."

Les's first team had coalesced to become one of the most competitive squads in the country, despite the devisive media around them. Les had to learn to look past the negativity and inspire the Wolfpack to play well when the initial jump-ball went up.

Even in later years when it appeared that Les was saddled with a depleted squad that was supposed to compete against the ACC thoroughbreds, he pulled off some huge wins. He had the two previous NC State coaches mentoring him during those difficult times—Norm Sloan and Jim Valvano. As National Championship coaches [1974 and 1983], they had raised the bar substantially.

The press was both excrutiating and empathetic. But the story of Les's first year at the helm was relinquished to the back page. Other meaty stories persisted.

As a direct result of the academic shortcomings of a few previous Valvano rosters, the university's academic restrictions became the most stringent in the ACC. Les was doomed to perform with considerable handicaps—like swimming with a bowling ball.

The NCAA's restrictions and the penalty of losing postseason eligibility were mindful of what Les had already experienced at East Tennessee State. He knew the sheet music to this song by heart when he arrived in Raleigh.

"Unlike the situation at ETSU where I had no idea of the former coach's transgressions and what might happen, I knew what was going on at NC State before arriving. But this was my career ambition job and I was prepared to deal with whatever might happen. We had to weather the outside noise and focus on basketball. We did that in the first year," Les details. "But the next two seasons meant that I had to coach past the distractions and the fallout from the administration's own directives."

The Wolfpack dropped off to 12-18 at the end of the 1992 season and 8-19 in 1993, both years tinged by scholarship losses. The 1993 season was the worst in modern era for Wolfpack basketball. Les only had seven players on scholarships [when 13 were allowed]. One of those seven became injured and missed several games. So he played with six.

"I never expected to coach at that level with half of a roster. But those were the cards I was dealt. I couldn't lead the players into a game without adjusting my own mindset to do the best we could do—believing we could win under those circumstances," Les realized. "And we did win a few games we had no business winning."

The higher academic standards were also taking their toll. Players that could have been recruited by Virginia, Duke, and North Carolina could not meet the enhanced academic standards set forth by the NC State administration. Les had gotten to the top of the food chain in basketball, but had similar difficulty finding the right fit for the Wolfpack as he had at The Citadel years earlier. At The Citadel, they had to adjust to a military environment. There were no junior college transfers, and the school's honor system gave no second chance. The college required a different type of recruit than could be readily found at most high school gyms. At NC State, he had encountered a new dynamic—a most difficult task—finding outstanding scholars who could play basketball at the highest college level.

Losing 19 games in 1993 did not endear Les to the win-at-all-costs basketball fans but made the academicians happy. The Redcoats were there to support the program and found much inspiration in Les's abilities despite the obstacles. But, in the end, they just wanted to win.

He had recruited a potential Rhodes scholar, and several others whose classroom prowess far exceeded their court abilities. The 6'10" Todd Fuller would become a fine player who did receive the rare invitation to perform post-graduate work at Oxford, England. However, he declined the Rhodes scholarship to play in the NBA.

As he did at The Citadel and East Tennessee State, Les was building a good team from an adversarial beginning. His team in 1996 improved to 15-16, losing eight games determined by a last possession. They were back in the thick of top competition despite the setbacks and near-impossible academic restrictions. Les could take no chances on borderline students.

"I had some very difficult circumstances that I had not anticipated. But I had been able to compete in the past with similar adversity. Though I was used to the conditions from before, trying to build a winner in the ACC in the face of the obstacles from the administration might have been foolhardy. It was my job to look ahead and get past it. I did all that I could do and now I look back with no regrets," Les explains. "Complaining or making excuses was not something I had ever done before. I never liked complainers. Along those lines, I did not like to hear the excuses from our fans and I didn't want the players hearing them either.

"Our charge was to win games despite the distractions," Les concedes.

Les was chosen to guide the university's flagship program back to impeccable order and with the expectation of new successes with top-level student athletes. Les knew that the normal mission of winning championships was on the back burner with the NC State administration. He had to get the program back to a higher academic standing and navigate the looming concerns from the past revelations. In summary, he had to win back the confidence and respect of all—the players, the faculty, the fans, and the NCAA. It was a lot to ask. The program was in shambles.

"When I came, the administration of NC State was not in a mood to allow much latitude. I was hired to fix the program, regardless of the cards dealt to me. I had proven it could be done by virtue of the progress we made at East Tennessee State over the five prior years."

At ETSU, a team beset by unexpected sanctions, Les was able to take the progression of success from 7 wins to 14 to 20 to 27. On the way to two consecutive NCAA postseason appearances, he had beaten other major conference teams besides Valvano's Wolfpack club in Raleigh. As the pressure kettle began to boil, things got worse for Jim Valvano. Les's name, as a former player, began to surface. He was a natural choice to come in and guide the program.

In his first year, 1990-1991, he assumed he had some fine players returning, courtesy of Valvano. He may have had the best guard tandem in the ACC, Chris Corchiani and Rodney Monroe. But it got back to him that both were dead-set on leaving—Monroe to the NBA and Corchiani to another college.

Chris Corchiani stated that he would not be the only player leaving if Jim Valvano were dismissed. He intimated that junior guard Rodney Monroe, the team's leading scorer, along with sophomore forwards Tom Gugliotta and Bryant Feggins, Mr. North Carolina Basketball, would also leave if Valvano were pressured into a resignation.

Les had not planned on re-recruiting all of the players.

Convincing Corchiani and Monroe to stay for their senior year was as hard as recruiting blue-chippers from a five-star camp. Both had received bad advice from outside sources that made them believe their stock was at its highest. Les had to disprove the logic. Les's pragmatism would be essential.

Les's approach was to get one senior guard to stay so that the other would reconsider. He did so by approaching the streak-shooting Monroe, who was planning on declaring for the NBA draft under the player hardship rule. Monroe had averaged 22 points a game as a junior and felt he would be drafted early. Les had spoken to NBA personnel and knew differently. That gave him a reason to conference with Monroe.

Les approached Monroe soon after taking the position of head coach. He told him what he knew—from top NBA people like Rod Thorn, Jerry West, and Rod Hundley. These were his West Virginia connections that had top positions with NBA teams. These are people who knew Les well enough to not only take his call, but to give him NBA insight into any player they were evaluating. Those relationships could help steer Monroe.

After Les set the conference with Monroe with just the two of them speaking candidly, Les posed the NBA option to him as a financial choice.

"Rodney, before you leave money on the table, I feel I should point you to a direction so that you will have all of the input that I have," Les started. "I'm not going to bullshit you like some of the agents and others that stand to gain when you go pro. I'm going to tell you the truth," Les started.

Monroe's interest was piqued. His concern showed.

Les began with the facts. "First of all, my sources tell me that you will not be drafted in the first two rounds because you are a defensive liability. They would also like to see you bulk up a little more to play the 2-position. You're too small for the league at 6'3", so you will have to be quicker and stronger than what they see on film." Les related. "Your range for the NBA is suspect, too. You need to get stronger and demonstrate better range for your shot. Your footwork in the league will need to be better to defend. You do not come off switches well. It's all over the film. I saw it when I coached my team against you. I'll make your defense better by making you a smarter defender. But I need to know if you and I agree to bump up your stock that you will listen to me and work hard to get better."

Monroe was intrigued. He thought he might be selected late in the first round of the 1990 draft. He had a deft touch and was a fine free throw shooter.

"You know some of the NBA scouts. Give me one that you trust, and I'll call him right now," Les offered. "You can hear it from them."

Monroe declined.

"I can't promise you anything by staying another year, but I can promise that after a year with me, you will be a better player for the league because I will get you ready. I'll work with you to improve your defense, your decision-making and importantly, your strength. Those things will help me, too, because it will make our team that much better."

After a short consideration, Monroe decided to stay. And Les delivered his promise.

Monroe averaged 27 points per game his senior season, becoming the Player-of-the-Year in the ACC for 1991. He broke David Thompson's NC State all-time scoring record. He moved to 4th on the ACC's scoring list (with 2,551 career points) and helped elevate Les's first NC State team to a 20-11 season and into the 2nd round of the NCAA tournament the following March. Monroe's stock rose, and he was drafted early in the second round as the 30th player overall. The year before, Les's sources indicated that he would not make it into the first two rounds.

Once he had convinced Monroe to stay, he had a reason to open a conversation with Chris Corchiani. Corchiani's father was already shopping Chris to other programs. This was going to be a "hard sell." But Les had other ideas. He went to the gritty playmaker with a plan.

"Chris, only a fool would *not* try to keep you here for your final year," Les started. "Not having you here creates a big problem for me because I'm going to up-tempo the game and get more possessions. You are the perfect fit for my tempo. I've studied the film. You defend, you penetrate, you do not turn it over, and you find shooters. There's nobody like you on any other roster in America, much less on ours. With Rodney committed to stay, I need somebody that will have a feel for the floor and set up the conference's best scorer. If I don't have you back, it will surely affect Rodney's production and maybe his draft status. You two are the best in America. I want to have a chance to showcase both of you. But I will need you to commit to me that you can handle the pace."

Corchiani had been the leading voice in a mass exit strategy of other players. His decision to stay with the Wolfpack would impact the two sophomores, Gugliotta and Feggins.

In time, and with other discussions with Corchiani's father, the matter was settled. Chris Corchiani was coming back for his senior year. It was the best sales job of Les's career. He had them both, "Fire and Ice." The bonus of keeping the two sophomores, Gugliotta and Feggins, was not a given and required other separate conversations. Corchiani's leadership skills would resolve much of the discontent in the locker room.

Les still needed to improve the supporting cast. Having both Corchiani and Monroe meant the coming season would foster high anticipation for the fan base. This team would be fun to coach. With the NCAA and administrative restrictions in process, it would be difficult to bring in players with those basketball skills in the next two years. Les needed to maximize the potential for the roster he had for 1990.

"If I had players like that every year, I could become a great coach!" Les offered. "I didn't recruit either of them, but re-recruiting both in the short time I had was as difficult as going to sign any of the big names other programs were courting across the prep basketball world."

Corchiani's decision to remain as the Wolfpack point guard delivered other basketball notoriety. He became the all-time assist leader in the history of college basketball that season with 1,038. In June of 1991, he was drafted 36th overall—just six positions behind Rodney Monroe in the second round. It was an unexpected result for a profoundly deserving player.

With Les's first season in the books, the news that there would be more sanctions related to the Valvano years went beyond what Les expected. And those sanctions did not all come from the NCAA. The university imposed the strictest academic guidelines in all of college basketball. The Wolfpack recruiting would suffer. The administration, if anything, over-corrected the mistakes of the past with the most difficult rules any coach in the ACC would face. The admittance requirements for the basketball team exceeded those of Duke, Virginia, Wake Forest, and Blue Heaven over in Chapel Hill. Les had to find top students that could compete at the ACC level to bring them to a program that had less scholarships and more oversight than any of their opponents. It was a daunting task.

Les was, in effect, paying the bill for the filet mignon eaten by an earlier diner while he was being served a side-salad. And he had no input into the decisions. He was directed to straighten out the program and compete at the highest level with restrictions incompatible with either mission.

The administrative vice-grip became tighter in the second season. Les had one legitimate performer coming back, Tom Gugliotta, a 6'10" player who grew five inches after his freshman year. In Les's up-tempo style and with Corchiani at the point, "Googs" averaged 15 points a game. He had emerged. As a senior, he averaged 22 per game. But the team only won twelve games with a noticeably depleted bench. They did manage one of the great upsets of the year by beating their biggest rivals, the Tar Heels of North Carolina. This was all-the-more stunning since the Pack was reeling from an eight-game losing streak. Gugliotta had 38 points that night.

In the toughest league in the NCAA, Les's teams desperately needed more depth and less bragging about their academic prowess by the college deans.

Gugliotta was selected 6th overall in the 1992 NBA draft, by the Washington Bullets. He went on to a fine NBA career, averaging more than 20 points per game twice and becoming an NBA All-Star.

By Les's third season, the vice had exacted a full measure of pain. Les's roster only had seven scholarship players and one of them became injured and out for the rest of the season. For many games the Wolfpack only dressed seven players, including walk-ons. They suffered through an 8-19 campaign; but they had the best SAT scores of any ACC team. Les's team would only win eleven the next year and twelve after that. In his final (sixth) season at State, he won 15, losing 16. Nine of the losses were by four points or less. His last game was in the second round of the ACC tournament, losing to his good friend Bobby Cremins and the 1996 Atlantic Coast Conference Champion Georgia Tech Yellow Jackets. It was a fitting end.

Les summarized the composite experience.

"I never made any excuse to our alums, not even privately, about the rules I worked under. I figured that I had spent my career winning games in the face of adversity—at Cedar Key, at The Citadel, with the probation at ETSU, and now at NC State. I just coached the game I knew with the resources I had to the best of my ability. Timing and luck played a role, yes, but I never believed anything but making your own luck from hard work. It was one the lessons my father taught me. We always played to win, and I felt I always got the best out of my players," Les summarized.

"So, when I look back, especially at State, I completed the task of which I was asked and was still able to be competitive. My last year was tough because I thought we had turned the corner—and we did. But we lost more than our share of close ones that year."

What wasn't said was that Les was forced between two opposing forces, the fans and the administration. The administration was determined to bring the academic reputation of the institution back to the top. Most of the fans had no concern about the academic reputation. They only wanted W's. Les did all that he could with what he had admirably.

There were other difficult moments.

The year before Les took the reins at N. C. State, Jim Valvano had re-cruited and signed 6'9" Tony Robinson from Havelock High School near Camp Lejeune, North Carolina. Coincidentally, Les had recruited one of Robinson's high school teammates, Alvin West, during his tenure at East Tennessee State. But Les had passed on the gangly Robinson. Tony Robinson was a fine student with high testing scores. However, Les did not see him as a good fit for his program at ETSU and the Southern Conference. Owing to the academic pressure in his last year, Valvano brought in Tony Robinson for his potential GPA upside, but he had only averaged one point a game in his twenty Wolfpack appearances during Valvano's last season. Les in-herited the player he had passed on recruiting at the Southern Conference level three years earlier.

"Tony Robinson was a fine person and a kid with whom I had a great rapport. He used to joke that I was his uncle," Les recalled. "He really didn't have the skills needed to compete at the ACC level, but I got him into a few games. Tony may have been one of those kids that was tall but really wasn't inspired by the sport of basketball. Yet, he did have some skills. Besides that, he was likeable. The team liked him. The professors liked him. The assistants liked him. I liked him."

Tony Robinson logged very few minutes over eleven games during Les's first year, Tony's sophomore season. He fit with the team well and was admirable as a bench player in the locker room.

"He never sulked or complained," Les stated.

"He was a bench player, but never a kid that grumbled. He came to some practices late because of afternoon labs. He certainly was one of the guys that raised our team GPA. And he seemed to always have a smile. So, I could never say anything but compliments about Tony. He was just one of the guys you couldn't help but like," Les stated. "He was serious about his school work. And his demeanor never changed much. If anything was eating at Tony, you'd never know it."

But on Monday evening, November 23, 1992, the always-reliable Tony Robinson was not available for a scheduled exhibition game in Reynolds Coliseum. Les was not overly concerned because he had been late before because of late afternoon labs. He had not been at the pre-game meal. When a manager was sent to check the locker room and the trainer's room shortly before the game was to begin, the young player was not to be found.

"I sent the manager to his dormitory room assuming that he may be sick or asleep. But the manager returned telling me that the door was locked and that nobody answered. The exhibition game was underway."

"I quickly decided to have the manager seek the campus police to unlock the door, still not in the least concerned that Tony's absence could be attributed to anything serious. Tony had a level and productive attitude. I was not even remotely concerned about drugs or foul play. Tony was a good kid. It was a mystery that he would miss the game.

The exhibition game moved towards halftime. Just as the first half clock expired Les was about to follow his players into the home locker room.He saw his Athletic Director, Todd Turner, and the NC State Chancellor, Larry Monteith, standing together on the floor waiting for him.

The news was devastating. His reliable young player, Tony Robinson, had inexplicably taken his own life. He shot himself with a .25 caliber handgun in his dorm room just hours before.

"I was completely shocked. I knew right away it wasn't about basketball," Les remembered. "And now I had to go into the locker room with that news. I decided not to wait, and I broke the news to the players. We all cried. Basketball was not important. This kid that was practicing the day before and joking around with the other players. Yet he had decided to end it all. We were all in disbelief."

"There were no signs that Tony Robinson was suicidal," Les established.

Les fielded a litany of questions from the press.Indeed, there was no indication that foretold this among those that knew him best. It made no immediate sense.

The incident occurred near the Thanksgiving break and Les had a handful of new roles to fulfill. He needed to comfort his team and approach the news for its profound revelation. Basketball is a game. There is much more to life.

More reporters came in. They had created the supposition of some discontent in the locker room that Les needed to address and dispel. There were the conversations with the assistant coaches, Buzz Peterson, Al Daniels, and Ed Conroy. There were questions and reports for the university, for the trustee board, for the Wolfpack Club, and for the alumni.

Les thought of Tony's family and focused his efforts to assist Tony's parents in any way possible. His dad was on active duty in the United States Marine Corps. They wanted Tony's funeral service and interment performed in Raleigh. Les personally found a church official and a burial site at the Mount Hope Cemetery for the family. The funeral was on the following Monday, November 30th. Les also accompanied his parents to Tony's dorm room to recover the player's personal belongings. It was too sad for words.

The team schedule, including practices, had to be re-worked during this difficult bereavement process. The players admired their teammate and dwelled for a time upon his empty locker. It was a sullen time in Raleigh. There were no immediate answers to the question "Why?"

It wasn't until a few days after the funeral that two students had asked to see Les at his office. Les had always had an open door policy for anyone who wanted to see him and was not sure what the meeting was about. His office assistant, Beverly, had set up the meeting before an afternoon practice.

Les recalled the office meeting.

"These were two students who, I'm sure, made a most difficult decision to come and see me. They opened the meeting by telling me that they were both gay," Les shared. "But the next thing they told me was that they both felt responsible for Tony Robinson's suicide. Of course, I was immediately curious of their affiliation with Tony. Then one of those young men spoke up and said, 'Coach, we had been pressuring Tony to step forward and come out of the closet. Tony was gay. He had so much trouble dealing with it and especially trying to reconcile this with his father, his family, and the team. We pushed him to set the record straight. We constantly told him of its importance and never realized how difficult it was for him.' I was completely surprised at this unconsidered answer to the reason of the suicide. I'm certain that no teammate knew the reason or Tony's lifestyle choice. It was truly tragic," Les laments.

In the aftermath, Tony Robinson left other indications including a note in his car that made it clear that the suicide was about the fear of acceptance for his lifestyle.

On April 29th, 2013, Jason Collins of the NBA's Washington Wizards did the unthinkable. The 6'10" defensive specialist from Los Angeles by way of Stanford University came out publicly and told the world that he is gay. His many supporters congratulated him for his bravery. Prior to Collins' declaration, it had been quite abnormal for an active player in any major sport to stand up and profess such an intimate side of a personal life. The revelation had a reverberating effect upon professional sports. It also brought the pangs of loss for an athlete that Les Robinson remembered at NC State. The Jason Collins revelation may have been the event that could have saved Tony Robinson years before. Tony Robinson was only 22.

In the basketball world, there are success and tragedies well beyond wins and losses. There are also divergent factions that are not always cohorts for a common cause.

Les would never forget the amiable tony Robinson or the sadness of the aftermath. The loss was devastating to the team, the university, and to those that cared about a special person who brought smiles with him everywhere.

Immediately after the loss of Tony Robinson, the season began. The team had to pull together. The coaches needed to break down film. The academic work had to continue at a high level. The season is also a time to look at high school juniors and uncommitted seniors. There is little personal time and basketball wives become basketball widows until April. The demands are suffocating.

Les was able to find several players who could excel in the rigorously academic strategies imposed by the university. The requirements were spelled out in Les's contract. He faced the ACC recruiting wars like a marathon runner with a boa constrictor in his knapsack.

One of Les's recruits, Todd Fuller, was Les's greatest success in pleasing the differing factions on campus. He was an exceptional person, talented athlete, and a brilliant student. At first, Les believed the student side of Fuller would be his legacy. Fuller only recorded one grade that was less than an A in his academic career through every level of his education. It was a B+. Fuller had a personal work ethic that made him an exceptional college basketball player.

In Fuller's senior season [1996] he led the league in scoring at 20.9 points per game while also pulling down 9.9 rebounds per game. He was a complete player. He was an Academic All-American and was inducted into the exclusive Phi Beta Kappa Society. He earned his degree in Applied Mathematics. His basketball ability made him a 'lottery pick' as the eleventh player taken in the draft by the Golden State Warriors. The postscript is that Todd Fuller turned down the highest honor of the prestigious Rhodes scholarship to play in the NBA. Fuller became the poster edition of Les's answer to all factions—the fans, the alums, the league, and the faculty. Fuller was a special player.

But, there were not many Todd Fullers to be had. Les had learned to assess players and if he were to err, his mistake would trend towards academia. He had more than one player that he took as a "project" because the player's academic profile matched the university's requirement. A few roster positions would have to be filled by players whose basketball skills were minimal by ACC standards. He had no trump card of asking the administration for an exception so that he could bring in a blue-chipper or two. The results bore out the dilemma.

Les's friends, Bobby Cremins and Gary Williams, were able to bring in the players Les had to pass on. Dean Smith and Mike Krzyzewski were feasting in "The Triangle" on the period when NC State was not in the hunt for the best in the land. There were no David Thompsons, Hawkeye Whitneys, or Kenny Carrs—players that could bring the program up to compete with the top teams in America. And unfortunately, there was no Jerry Stackhouse. It might have been Les's biggest disappointment that Jerry Stackhouse was not a Wolfpack recruit.

Stackhouse, the best high school star in America, had narrowed his choices to NC State and North Carolina in 1992. He was thought to be all-but-wrapped-up by Les in a recruiting war with Dean Smith. His mother, Minnie Stackhouse, liked Les and even baked him a birthday cake during a September recruiting visit. Going into the last week before the signing, Robinson truly believed he had beaten the Dean over the most exciting prep player in America.

"But Dean Smith 'pulled out all the stops,' When it heated up, I knew that the one player who could have 'turned up the W's' at State was not coming.I was devastated that he would be playing for our major opponent nine miles away, the North Carolina Tar Heels," Les relates. "And I knew I had been beaten in the one-on-one recruiting challenge by the best in the business—Dean Smith. He had tools that I hadn't imagined. It took Bobby Cremins and Mike Krzyzewski to make me understand what happened.

"This was another time when Bobby Cremins brought me back to reality," Les recalls. "We were at the coaches meeting in the preseason and I saw Mike Krzyzewski. I was curious about why he was not in on the Jerry Stackhouse recruiting. So I went over when I had a chance to ask him. Mike said he knew that Dean had put all of his energy into getting Stackhouse. He figured it would be a waste of his time to fight Dean on this one. He was nonchalant about the fact that he had gotten out early. It was like he knew something that I didn't. I thanked him for letting me know.

"When I told Bobby Cremins about the conversation, he answered in typical Cremins style. He said, 'Les, you dumbass, Mike pulled out early when he saw what Dean was up to. Even Mike knew that Dean was going 'all in' on Jerry Stackhouse. That means you're recruiting against every major star that ever played at North Carolina, including Michael Jordan. Stackhouse was going to get a call from Jordan, from Walter Davis, from Sam Perkins, from Bobby Jones. Even I know that.'

"Bobby was dead on. I had gone all the way down the road and was left with nothing to show but a bunch of trips to Oak Hill Academy and Kinston, NC—and a birthday cake.

"Stackhouse could have gotten calls from NBA Coach George Karl or Laker's GM Mitch Kupchak. There is nothing illegal in that. They would feel, if asked, like they owed much to Dean. Dean had more influence in the basketball world than anybody. I found out later that there was a back-story that few knew in the Stackhouse sweepstakes. Stackhouse had a half-brother, Tony Dawson, a 6'7" forward who had played at Florida

State University for Coach Pat Kennedy. Dawson had much input into the Stackhouse decision. He was on the rosters of several European professional teams. He was not a bad player but was probably not an NBA talent. Through former North Carolina Tar Heel and Milwaukee Bucks Coach George Karl, Dawson was offered a tryout during the recruiting period for Stackhouse. The timing was perfect, and it was certainly legal. That timing brought to light the immense impact of the Tar Heel family and Coach Dean Smith's influence upon the college game. I had the utmost respect for Dean. He could move mountains. But not getting Stackhouse was probably my greatest setback as a recruiter.

Tony Dawson was a borderline player who later got another tryout and 10-day contract with the Sacramento Kings and the Boston Celtics. The opportunity with the Bucks came at the right time and was a clear factor in Stackhouse's decision.

Les always contended that the veteran coaches in the NCAA who had earned the resources and former player contacts to influence basketball recruits legally had every right to do so. Admittedly, the rich would always get richer. But it was still difficult to lose the star player he needed to elevate his program.

By the time the books were closed on Les's sixth season at NC State, he had decided to assist the "Redcoat" fans and the university by stepping aside so that a new coach could begin the next chapter. He had done as commanded years earlier. He restored the academic and ethical reputation of the Wolfpack basketball program. He had the best students in the conference. He was offered and accepted the role as assistant Director of Athletics. When, in short order, AD Todd Turner left for Vanderbilt, Les was named Interim AD, then as permanent AD—a position he held from 1996 until 2000.

His legacy as a head basketball coach is that he reversed the lingering issues created by his predecessors to restore legitimacy to programs at three Division-1 institutions. His legacy as a Director of Athletics—at ETSU, NC State, and The Citadel, became an even greater triumph. He directed record fundraising, major construction projects, and the hiring of substantial coaching choices across the entire spectrum of their respective sports programs.

These truths became most evident at his alma mater. It was where he had his greatest response to the most troubling adversity. At NC State, they bled red.

"There was bleeding over at the administration because of the unreasonably high academic demands they instituted for basketball only. There was bleeding from the chancellor over raising the somewhat damaged reputation of the college. There was bleeding in the alumni base— the Redcoats—who wanted to win, regardless of the circumstances. They longed for the special days when Jimmy Valvano slayed all of the giants. Then there was internal bleeding. That was from our own athletic department. We had endured so much oversight daily and the demands were too high. 'Bring in solid A students and beat North Carolina and Duke,' seemed to be what they wanted. 'Win with only seven scholarship players on the roster,' was another between-the-lines command. To some degree I was able to do that; but to win consistently, we needed to have all of our scholarships and be able to recruit C students, too. Heck, I was a C student! The ruptures were great. There was every opportunity that we could bleed to death before we could turn the program around."

An enduring friendship was born in 1976 when Les and Bobby Cremins faced each other in SoCon battles. They remain close friends in their retirement. Photo courtesy Georgia Tech University.

CHAPTER 22

BOBBY CREMINS

Les has a close friend who does not call him "Les." It comes out as "Lez."

His best friend in coaching, Bobby Cremins, coached at the College of Charleston for six years prior to his retirement. He returned to coaching after a six-year hiatus to a city that he had visited often to see his friends, Les and former University of South Carolina teammate and roommate Corky Carnevale. The interaction between these two fierce coach-competitors began in 1975, Cremins' first year at Appalachian State University. Robinson was in his second year as Head Coach at The Citadel.

Les and Bobby had some interaction when Cremins came to The Citadel Basketball Camp to work in 1970. Les was a new assistant to The Citadel's Coach Dick Campbell at the time. Bobby was at the end of his college career where he had starred for Coach Frank McGuire's University of South Carolina Gamecocks. Meeting as Southern Conference head coaches five years later came with some trepidation.

Cremins' wife Carolyn recalls the story of their friendship beginning awkwardly at the pre-season Southern Conference meetings.

"Les called our room and asked about he and Barbara getting together for dinner or a beer," the hesitant Mrs. Cremins recalled, "but Bobby was not in the room at the time, so I told Les that Bobby would call back upon his return. When Bobby returned, we must have spent ten minutes trying to figure what angle this opponent coach had and if he was trying to spy on our recruiting information or our style of play or some other advantage that he could get from meeting Bobby for a beer. We had no idea that he had absolutely no ulterior motive whatsoever. He was just a sincere man who wanted to forge a new friendship. He and Barbara met us for dinner and the rest is history. Those two may be the nicest couple in the business. We have much in common. We've been inseparable ever since."

Cremins won 570 games, only losing 367 over his career at three colleges. His career produced three Southern Conference championships at Appalachian State University, two ACC regular season championships at Georgia Tech along with two more tournament championships, and another Southern Conference regular season championship at the College of Charleston.He was his conference coach-of-the-year seven times (4 SoCon, 3 ACC), and his teams made eleven NCAA tournament appearances, making it to the Final Four in 1990.

Bobby Cremins was the James Naismith NCAA College Basketball National Coach- of-the-Year in 1990.

Cremins recognized talent and was an amazing recruiter. Prep stars loved the easy-going coach for his sincerity and knowledge of the sport.

Cremins' dossier of recruited talent at Georgia Tech included players like Stephon Marbury, Duane Ferrell, Dennis Scott, Matt Harpring, Mark Price, Jon Barry, Kenny Anderson, Travis Best, John Salley, Tom Hammonds, Brian Oliver and Jason Collier. He ran one of the finest program in America and gained a reputation as being among the most energetic recruiters.

In 1989, Cremins would be supplied with college basketball's top talent to evaluate and assemble a team to compete. This would be international basketball's most important qualification event. Every zone of the world has these games to graduate teams to the World Games and eventually to the Olympics. The annual tournament is run by FIBA, a French acronym (*Fédération Internationale de Basketball*) that organized international basketball rules and tournament play.

Cremins and Les would often arrive at NCAA meetings together, play tennis, have a beer and take their wives out to dinner. Their innate respect for each other's abilities was always evident, except when they were in front of each other. Then, it was a time for mutual annihilation. They did it with humor.

"Cremins and I seemed to always bust on each other, especially when we are around other people. One of the best I ever got him was when he was coaching his first year at the College of Charleston and was invited, like me, to attend the Hibernian Society of Charleston's St. Patrick's Day formal banquet. He was sitting at a special table up front next to me," Les started.

The Hibernian Society of Charleston is one of the most exclusive and unique Irish organizations in America. It was founded in 1799 for charitable purposes and hosts an annual banquet each year on St. Patrick's Day. The event is formal and attracts a wealth of local and statewide personalities. Annual banquet speakers include U.S. presidents, business and industry giants, top politicians, and military leaders.

"Bobby started out talking about how nice the banquet was, who was there—like the governor and both U.S. Senators—and a virtual *Who's Who* of Charleston. He said, 'Man this banquet is nice; this is first class," he repeated with eyes wide open.And then he asked me, "Lez, you were here in Charleston every year, when Coach Frank McGuire was still coaching. Him being a proud Irishman, he would have loved this! Did Coach McGuire ever come down to this thing?"'

"I thought fast, and I said, 'Oh, no, Bobby. I don't believe he ever made it down here.' I added, 'He was always working during this time of year coaching in a postseason tournament.' Everybody around Cremins broke out laughing. And Cremins got it, then smiled for a moment just before he announced for the one thousandth time that I was an asshole." Les recalled.

They had gotten each other many times over the years and each incident bred another.

"One of the best stunts ever pulled on Bobby Cremins was done by Jim Calhoun and myself," Les attested. "It was a classic."

"We were in Albuquerque, April of 1983, just after Jimmy Valvano's Wolfpack had upset the heavily favored University of Houston and *Phi Slamma Jamma* to win the National Championship. We had agreed to meet at the hotel bar after the game with Cremins. Because he had turned around the basketball program at Georgia Tech, Bobby had won the Atlantic Coast Conference's Coach-of-the-Year Award. The ACC had sent out the press release near the time that the NCAA tournament was winding down, just days before our meeting in Albuquerque. I had already congratulated Cremins for the great work he had done to bring Georgia Tech back near the top.

While Cremins had stepped away, Calhoun and I cooked up a plan to get Bobby to agree to relinquish his Coach-of-the-Year award to Valvano since Jimmy had just won the NCAA tournament. This would not be possible with any other coach, but we both knew that Bobby was naïve and sincerely cared about others. He is truly selfless.

"When Bobby came back to the bar, Calhoun asked the planted question, 'Les, what a great game! That team was motivated and never believed that they were out of the game. That took great coaching, since they were such heavy underdogs. Wasn't Valvano the ACC Coach-of-the-Year?'

"I responded in a monotone voice, 'They pick that award early and it was before the tournament wins. Bobby won the award in the ACC. I deadpanned that Bobby was most deserving, too. But I continued the thought as planned by saying, Valvano would have been a great choice once everybody saw what he was able to do in the tournament.' Bobby bit. He immediately agreed."

"As if cued in at the perfect time, Calhoun noted that 'in the Big East, they'd simply give it to the guy left standing at the end of the year. That's the fairest way.' Bobby again agreed. Calhoun kept a straight face. So, Calhoun continued by saying 'You know, Bobby, it could still be done.'"

"All you have to do is call your Sports Information Director, get him to call a press conference when you get back to Atlanta and relinquish the award in favor of Valvano," Calhoun posed.

"Cremins thought about it," Les recalled. "I added that 'it would go a long way with the other coaches' for Bobby to step forward and offer to give the award back. As competitive as Cremins had always been, he has this tremendous and likeable side to him, much like Frank McGuire. He is always a perfect gentleman. I knew that being a gentleman superseded everything else. So, we were playing on his sense of fairness and his deep convictions of always being the consummate gentleman."

Les added, "You have to know Bobby. He is one of the most genuine people on the planet."

"He started talking himself into this set-up. He said, 'You know Jimmy did a great job. He won several huge games in the tournament. He has a great ability to motivate his players to step up. Do you think it would be okay with the people at Tech for me to give the award back?' Both Calhoun and I nodded. He was taking the suggestion seriously just as we figured. By this time, Cremins was convinced that he should call his SID and his AD the next day and then schedule press conference in Atlanta on Wednesday to relinquish the award!"

"We continued to fuel the idea for quite a while, but when we bought our last round, we had to come clean," Les divulged.

"I said, 'Bobby, Jim and I are just busting on you. You can't give back an award even if you wanted to! Calhoun shook his head as he laughed out loud. Cremins called Calhoun and me a few choice names he knew from his days back in the Bronx while we just stood there laughing. Bobby still hates when I bring that story up."

Some of the stories happened because Les was in it. Others happened because he confided in Les.

"Bobby Cremins has always had a habit of asking questions that were not exactly what he meant to ask. He'd ask the question sincerely, but they were postured in a misleading way many times. There are two stories about his questions that illustrate this quirk," Les tells.

"Once we played tennis at Wild Dunes Racquet Club on a court right next to a very famous retired tennis pro, Rod Laver. I knew it was Laver without a doubt and I think Bobby knew who it was, as well. When we took a break, we had a chance to introduce ourselves. Knowing that he was Australian, I knew he probably had no idea that he was with two basketball coaches, so I introduced Bobby and myself. Right away Bobby asked him, 'Did you ever play in any big tournaments?' I nearly rolled over. I knew what Bobby was meaning to say: 'Tell us about playing in the major tournaments.'

Laver was nice about it. He told Bobby about the French Open, Wimbledon, the U.S. Open and the Australian Open in enough detail to make Bobby comfortable even though he had asked a laughable question.

"Rocket Rod" Laver was the only male (or female tennis player) to win two singles Grand Slams within the same calendar year. He was the world's top player for six years and won 200 career tournaments. He won eleven Grand Slam events in sixteen tries, winning all four prestigious tournaments in 1962 and 1969.

"After we got through talking with this sports legend, I laughed again at Bobby's initial question. He laughed, too. I said, 'Bobby, he not only played in the big tournaments, he won 'em all several times. He was the best in the world, you dumbass.' We have both laughed about that for years."

Les told about his other bumbling question that was mis-worded.

"Bobby self-confessed a similar story. He grew up in the Bronx as a New York Yankee fan. His favorite player was Mickey Mantle. He was not just another Yankee fan, but a *huge* fan whose childhood revolved around the Yankee's game schedule. Later in life, when he was the head basketball coach at Georgia Tech, Bobby was asked to play in a celebrity golf tournament in Atlanta. Mickey Mantle was playing in the same tournament. Bobby couldn't wait to meet his childhood hero. So when the opportunity presented itself, Bobby became Bobby again.

Mickey Mantle came to the New York Yankees in 1951 out of Commerce, Oklahoma. Casey Stengel was the Yankee skipper and immediately saw Mantle's raw power, speed, and ability. Despite his rough start in the Majors, Stengel stuck with the young switch-hitting phenom to build his confidence as a major leaguer. Stengel managed Mantle for his first ten years. The Hall-of-Fame player won the Triple Crown in 1956, played in twelve World Series, and won seven World Series Championships. He played in sixteen all-star games and was named the league's Most Valuable Player three times.

He shook hands with the Mick and asked, 'Did you ever know Casey Stengel?' He says that what he meant to say was 'Tell me what kind of manager Casey Stengel was.' But that's not what came out."

"Again, Mantle was congenial and respectful. He told Bobby that Casey Stengel was like a second father to him and that he was a great manager. Bobby got the answer he wanted from a question he didn't know how to ask!"

Les continues, "I hear some second-hand stories from Atlanta because we have a mutual friend there. Bobby and I have the same sports agent, Atlanta lawyer Richard Howell."

Howell represented both Bobby Cremins and Les Robinson as a sports agent over thirty years. A contract lawyer and Princeton University graduate, Howell made the transition in 1984.Among his first three clients was the Georgia Tech basketball coach, Bobby Cremins.

Howell tells of their mutual esteem.

"Marty Blake, the Hawks GM and a man considered an expert in assessing basketball talent, was the man who first proposed that I contact Les Robinson. It was about the chance to represent a very talented player from The Citadel, Regan Truesdale. Blake said that if there was any place in the country that had a clean record and no funny business going on, it's at The Citadel. Les told me that Truesdale already had five people he was talking to about serving as his agent. I told him, 'he really needed to have six!' In the end, I became Truesdale's agent. I had never met Les.

"I called Bobby Cremins because I figured he might know Les. Cremins lit up when I mentioned the name and told me that Les Robinson was one of his best friends. In a few months, Les left The Citadel to take the job at East Tennessee State. I became Les's sports agent because of Bobby. I ended up assisting him with his contract at NC State and then as AD at NC State and The Citadel."

Richard Howell had always been a low-key tell-it-like-it-is guy. Honesty mattered. His list of clients included the Dallas Cowboy's Emmitt Smith, the San Francisco 49'ers Garrison Hearst, along with NBA players like Tom Gugliotta, Mark Price, Latrell Sprewell, Todd Fuller, Kenny Anderson, and Jason Collier. Howell recognizes character.

"Sometimes in our business, it is important to recognize reality, and even the lack of character. You can get pretty good at it after a while," Howell suggested.

"People like Les and Bobby are special. They both get along with people in sports that may not otherwise get along with each other. Neither has sold their souls for short-term benefits in what they have done both inside the sport or in their personal lives. Where would you ever find two guys that are universally liked and admired by everyone else in the profession?"

"Les can recall every detail of story that might have happened forty years ago. Bobby will remember a great story, but usually only when Les prompts him. When you're with those two, you cannot help but be entertained," Howell summarized.

"Just about everywhere I went as representing The Citadel, East Tennessee State, or NC State, there was either a situation when I had Bobby with me or his name came up related to a story about something we had done that humored an audience. You have to understand Bobby as I do. He's a fierce competitor. Losing is not an option. His instinct is that everybody he meets is a friend because that's how he was raised. He is honest, and he is sincere. People say that about others; I know, but Bobby is the epitome of both of those qualities. The trouble is that he is so sincere that he has a tendency to have people take advantage of his good nature. If anything, it has made him legendary in the coaching ranks because he has the character and personality that every other coach most admires. Some of that came from his upbringing, I'm sure, but a lot came from his mentor, Coach Frank McGuire."

In the ACC Bobby's inherent honesty would serve to humor the other coaches at meetings all-too-often. Les set up one situation, and with Bobby near, the Bronx smile widened.

"You can't make this up. This story involved Bobby coming in late to the annual ACC meetings. Bobby always tells the truth. Count on it. But often he tells the truth at precisely the wrong time.

"The meeting had been going on for forty-five minutes; but inexplicably there was no Bobby. I was sitting near Dean Smith and Mike Krzyzewski. Gary Williams was right behind me. All the coaches were listening to the commissioner when Bobby suddenly appears—and typical of Bobby—he sincerely apologizes for his tardiness. But he goes further and tells us, 'I got held up at a player's home who he was recruiting. The parents had a lot of questions.'

"Dean turned to look at Bobby as if Bobby was joking. Mike put his head down into his hands because he knew that Bobby was telling the honest truth. Gary Williams couldn't hold back from laughing. Bobby sat down after the explanation. I leaned over to him and said, 'Bobby, you know we're in a dead recruiting period, right? You just told the league office and all the other coaches that you've just committed an NCAA violation. Bobby really didn't know he was not supposed to be in player's homes when he admitted that was precisely where he was coming from.

"Now, here's the real irony. After he retires, he gets a call from the NCAA headquarters in Indianapolis. They want to put him on a select committee to oversee NCAA rules and infractions. He accepts. He calls me to tell me about it. I broke out laughing. They couldn't have found a more forthright and honest coach who knew less about rules and infractions than Bobby. I bust him about being on that committee frequently. When a coach or a program gets out of line, I try to ask him what exactly they did wrong, based on the rulebook. I don't believe he's ever read the NCAA rulebook. But, then again, most coaches haven't. They leave that up to the ADs and the NCAA compliance coordinator. Besides, Bobby is like me in this regard. He doesn't want to build animosity with other coaches. In that sense, he may struggle on the Rules and Infractions Committee. But he is just too polite and accommodating to others to refuse to help."

Les gave another example of busting on his most trusted friend.

"A few years back, Bobby and I were together on a panel of former ACC coaches reflecting the past. The event was built for the unique humor that the coaches exhibited while cracking on each other. It was a fundraiser, so we were all having fun with the panel format. One of the audience questions directed at me was to elaborate about my two best memories as a coach.

"I told them that my first would have to be a memorable win against top-ranked North Carolina. They were better, but we played up and we upset them. I had supposed that the win was especially gratifying since nobody would have figured we could win that game but me and the players."

Les pointed to his second memory as his last game as head coach of the Wolfpack.

"I answered, 'It was just after we won the first game in the ACC tournament the night before. We were on a natural high and I tried to bring the players back to earth. We promptly played a poor game and we lost. I felt sick about it. I went into the locker room and ranted about our losing performance against an awful team that was poorly coached. I just couldn't understand how we could lose to that coach and that team.'

"Naturally, the follow-up question was 'Who did you lose to?'

"I answered, 'Georgia Tech,' and looked over at Bobby. Of course, the whole place broke out in laughter." Indeed, it was Les's last game as an NCAA head coach, losing to Georgia Tech, 88-73.

The Cremins-Robinson relationship is built upon a quiet respect wrapped around a very public banter. They have endured as best friends.

Brazil's Oscar Schmidt has scored more points than any player in Olympic basketball history. Drawing by author.

CHAPTER 23
ADIOS, MEXICO CITY

"When Bobby Cremins was appointed by the USA Basketball Committee to the duties of head coach for the World Basketball qualifying games in Mexico City, he honored me by calling and asking that I join this effort as his assistant coach," Les recounted. "It was in the summer of 1989. Bobby had built Georgia Tech basketball into a perennial national power. In fact, it was after the next season (1990) that Bobby was named the James A. Naismith NCAA National Coach-of-the-Year. Bobby had gained a reputation as a top recruiter and—in my opinion—his ability on the sidelines was as good as anyone I knew. He was very much underrated during his career for his knowledge of the game and ability to outmaneuver other top-level coaches. He learned much of this by studying his mentor, Frank McGuire."

Les, beginning his fifth season at East Tennessee State University, would assist Cremins along with Indiana University assistant coach Joby Wright. By the time the team departed for the games in the world's most populous city, the team roster had been chosen. It featured Billy Owens of Syracuse, Lionel Simmons of LaSalle and Christian Laettner of Duke. The team also had two players who would later play for Les, Chris Corchiani and Rodney Monroe from NC State. His East Tennessee State team was well represented by 6'11" scorer Greg Dennis.

"Even back in 1989, they told you not to drink the water in Mexico City. The first night we were there, Bobby and I met downstairs at the bar for a quick drink and short discussion about our personnel. I ordered a Corona. Bobby ordered a mixed drink. As he was drinking it I reminded him that ice was made from water—and they told us not to drink the water.

Bobby was sick for four days," Les related. "He was struggling, and I was just smug. We laughed about that awful circumstance years later, but at the time he was really sick.

"We went to the initial coach's meeting to get the rules and study the brackets early on. Those other teams and their coaches, understandably, had a disdain for USA basketball because we won so often. Most of the teams were from Central and South America. The qualifying tournament determined who would play in the FIBA World Games the next summer— and to an extent—our Olympic pool seeding for 1992 would come from that showing. If we were eliminated, all of that would come crashing down. Those officials in the coach's meeting seemed to have a scheme to make that happen," Les recalls.

"Neither Bobby nor I were conversant in Spanish. We thought they would have an interpreter there, but they didn't. They would say something that we didn't understand and look at us and smile. Some would even laugh. We both got the message. They were all plotting in the brackets to give USA the worst draw. We left that evening not knowing what information was decided, what rules changes there were, but knew exactly what our schedule was. We had our first two opponents lined up—the Dominican Republic and Puerto Rico. They were the other favorites besides us—in addition to Brazil. They were laughing about setting us up to fail," Les tells.

"I knew we had a good team and that Bobby would be a great coach. If we were truly playing our best, who we played whenever would not matter. Given that, there was no doubt that international basketball had improved significantly in the 1980s. Its popularity was at an all-time high. Every team we would play was a professional club and had played together for a while. What they didn't know was that Bobby and I were both concerned about our team chemistry going into the tournament. We had not been together that long. Chemistry is as important amongst great players as it is at any other level. So, those first two games would determine our advancement eligibility to the winner's bracket. In other words, you had to win one to advance. If you lost both, you played it out, but would not qualify for the World Games the next summer. That would be incredibly disastrous for USA basketball—and for our coaching careers, as well!" Les assumes.

The USA squad had not played cohesively enough to meld together a team chemistry or to get a feel of the pace of international play early on. There was always the added confusion with international rules. Because there was adequate depth, Cremins selected a starting lineup that had Gary Payton from Oregon State and Rodney Monroe along with Billy Owens handling the ball. They augmented these three with Christian Laettner and Doug Smith, a 6'10" inside player from Missouri. Antonio Davis from UTEP, Jason Mathews from Pittsburgh, along with Chris Corchiani and Lionel Simmons would log many minutes and add much punch from the reserves. That first game would tell the coaches much about the team's abilities and address the chemistry that the coaches sought.

Fatefully, the USA team was upset by the Dominican Republic, 116-108. The USA team defense was atrocious. They made too many crucial turnovers. Officiating would be a thorny issue throughout—especially given the language barrier. The chemistry that Cremins and Les had hoped for the team was awkward and hesitant. And they would have to be back on the floor for the next day for a game against a very good Team Puerto Rico to avert a major embarrassment.

"Neither Gary Payton nor Christian Laettner seemed to fit in with the rotations or the game plan. Lionel Simmons had a fine game with 24 points, but it just didn't seem that the team was as inspired as it should have been," Les recalled. "We needed to regroup and change our player rotation and make some adjustments on defense."

"Dave Gavitt was there. He was the former head basketball coach at Providence and helped put together the Dream Team for the 1992 Olympics. He was in charge of USA Basketball at that time," Les recalled. "Gavitt came to me after that awful showing and told me I would need to play the bad guy in the locker room. He knew Bobby was a serious competitor and a fine 'X's and O's' coach, but that I would have to be the one to bang the locker and threaten the players. That was not how I coached either, but I took his advice because I figured that he was right. I spoke with Bobby giving him Dave's suggestion. Bobby concurred. We needed to be challenged."

"I took on that role and became a scourge to the players. It was not my character, but it was what the team needed—somebody to get into their faces and make them wake up. Probably to this day those guys think I was a hard guy to play for.But I needed to do everything I could from every angle to support Bobby and keep our team focused. Bobby then showed me, the team, and the world why he is such a special coach. Team USA responded."

Les spoke about the strategy for the team to respond under pressure.

"Now Bobby and I talked after the disappointing loss. He felt that we needed a change to our line-up and even the game rotation by changing some player roles before we played Puerto Rico next. One of the changes he and I discussed was to bring Christian Laettner in off of the bench instead of starting him. It was not because of Laettner's ability or attitude, but because we both noticed the others would not pass the ball to him. It was likely that the 'Duke thing' took over—where other players just hated to feed the legacy of that college's best player. It was the wrong time to be envious or jealous. But the time was short, and we needed to fix the problem. I felt like—with Bobby coaching in the ACC the next year against him—that I should bring it up to Laettner as my idea, not Bobby's. Bobby didn't care about the repercussions or who talked to Laettner; he just wanted to win. The change would benefit all, including Laettner. So, I went to Laettner's room and sold him on the idea that he would help us more in a 6th man role. To my surprise, he agreed. As I was leaving his room he added that he wanted me to ask Coach Cremins if he could talk to the guards about getting the ball to the inside more often. Evidently, he did not pick up the vibes that Bobby and I had noticed. The reluctance of the other players to get the ball to him was hurting the team. It certainly was not his fault. We had no choice but to reshuffle the deck."

Laettner and company came back the next night to knock off the other pre-tournament favorite, Puerto Rico, by a score of 105-92. The big men— Laettner, Owens, Davis, Smith, and 6'10" Matt Bullard from the University of Iowa played extremely well throughout the crunch moments of the tourney. Amazingly, as a group those inside players shot an astonishing 60% from the floor for the tournament between them.

Les explained the change in strategy and how it changed the result.

"It was the big guys that got the job done in Mexico City. And it was Bobby Cremins' ability to use that talent smartly," Les said. "Cremins was, by the time we left, greatly admired by the players. They knew he was a solid coach. And we had become the best team we could become.

"Puerto Rico was an outstanding team and well coached. We were definitely in danger of losing had our team not given a stellar effort," Les said. "We really felt like Puerto Rico was much better than both Brazil and the Dominican Republic. But all three had the ability to take us down."

Billy Owens poured in 26 points against Puerto Rico and established himself as a go-to player throughout the tournament. Importantly, with the win, the pre-tournament coalition of Hispanic teams bent upon the upset of USA basketball saw their strategy backfire. Team USA qualified for the winner's bracket, which was—in reality—the seeding round. The rest of the tournament would be played to raise the team to its best possible seeding.

"After the huge win over a very good Puerto Rico team, Bobby felt that we had some work to do to keep the team playing well. Laettner did a fine job in his new role. And the players got used to him as an asset we needed to help us win. We had a few problems with Gary Payton early on. He was young and could be disruptive sometimes to what we were doing. Bobby handled that masterfully and knew how to shuffle him in as the situation arose. We needed his best effort, as well. He played fine defense for us but had a poor shooting tournament. That part of his game got much better as an NBA player. Not surprisingly, Payton led the team in steals and Bobby saw the he could use him to shut down somebody on the other team."

Indeed, the team reeled off six straight wins and qualified for the silver medal. But one particular win stood out.

"We beat Brazil in a very close game, 99-96. They had the great Oscar Schmidt. He was unstoppable. But there was a riot at the end of the game and Oscar Schmidt was about to nail one of our players when Bobby tackled him," Les recalled the scene. "Soon the police and security had everything under control, but it was definitely an ugly ending to a great win. I believe Schmidt scored 44 against us that night despite our best effort to keep the ball from him. He was a very confident offensive player but did not defend well—something we tried to exploit."

Brazil's Oscar Schmidt could play in any league. He scored 49,703 points professionally, more than any NBA player—ever. He is the only player to have scored over 1000 points in Olympic competition. Schmidt famously did not play much defense, and by that alleged reputation, only raised his arms to receive the ball on the other end of the basketball floor. He gave his arms a rest while defending.

Schmidt had averaged 41.9 points per game for Brazil in the 1988 Summer Olympics played in Seoul, South Korea. He was the one international player who even the television pundits agreed was well worth the price of the ticket.

Schmidt is considered the catalyst of the USA Basketball decision to select the 1992 Olympic Team from the NBA player pool. No American college player could guard the great Oscar Schmidt. Perhaps that kind of defense could come from the NBA. In the 1987 FIBA games, played in Indianapolis, the 6'8" Schmidt brought the Brazilians back in the finals against Team USA to win the gold for Brazil. He scored 46 points in their 120-115 victory. They were once down by 18 points. With many NCAA and US Olympic officials watching the disappointing loss, Team USA would need to make a statement to regain respect in world basketball. The 1988 Olympics edified the sentiment. The collection of America's best college basketball players that year could win only the bronze medal in Seoul.

The NBA's "Dream Team" was the timely answer for the 1992 Olympics. Interestingly, that team's only 'token' college player was Christian Laettner, recently of Duke University, who had won the John Wooden Award as national college basketball player of the year. He had handled being a 6th man in Mexico City in 1989 quite well. He would be a much deeper bench player on the star-studded Dream Team of 1992.

The 1992 Dream Team included Larry Bird, Magic Johnson, Michael Jordan, Charles Barkley, Karl Malone, John Stockton, Chris Mullen, Scottie Pippen, Patrick Ewing, David Robinson, and Clyde Drexler. Christian Laettner was chosen over LSU's Shaquille O'Neal for the only college roster spot.

Duke University's Christian Laettner played solid for the USA team.
Photo courtesy Duke University.

Whether Oscar Schmidt could play in the NBA was not a question for Les. There were plenty of NBA players with lesser skills and an aversion to playing defense. Schmidt was a great international player and he was also someone whom Les felt pretty good about even after the craziness of the competition.

"He could play. He was fun to watch; and wherever that Brazil team went, he was a celebrity. You always saw him smile. He liked a crowd," Les recalled.

"After the game with Brazil that night, Bobby figured there might be a problem since we stayed in the same hotel with a couple of other teams. Brazil was lodging in our hotel. The morning routine was to go downstairs and enjoy the buffet breakfast and chat with other players and coaches. After the fracas and Bobby's tackle of Oscar at the games' end, he was hesitant to further provoke this big burly player that quickly the very next day. In college at South Carolina, Bobby was a street-smart Bronx-attitude player who feared no one. But the game and the fight were still fresh. Bobby simply did not want a press-worthy follow-up incident at breakfast.

"Bobby called my room and asked if I was going down. Bobby, being the caring and courteous guy that he is, was concerned that he might incite a reprimand with Dave Gavitt and USA Basketball should something else happen. So, I went down with the intention to call Bobby if I did not see Oscar. As fate would have it, Oscar was down at the buffet and near where I was in the line. We exchanged a nod and then chatted a moment. We ended up sitting near each other. He laughed about the postgame rumble. Now, I didn't call back up to Bobby to tell him that the coast was clear. I really wanted him to come down and see me at the table laughing with the big guy he had just tackled several hours before. But Bobby waited. Oscar went on up, and I called Bobby then. When he found out what I had planned, he got this big smile and just called me the name he has always called me in that famous Bronx accent— 'you asshole.'"

USA basketball was changing. It may not have changed any quicker had the USA team been eliminated in the Mexico qualifying tournament in 1989, but it certainly would have changed two careers—that of Bobby Cremins and his best friend in basketball, Les Robinson. The deft work they performed in Mexico City was a catalyst for Team USA into the 1992 Olympics. There may have been as much as a half billion dollars of advertising revenue riding on their coaching abilities. They had effectively paved the way for modern pop culture, the rise of the City of Barcelona, and the incredible marketing opportunities of USA's 1992 Dream Team.

The postscript of that 1989 Mexico City experience was that the U.S. Olympic Committee called upon Bobby Cremins again. He assisted USA's head basketball coach Lenny Wilkens. They captured the gold for Team USA in the Atlanta Olympic games of 1996. Among the NBA stars on that team were Shaquille O'Neal, Hakeem Olajuwon, David Robinson, John Stockton, Scottie Pippen, Karl Malone, Charles Barkley, Grant Hill, Anfernee Hardaway, Glenn Robinson, Reggie Miller, Mitch Richmond and a much-matured Gary Payton. They are commonly referred to as "Dream Team II."

Les was called upon again, as well. His goodwill tour of Europe in 1994 with an Atlantic Coast Conference All-Star team did much to elevate the game of basketball.

"Assembling great talent to play in these formats would seem like a dream job that any coach would revel in, but there is much more to it than meets the eye," Les details. "A player's natural aversion to something is exposed. So, a coach has to not only assess the strengths, but also hide the weaknesses. It's not as easy as it looks!"

Just as Les found great favor as an NCAA selection committee member and subsequently served on the NIT selection committee, Cremins was named to the NCAA Committee on Rules and Infractions. Note: Both former coaches ended up on the barrier islands of South Carolina, where it is safe to drink the water!

A coaching fraternity. *Les's record against Dean Smith during his six years in the ACC was better than any other coach in the ACC during that time. Smith recruited Les out of high school. Their relationship was as mentor-student. Photo courtesy Greg Blatt and Robinson family archives.*
TOP: Gary Williams, Les Robinson, Jerry Green, Lefty Driesell, Lloyd Carr.
BOTTOM: Johnny Orr, J. Boeheim, Roy Williams, Dean Smith, Bill 'Clem' Foster, Johnny Unitas, Eddie Fogler.

CHAPTER 24
COACH DEAN SMITH

"I've been asked many times 'Who are the best coaches in America?'" In my coaching experience and being around some of them as I did, I can answer that in several ways. I like to put them into categories.

"The best teaching coach in America is Mike Montgomery. His ability to instruct elevates the player and the team. He is a great floor coach that gets into the moment with the player and makes that player much better."

He continued to another category.

"Because of what he does with his kids, Tom Izzo from Michigan State has to be in that conversation as a top coach. I've always been impressed with what he can do over the course of a season. He gets a lot out of his kids and they believe in him. So, I would say he is the best at taking raw talent and making them into a cohesive team."

He continued. "Bobby Knight has to be up there, of course. People might not like his method. He's a hard-nosed SOB—but maybe one of the smartest of them all. That's saying a lot. Look at the intensity his teams played on defense. That came from Knight. If you look back at his career, you have to conclude that he is among the brightest ever. In my mind, Bobby Knight is probably a genius. He's one of those guys like the author Pat Conroy or the columnist George Will who is extremely bright in what he does, but is, maybe, not normal like most of us. Pat Conroy is an unbelievable author; but is not really a normal person. He's different. He's a recluse at times. He makes unusual decisions sometimes. It's the same with George Will as an intellectual. He's at a whole different mental level than the norm. They are abnormal in their mental abilities beyond most everyone else in their field. From what I've seen over the years, Bobby Knight is college basketball's abnormal genius.

"Mike Krzyzewski is very bright, and he is, next to Jerry West, the greatest competitor I've ever known. You could probably add Norm Sloan into that group, too. Sloan was so driven to win that he became an amazing head coach. Coach K has that steely-eyed will to win and that's a tremendous advantage when he can channel that into his players. There's no question that he will end up with more wins than anybody in the history of the game. I admire and respect his career, especially when you look at the awful start he had at Duke. And I like him as a person because he is genuine.

"Recruiting, attitude, player's coach—you can make an argument for Bobby Cremins. I know I'm biased because we're close friends, but Bobby Cremins was a refreshing figure for the NCAA. He's the one coach in hundreds I've known that all other coaches both respected and enjoyed. And his players would go to war for him.

"There are others I've always admired like Terry Holland, Larry Brown, Jim Harrick, Dave Odom, and Roy Williams. All of them had unique abilities and furthered the profession.

"The total package had to be Dean Smith. He had high regard as a teacher, recruiter, diplomat, innovator, and competitor. He was also a great chess player. He did things yesterday to get a result tomorrow.

"Knight could be brutal to his press and fans. It might be a fan asking him something about his zone defense and he'd likely get this kind of response: 'Why the hell are you asking me about what defense I run. You're a banker. I don't ask you about interest rates, so what the hell do you know about defense?'

"Dean Smith would answer that same question pleasantly and with the ability to make the banker feel good about being a Tar Heel fan. He might be irritated or thinking like Knight, but he would have the diplomacy to answer like an ambassador for the university. His response would be, 'You, being a great fan of the game probably saw that our big guy was in foul trouble and we needed to zone up to protect him.'

"Keep in mind that when I first met him, I was a player at NC State when he was an assistant to Frank McGuire at North Carolina. His memory was unbelievable. He knew who I was and where I was from as an opposing player and always greeted me when I was freshman coach at State. When I took over in 1974 at The Citadel, I called him. I wanted to run the motion offense and he was the best in the business at the time. We met at a clinic and he spent two hours with me teaching that offense. Here I was, a State grad, learning from the best in the business who was also my greatest rival in my playing days. But Dean cared about me as a person, and we maintained an excellent relationship over all those years.

"Dean Smith was the most organized human being I had ever met. I have a personal story demonstrating this from my early coaching career. It illustrates his planning, diplomacy, and brilliance. I was coaching at The Citadel. We played in the North-South Doubleheader every year in Charlotte. Two SoCon teams, The Citadel and Furman, would play North Carolina and NC State on back-to-back nights. It was great for the Charlotte area to see these two major programs and it gave us and Furman a chance to test ourselves against the best. Our fans loved that weekend in Charlotte, as well."

Originally South Carolina and Clemson played the two North Carolina juggernauts, but pulled out because of their poor showings. Furman and The Citadel jumped at the opportunity. The tournament was played for 27 years at the Charlotte Coliseum. It ended because of the NBA coming to Charlotte in 1988.

"The ACC was the first to experiment with a shot clock back then. But the clock was in transition for their league. The Southern Conference did not have the shot clock, and the NCAA was a year away from utilizing the 45-second version in the tournament at the end of the year. The shot clock was going to become a reality in the NCAA and all the coaches knew this. The shot clock came in to counteract the slowdown games in which the Davids of college basketball were trying to compete with the Goliaths," Les explained.

The mismatch would compel coaches to try to slow it down to a dozen possessions or so to pull off an upset. You'd see scores – like in the 1966 ACC tournament semi-final – NC State 12, Duke 10. Duke was the sixth-ranked team in the nation at the time. Other near-upsets of this vintage were occurring frequently. The shot clock would force teams to play and take away a very unpopular coaching strategy. The fans were demanding the shot clock, as well.

"By chance I attended a coaching conference before the 1981-1982 season. Every year the Division 1 coaches would meet without the NCAA and the ADs. This meeting was in Chicago. It was at a hotel near the airport. Coaches could speak their minds and bring up current concerns and issues. Bobby Cremins and I had become great friends and we met there. Dean Smith was an attendee, as well. At a break in the conference, we were coming out of the restroom when Coach Smith asked if I had a moment to go over something.

"He started, 'Because the Southern Conference had a different rule, no shot clock, it would be up to the home team to decide to use or not use the shot clock when two different conferences met.'

"In this case, it was Coach Smith's decision for our February game. He had Sam Perkins, James Worthy, and Michael Jordan was a freshman. His role players like Matt Doherty and Jimmy Black were better than anyone we had in our program over the last forty years.

"The conversation went like this: 'Les, you know we can either use the shot clock in Charlotte or do away with it. I thought, before I made a decision, I'd ask you what you'd prefer to do.' He was asking me for my preference, which didn't matter. It was his call.

"I knew Coach Valvano at NC State was not even considering asking me that question for the first game on Friday Night. We would have to play with a 45-second clock. (The possession time clock was later shortened.) Jim Valvano was a great guy, but he wasn't going to give me that opportunity to slow the game down.

"Dean Smith, a man of tremendous anticipation, made it a point to option the shot clock rules to an opponent for one game that would benefit his team for other games months later. Only Dean Smith would have the foresight to plan challenges for his team.

"I answered with a smile, while questioning his motive in my mind. 'Coach, you're asking me if I had a choice to use the clock or not? Let me get this straight. I get to make that choice for our game?' I restated the question back to Smith to make sure I was hearing it right.

"He answered, 'Yes. I'll do whatever you decide, Les. It's your call,'

"'Well, Coach, you actually have the choice the way the tournament is set up. So that there is no misunderstanding—are you sure you want to pass that choice to me?' I asked.

"He said, 'It really doesn't matter to me, Les.' We'll adjust either way. I don't want to sound presumptuous, Les. God forbid. But we plan to be in the NCAAs a month after our game with you. There will be no shot clock rule there. In the first round, we may run across a smaller, well-coached opponent that may be much like The Citadel. We have to be ready to play without a clock under those circumstances. Again, not being presumptuous, but I assume that you will spread the floor and make us defend away from the basket. Looking at our schedule, that's the only opportunity I'm going to have before the NCAAs to chase little people with big people.'

"I grinned. Before answering, I thought through his next response to cover other angles.

"I answered this way, 'Now, if you are okay with it and this does not mean we will not get invited back next year, and that we will remain friends, I would much prefer to play without the shot clock. And I want to thank you for letting me have some input since you know it will help our program.'"

They shook hands and went on back to the large conference room. Les felt as though he had just gotten the break of his life against what would prove to be the best college team in the nation that year. Smith won it all in the NCAA tournament with a freshman sensation, Michael Jordan in 1982.

Les continues, "Bobby Cremins happened to catch part of the conversation about the shot clock as he waited to go back into the meeting with me. He witnessed the end of the discussion quietly. As we walked back towards the conference, Cremins asked, 'What's up with Dean?'

"You wouldn't believe it, Bobby. Dean knows his schedule and is asking me before the season starts if I would prefer to hold the ball against him next February. He let me decide on the rule when it is actually his call. Of course, I can't compete with his team with a shot clock. They'd kill us. He just cut me the biggest break ever. I'm stunned,' I detailed to Bobby. 'This was an unexpected gift,' I said, 'Dean Smith is one helluva good guy.'"

Cremins brought Les back to earth.

"Cremins said, 'You dumb ass! Dean just told you that he's going to kick your ass whether there is a shot clock or there isn't. It doesn't matter what ball they use, what time they play, what gym they're in or what color uniform they wear. They're going to kick your ass, period.'

"I answered, 'You know, Bobby, you're usually not that observant,' Les replied. "But you're right. They will probably kick our ass anyway. But with no shot clock, it will not be as bad as it would be with a shot clock. It's still a break I wasn't expecting.'"

As it turned out, Dean Smith proved his genius. The Citadel played three guards in that February game, two at 5'9" or less—Greer Huguley and Eddie Paone. The match-ups were hilarious. Wells Holland, The Citadel's tallest player at 6'6" handled the ball out at half court for much of the first half, covered tentatively by the 6'11" Sam Perkins. James Worthy at 6'8" was covering little Eddie Paone, 5'9". There was nearly a ten-inch height mismatch at every position except center. That was the scant five inches Holland gave up to Perkins. Les directed the underdog Bulldogs to work the clock with deft passing and back cuts, frustrating the #1 ranked Tar Heels and their thousands of fans. Coach Dean Smith countered with smaller second-team players to defend the little dribblers The Citadel had on the floor. Worthy sat for a good portion of the first half. The Citadel went into the locker room at halftime with a surprising 17-14 lead. Tar Heel fans at the Charlotte Coliseum were buzzing, wondering if the Heels would shake off the pesky Bulldogs. They had no idea that this situation was exactly what Dean Smith wanted.

Dean Smith had let his team try to figure it out for a half. They saw that anybody on any night could compete and frustrate their high-flying superstars. The lesson they needed for the NCAAs a month later had been taught by Les Robinson, as ordered by Dean Smith. Now the Tar Heels had to get down to business.

"Dean Smith came out and immediately employed his patented half-court trap. We had anticipated it and scored off of the trap a few times, but Dean had effectively changed the tempo. Once they got up a few buckets, we lost some of our composure. They became North Carolina again and raced out to a 67-46 win. The brilliance of Dean Smith to set up that first half proved beneficial on down the road as they played teams that held the ball in the NCAAs," Les confides. "And that's why when we talk about the great coaches, you have to hand it to Dean Smith. He was the full package. That little bit of preparation was a detail that nobody else, but Coach Smith would even consider."

The records are all made to be broken. Dean Smith completed his career at 879-254, a 77.6% winning rate in what many would consider the toughest league in the land. Upon his retirement, he had become the NCAA men's basketball coach with the most wins ever, surpassing the great Adolph Rupp of Kentucky.

During his six years as head basketball coach at NC State, Les's record against Dean Smith was tops in the conference—ahead of Mike Krzyzewski, Bobby Cremins, and all others. But Les knew that Coach

Smith was a mastermind and that everything he did with his teams seemed to be for a reason—a life lesson, a unique experience, or for a future win on his schedule. He was universally respected as not only a great coach, but also an outstanding role model. Les's admiration of Dean Smith began in his playing days at State when Smith was coaching against the ACC's first coaching legend, Everett Case.

The slowdown game at the North-South Doubleheader came up many years later in another venue. Les had gone to the Coach K Children's Classic in Durham, hosted by Mike Krzyzewski. It raised money for the Children's Hospital and showcased some fine athletes and coaches from around the country. Some played in the golf tournament. Les and Bobby Cremins played in the tennis tournament. It was the same weekend as the Kentucky Derby.

"We had some of the coaches and pro basketball stars go over to the host hotel to have a beer and watch the race," Les retold. "Everybody put up five dollars for the race, the winner or winners splitting the pot. We sat at a booth with James Worthy, who was by that time a celebrity star NBA player with the Los Angeles Lakers.

"Worthy started the conversation, 'Coach, I know you were at East Tennessee State and Buzz (Peterson) came with you to NC State and all, but where were you before you came to East Tennessee State? I didn't know you before then.'

"I knew maybe he didn't know about The Citadel, but I figured he might remember the game in Charlotte against us," Les recalled. "I couldn't wait to tell him about The Citadel and the Dean Smith slowdown game. He was going to flip out when he found out that Coach Smith planned the whole thing.

"I answered sheepishly, 'Well, I was at this little school you probably never heard of. A small military school down in Charleston—The Citadel.'

"And he went, 'The Citadel!' And he immediately realized that he played in that crazy game in the early 1980s against us. He went nuts."

"'Were you the coach when we played in the North-South, in that double header down there in Charlotte?' he asked."

"And I said, 'Yes.' I knew where this was leading." Les smiled.

"And he said with a loud laugh, 'I hated that game! I hated that game! The Citadel. Wow! I didn't get to play because of you. Coach Smith benched me because I couldn't cover a midget.'

"He said, 'You started three little guys—and see—I had to play against some tiny guy who dribbled everywhere and ran me up and down from baseline to half court. I felt like a fool. Coach Smith put a guard in for me and I had to watch them dribble and pass and put us to sleep and then someone would backdoor us. I was pissed.'"

Les could see that Worthy was becoming excited in his realization.

"I had to tell Worthy the whole story. 'I knew the deal. I had not figured that Dean would take the potential national player-of-the-year off the court. But he did.' Now Worthy was catching on and I had to go back and tell him about that decision was done in Chicago months earlier. Dean set it up and I was the beneficiary. Worthy got the short end out of that agreement."

Worthy, still perplexed by the revelation, continued the questioning.

"'So you're telling me, he knew before that game, it was like a setup that ya'll were gonna hold the ball? Right? Coach knew you were going to spread it out in our locker room before the game?' Worthy asked me, more as a statement than a question."

"He thought out loud to me, 'I knew Coach Smith was a control freak, but I had no idea he had the ability to control our team *and* the other team, too! He was setting us up while planning the strategy for the team we were playing at the same time! That's brilliant!'

"And I said, 'Exactly...what I just said. Dean set it up.'"

"Cremins was dying laughing about it because he was there in Chicago, too. Remember he said Dean was going to kick our ass in every circumstance."

Les described the revelation as it had shown on Worthy's face.

"Worthy grinned at me and Bobby. He was putting the details of the story back together in his mind. He realized how organized Dean Smith was," Les explains the setting. "He said that he couldn't wait to tell Sam Perkins and Michael Jordan."

"He added, 'This one is the best stories I've ever heard about Coach Smith. They're not going to believe it. But, knowing Coach, it makes perfect sense.'"

Worthy was fascinated. He was playing for the best coach of his time in America and had no idea to what lengths his coach would go to make a point or command a situation.

Les further added, "And Dean had a way of understanding situations, too. He was engaged into the plights of other coaches, especially the coaches he cared about. I was fortunate to be one of those."

"Years later, I had my worst team at East Tennessee. It was my second year. We were on probation. They had taken 5 or 6 scholarships from us so I'm playing with the left-overs of the team the year before. I mean the cupboard was bare. But I scheduled UNC when I first I got up there, thinking we were gonna' be fine, not knowing I would have to suffer the consequences of the previous coaching regime. Things were done there before I took the job that I didn't know about. I was left with an awful team, the worst I ever coached.

"We went to the Dean Dome. Dean's there in the hallway taking the last drag from his cigarette before the second half, like he always did. We are getting it handed to us. We had three minutes to get back out there. And he looked at me from down the hall like he was sorta' apologizing, and I nodded and said, 'We're just bad, Coach.'

"But we had a good relationship, and he said, 'Is there anything we can do?'

"Dean had one defense that I knew of, that didn't apply pressure of any kind. It was a point zone. I had actually learned it from my assistant Dave Hanners who played for Dean.

"Well Coach," I said, "since you asked me, I wouldn't mind seeing a little of that point zone.

"He didn't respond," Les grins. "He just winked. But I knew he was going to come out in the point zone, because I just knew the kinda guy he was.

"I walk on out, I get in the huddle, with the team—and I hated this team, too. They wouldn't listen, and they had given up. We weren't very good and we all knew it. They had a miserable year. It wasn't their fault because of the sanctions. That's a given. But we just weren't competitive, and we had some guys that just didn't want to play anymore, and some that just were obstinate. I needed some new faces, and soon!

"So, I get in the huddle and, I'm thinking, they're not listening to anything I'm saying. This team thinks I don't know anything about basketball. Dean had just given me a chance at credibility.I started speaking loudly with confidence, 'All right fellas, in this situation, I've followed Carolina for a long time,' I said, 'A lot of times they run a point zone to open the half.'I said, 'Look for a point zone and be ready to move the ball quickly to beat it.' In a point zone they actually point, cause it's a match-up to where the ball is."

"The second half starts and there it is. Dean Smith delivered a gift. My guys recognize it's the point zone and they look around and think, 'Coach knew what he was talking about!' Dean's point zone wink gave me a chance to take command, pull the team together and build a program. But I knew I was not going to be able to do it with the players I had.

"The next year is when we started building the program back to respectability with Mister Jennings and Greg Dennis. Though we had only 7 wins during that awful year with that awful team, we improved to 14 the next, then to 20 wins, and then to 27."

From that beginning, Les was able to build East Tennessee State University into a basketball powerhouse.They made it into the NCAAs his last two years at the helm. In a way, Dean Smith was the catalyst. He delivered credibility to Les. And Les never forgot the favor.

"He helped me at The Citadel and at East Tennessee. And Dean had a memory like no one else, either. When I was still head coach at The Citadel, we had just played Stetson and Boston University in a tournament down in Deland, Florida. We played well, going 1-1, beating Boston University the second night.It was midway through the 1976 season. We had bussed back at night—and we were playing Clemson in four days. We got into Charleston during the early morning hours. I hotfooted it up to Clemson later that day. They're playing North Carolina at Littlejohn Coliseum. I go in a side door with no ticket to a long tunnel-like hallway. The lockers were there. It was visitors on the left, Clemson's on the right. And I could see the clock, 2 minutes, and there's Dean puffing the last drag on his cigarette. I came up from behind him and said, 'Hey Coach.' We shook hands. And honestly, he just turned and said, 'Great game at Stetson last night on the road. Good win.'

"Now, he either just read it that day or remembered it from someone telling him. But he would look ahead, to see who might be coming to this game for different reasons, to scout because of his team. He had a very calculated reason for almost everything he did.

"Dean also usually had full control of situations, except maybe the one time I remember that the chancellors usurped a situation.

"I'm sitting at the table with some guys, and one of them was a big North Carolina fan and he asked, 'Weren't you coaching at State when State and Carolina played back to back?' And I said, 'Yes.'

"He said, 'That's the craziest thing I've ever seen—I wonder why they ever did that—why'd they do that—the ACC?'

"And I said, 'Well, you're talking to the guy that did it. I did that.'

"He questioned, 'You?'

"I said, 'Ultimately, I made the decision. And Dean was fine with it.

"And he said, 'How? I mean, why?'

"I said, 'Well, I'm a little bit of a gambler. You probably don't remember, but the first game….'

"And I went into the detail. Well, Desert Storm broke out. While we were riding over to Chapel Hill from Raleigh, the Gulf War started. It was announced on the airways. Mid-January 1991. But, we didn't know about it, we were on the bus. It's a 25-to-30 minute bus ride and it happened while we were getting there. The team gets off the bus and I'm getting off first. Dick Vitale is standing at the door and he's a bit more hyper than usual. He's going crazy. He's asking 'You gonna play? You gonna play?' Normally, coaches will give a briefing to the studio announcers. We would talk about injuries, the defensive schemes, and matchups. But I had no idea why he was asking if I was going to play.

"I thought Vitale was talking about some inside points he could make on TV. I answered him, 'I know it's a big rivalry, but I didn't know they get that excited about it.'

"And I said, 'Well, let me get in there and get my coat off or whatever and we'll sit down and talk.'"

"Vitale said, 'No, no, no, no—you don't know, Les. Are you gonna play the game?'

"And I said, 'What are you talking about?'

"And he quickly answered, 'you don't know?'"

None of the players or assistants knew about the war starting either. There were no cell phones, or text messaging avenues.

"He said, 'Desert Shield is now Desert Storm, a war's broken out. They're saying there might not be a game.'

"I said, 'Dick you know something I don't know. I don't know anything about this.'

"And about that time, we get to the Dean Dome entrance, and, boom. These two security policeman grab me and said, 'Coach, come with us.' And they take me down this hallway. We go through a couple of doors; I remember, there were a couple of other cops at this other door, and there were glass doors and Vitale was trying to go with them.

"This guy stopped him and said, 'No, you can't go in.'

"Vitale was still excited and hyper. He yelled, 'Les come back and tell me as soon as you know, come back...I need to know.'

"It was because he wanted to break it on ESPN. He was still hollering when we got to the elevator," Les retold.

"We go up. I'd never been to this area. We go into a dimly lit office. It's John Swofford's office, the UNC athletic director at the time."

Swofford later became the Commissioner of the Atlantic Coast Conference.

"Dean's sitting there. There's a couch and a chair. We shake hands and he motions to sit. Swofford asks, 'So what do you want to do?'

"I said, 'Well I just got off the bus. You know I had no idea.' It's a 9 o'clock start. Nationally televised. And obviously, it's gonna be a sellout. This is when I have Corchiani and Monroe and a fine junior in Tom Gugliotta. North Carolina has a Final Four team. I can't decide what to do and say, 'This all happened so quickly, and I don't know who makes the decision— us, the league, TV, the Governor, the U.S. President or the fire marshal.'

"Dean laughed at my comment and said, 'Well, generally in these situations, the visiting team would make the decision. We'll leave it up to you. Whatever you think.'"

"I answered, 'You know,' I gotta get my NCAA rule book out. This is the first time a war's broken out and I don't know what the rule is on that.'

"I thought about it and said, 'Honestly, I can't make this decision.'

"And we talked there for a minute. And John Swofford was leaning toward not having the game. But, I think, Coach Smith wanted to play. And he finally said, 'Les, let's go down and see the chancellors.'

"The president of the North Carolina system was also there.

"Our chancellor hadn't told me he's going to the game. But I guess it would make sense that the Chancellor would go to *this* game; all of them get together, the president and the two chancellors. As Dean and I are walking through the Dean Dome, and we're going down another hallway, a different hallway, there's nobody around. It's dark, it leads to the floor, and I can see it's heading for another different area of the coliseum—yet another place I've never been before. The Dean Dome is named for the man I am walking with to get to the chancellors. He knew where he was going in the maze of hallways. I didn't.

"Larry Monteith, our Chancellor comes walking around a corner. He said, 'Les, I wanna' see you.' And, I said, 'Okay.' And Dean said, 'Who's this? Who's that guy?' I said, 'That's our chancellor.' Monteith was relatively new at the job. Just like I was. And I said, 'Excuse me one second, Coach.'

"I went over a few paces from Coach Smith. He could not hear the conversation I was having with our NC State Chancellor."

"Monteith started, 'Listen, the chancellors and the system president decided we're gonna postpone this game.' He said it just like that. As a matter-of-fact. And Dean's was just over from us, but he didn't hear Monteith. For just about 30 seconds I think, 'Good heavens, I'm in the Dean Dome, a place named for the legend I'm coaching against. Coach Smith is the one person who is always on top of every situation and every detail. He's a master at knowing every piece of information in every circumstance. And I find out that the game has been postponed before he knew it. It's truly ironic that I'm going to have to be the one to tell him.'"

Les laughed at the irony.

"So, Larry Monteith leaves. I'm going to get to break it to Dean Smith in his gym. This is really unusual. Here's an idol of mine, Dean Smith, who is the coach that is the biggest control freak in the business. He plans everything and has control of every element it seems. But he doesn't know what I know. He can't control the decision that's being made in the moment. I let that short time that I had control of an outcome—and he didn't—savor for as few precious moments. I say, 'Uh, Coach, the system president and the chancellors decided that we'd play this game at a later date.'

"He said, 'I figured they'd probably do that.'

"I shook hands with him and said, 'Alright I'll see you whenever we play.' We got on the bus and went back to Raleigh.

"Years later, I tell Mike Krzyzewski this story and he broke out laughing because he knew exactly how Dean was. Dean had to have total control. In another irony, Duke played the night that the war broke out in a place I knew well. He was on the road at The Citadel in Charleston."

Duke beat The Citadel 83-50 that evening. A week later, Duke lost to NC State 96-91 in Krzyzewski's first game against Les. Krzyzewski's teams won a host of other games on the way to its 1991 NCAA Basketball National Championship.

NC State and North Carolina officials—ADs and coaches—couldn't decide on a make-up game date.

"Later, they gave us a date. We gave them a date. That was what the ACC Commissioner, Gene Corrigan, asked us to do to resolve it."

"The date they gave us, was after road games at Duke and Connecticut in front of their game. I'm thinking 'at Connecticut, at Duke, and at Chapel Hill.' The date I gave them was probably as bad. I don't remember, but we weren't giving each other good dates. So, the NC State AD came in to me and says, 'Les, no one has agreed on these dates, the conference office said we've got to come up with something soon.'

"I replied, 'I looked at the schedule. We both had a few days off, after our game with UNC at our place. Let's just play the next night at their place.'

"Todd Turner, our AD, shot back, 'Are you nuts? Back to back!'

"I said, 'Yes, I'm nuts, but I think that will be unique in college basketball. I doubt it has ever been done before.'

"He said, 'Yeah, but Les, it's Carolina.'

"I said, 'Well, I'm gambling. State wins over there one in nine years or something like that. I had looked it up. They don't win over here that often. I believe we can win here. We're good enough to beat them here. What better chance are we going to have to win there, if 18 hours later we walk in over there, having just beaten 'em?

"I said, 'And the worst-case scenario is that we lose both to one of the top teams in America. Dean knows he's got a great team and, if they are playing well, he'd want to do back-to-back, too. He's thinking that if he beats us here and carries that momentum over there, that's a plus for the same reason that I think it is.

"Well, that's what we decided to do. We played back to back," Les concludes. "Dean was good with it just as I had figured.

"We do beat 'em in Raleigh, 97-91. And Dean Smith said in the pressroom that night, 'That's the loudest he'd heard a crowd anywhere he's played from start to finish— ever.'

"I was standing outside our pressroom at Reynolds Coliseum waiting to go in when I heard that.So, I'm playing with house money now. We were underdogs, but we won the first hand," Les reveals.

As an aside, Les did something that no other coach had been able to do to a Dean Smith team that night in Raleigh. He ended a Dean Smith innovation. He explains the background and circumstance.

"Dean Smith was a genius innovator. So much in basketball is attributed to this thinking man's initiative. He came up with the 'Four Corners' offense. When he earned a lead late against a good team, they held the ball. Because of Smith's 'Four Corners,' the NCAA developed the shot clock.

"Another Dean Smith tradition was to take a squad of five players from the far end of his bench and put them into a game for a few possessions so that he could give his starters a breather and he could simultaneously make game adjustments speaking to them together without taking a time out. The substitute squad was instructed to go into the game and create a frenzied pace while giving 100% effort. The crowd loved it," Les informs.

They became known as the "Blue Team."

When Les saw that the UNC Blue Team was coming into the game, he quickly instructed his players not to let the ball go out of bounds and not to foul anyone. He wanted the clock to move without game stoppage. This meant no turnovers or timeouts either. Les had been prepared to take advantage of the less experienced Blue Team that Smith had relied upon for many years.

"Dean inserted his 'blue team' with the score tied at 22 halfway through the first half. He took out the big seven-footer, Eric Montross. He took out a pre-season All American in Rick Fox, a big scorer in Pat Sullivan, and a lightning-quick point guard in King Rice. Their fifth starter was their best shooter, Hubert Davis. Every one of them would later sign to play in the NBA. I stood and reminded our players about that circumstance. We could build an advantage if we didn't stop the clock.

"We performed as we planned. With pressure, we got a few 'gimmies' and were able to score two quick baskets. Dean sent his five starters back to the scorer's table. Now it was important to run it out as long as we could without the ball going out of bounds. We turned them over again, then again. We ran nine straight points up on the board before they finally got their great players back in. The momentum shift had occurred because of the time the Blue Team had to play. Our strategy had worked. Dean saw the fallacy of the Blue Team playing critical minutes in a key game."

Les continued to recall the incident.

"By the time the starters with the All Americans came back in, we had become both confident and aggressive. We went on another streak, outscoring their rested starters 9 to 2. We were moved to being up 16 from the gift of the 'Blue Team' substitution—and by executing the strategy I had planned. We were able to keep the bench players in and the starters at the scorer's table. Dean knew exactly what we did. That night destroyed Dean's 'Blue Team' strategy going forward. And you can bet he did not use it the next night in Chapel Hill."

It was rare to see a Dean Smith innovation bested. That happened about as often as Halley's Comet.

"There was some downside to that first win on the back-to-back nights. All along, the ACC office was hesitant about the back-to-back games. But Dean and I both saw a benefit, or it would not have happened that way. The game was rowdy enough and the fans in Reynolds Coliseum got a little crazy. So, I got a call from the head of the officials, Fred Barakat, the next day. He started, 'Les, it got out of control last night.'

"Barakat continued, 'You were out on the floor last night, you were going crazy, etc.'

"I responded 'Wait a minute, Fred. I was thinking about the scene from the night before and I looked up and down and I saw players, fans, coaches, and managers all going crazy. "

"So, I asked Fred, 'How were my players on the bench?'

"He answered, 'Your players were fine.'

"I asked, 'How about my assistant coaches?'

"'Les, your coaches were good', Barakat answered quickly. 'No, we are only talking about you.'"

"'But me versus the whole screaming crowd?'" I asked, not expecting him to respond.

"Barakat answered, 'We'll handle the crowd; you just worry about Les.'

"'The rest of the outfit is okay. I'm the only one out of control,' I shot back.

"I got the message. They were going to call the next game very tight. I get it. The officials were going to be rabbit-eared. Barakat was giving me notice. He likely did the same for Dean. It was coming from the league office.

"So, we headed to the bus on our way to the game. Beverly, my assistant, came running to the bus. She was coming to the game in Chapel Hill but coming over later separately. She had a FAX sheet she handed me.

"She said, 'I thought you might wanna' read this.'

"It was from the conference office. It was Article 6, section 4—which is the sportsmanship and conduct section. The FAX said it is going to be highly enforced at tonight's game.

"I advised my team about a crackdown by the refs on the way over. No funny looks, no speaking to the refs, no anything, I said. 'They're going to call everything.'"

"I'm thinking, 'Keep your mouth shut,' to myself. 'They're gonna' be really tough tonight.'

"The game starts, a guard for Carolina has his hand on Chuck Kornegay as he receives the ball. Kornegay responds. 'Get your hand off of me.' He turned to the ref, 'Get his hand off me.' He pleaded to the official. Boom. Kornegay gets rung up for a technical. Ok, Kornegay looks over, and I said, 'What'd I say on the bus?' I told the bench. 'They're calling everything. Do not respond, dammit.'

"The ball goes up and down two or three times. Nobody's gotten in any trouble after Kornegay's technical. Dean Smith just stands up and motions traveling on a play away from the basket. That's all he did. He's done it a thousand times in his career, and not gotten a technical. They teed him up right away. We're shooting. It's a gift from the league office.

"The night before was physical. And we won. They basically were saying 'we're not taking any crap tonight.' But, I will say this. It shut everybody up. And I learned that night something I used in the NCAA meetings when I got on the selection committee. I had a chance to talk to officials at game sites. I told that story. You want to be in control of a game—call a technical on both teams within the first five minutes and you won't get any more crap.

"I explained. 'If you feel that there may be bad blood and something's going to happen, call technical fouls right away.' There was no more griping after that."

"Everybody played to the tight rules. We got a fair shake. They got a fair shake. We lost the game. They just flat outplayed us and we ran out of gas late. We shot like 28% over the last ten minutes. And frankly, they did not play that well either on the second night.

"It was strange adventure playing two nights in a row against the same team. But the strategy worked. We split with them and they were easily a top 5 team that year."

The Tar Heels' win the next night in Chapel Hill helped them to post a 29-6 record and play into another final four appearance. Les's Wolfpack went 20-11, losing in a heartbreaker in the Sweet Sixteen to end their season.

The North Carolina triangle boasts three major basketball powers: Duke, North Carolina and NC State. Between them they have won twelve NCAA Men's Basketball Championships since 1974. There is no other rivalry of that proximity in the country. Les was there coaching against two legends—Dean Smith and Mike Krzyzewski. Both legendary coaches rose to the top in career victories recorded.

Les and Dean Smith enjoyed a mutual respect. The fans of those three universities, among the utmost rivalries in all of sport, had been treated to an era of greatness.

It is not likely that North Carolina fans had any idea that Les Robinson and Dean Smith remained best of friends for over fifty years, each assisting the other whenever possible.

Les concluded, "I can say that Dean liked both me and Bobby (Cremins). He would help both of us in any way he could because of that relationship. And we thought the world of Dean. He was everything you read about and more. Even the wars he'd have with Mike faded away. Mike came to appreciate Dean in much the same way as we did."

Dean Smith passed away on February 15, 2015.

Bobby Cremins and Les drove to the memorial tribute together the following week. They were invited to attend by Smith's family.

Les's respect for Smith and assessment of his coaching ability across a career was well founded.

"There was nobody in the sport as detail-oriented—and yet, as considerate of others," Les resolved. "There was just one Dean Smith."

Les and Mike Krzyzewski played as partners for several years in the Make-a-Wish Charity tennis matches. Bobby Cremins enjoyed the competition as well. Photo courtesy Duke University.

CHAPTER 25

COACH K

Les had much more historical perspective than most for basketball in the state of North Carolina. He knew the dynamics all-too-well.

"Mike Krzyzewski has a unique situation in Durham as far as a following is concerned," he says, insightfully.

"Well, NC State and North Carolina have huge fan bases because they have enrollments of 25,000 or more. And they mostly stay home. Probably close to 80% of them stay in that state, no matter what career field they enter. Graduates of Chapel Hill and Raleigh usually stay in state. Duke is bigger in Chicago and New Jersey and New York City and San Francisco than it is in Lumberton, North Carolina. There was actually a story recently about the lack of media coverage Duke receives inside North Carolina.

"They're not as big inside the state. That sounds like heresy, but it is the fact. People do not understand that haven't lived in North Carolina. Duke is big nationally. They are huge. But they're not big in North Carolina. Mike was bitchin' about it the other day. A guy wrote a column about it, Kelly Sims. It made it into the newspaper up there. The column says exactly what people in North Carolina already know. It's very interesting about Duke. Their network, as far as radio stations in the state, people in Goldsboro, and North Wilkesboro, Hickory, Marion, and Salisbury don't care about Duke. They care about NC State or UNC. And their in-state media network— State's and UNC's— remains huge. Every little town's got a radio broadcast of every game they play. But Duke doesn't have a big following like that. Now, they've got a few little pockets of good coverage. But nationally, when we're talking basketball, they're bigger than anybody except maybe Notre Dame in football," Les detailed.

"Wake Forest is yet another story," Les elaborated.

"Part of the problem with Wake was that they moved. Now, their program has come back. But, I'm talking historically. Wake would have been a bear if they would've stayed where they were. They were in the research triangle. They were ten miles from NC State. They moved to Winston-Salem in the 1950's away from the town that still carries their name. So, they separated themselves.

"All the sudden it went from the big four to the triangle. Winston Salem is probably closer to Charlotte than it is to Raleigh. Winston Salem is right near the Virginia line. You go another 15 miles and you're at Powder Mountain and then you're at Mt. Airy, and that's right on the line just before you get to Hillsboro, Virginia. They have a great institution, but I believe they would have been better off staying in Wake Forest, NC. The town and the university have the same name but are in two different places.

"NC State is the largest university in the Carolinas and has been for a while—at least for the last dozen years.UNC is right there. They also have a huge student population. The in-state traditions run deep.

"So, Mike Krzyzewski has done all that he has done—in an absolutely incredible career—in a place where it would have been a lot easier to fail. His statewide coverage is so over-dominated by NC State and UNC that you would not know in places like Asheville or Rocky Mount that the guy has won five national championships. But you would know everything about his program if you lived in Newark or Milwaukee. That's a great comment on how special Mike is and how he has built maybe the best program in the country year in and year out.

"What I like about his program is that he has always been a coach that uses momentum as a feeder. He approaches a game by getting his defense to pride themselves on stops. By using solid defensive pressure, he can jump a momentum reversal.Guys get on breaks and fill lanes from turnovers. He is the best in America in creating and sustaining game momentum. That's his legacy. And it's a damn good legacy to have."

Les spent six years in the wars with Coach K, Bobby Cremins, Jeff Jones, Cliff Ellis, Gary Williams, Dave Odom, Pat Kennedy, and Dean Smith. One would be hard-pressed to categorize the team that had the best players on a yearly basis. There were traditions at North Carolina, Georgia Tech, Maryland, and Wake Forest. Florida State won 60% of their games under Kennedy. Virginia would enter the rankings often enough. Year in and year out, Mike Krzyzewski brought in players who stayed four years and dominated the field.

"Mike won two of his five NCAA championships during my six years at NC State. He was tough to coach against if you had a team full of blue chip players, and nearly impossible to beat with anything less. His players bought into his philosophy and played well as a team. I hated playing them, but when I got the schedule each year, I had them on there twice. It was not going to change," Les reminisced with a smile.

The NCAA Selection Committee brought Les in contact with Coach K more often in the postseason "Big Dance." Les was often in charge of a site for a first round or a Sweet Sixteen.

"Mike knew me well enough by then to gripe about a seeding, or the region he was playing in, or the neutral gym where he was sent to play," Les noted. "But he was Mike and that was his way. I knew that he looked to get any little edge, even if it was just to put it out there so that he'd get a better break the next year. And, though I was always a rival of his—and Dean's—I did my best to make sure their storied programs were treated fairly. They had earned everyone's respect."

Les began on a positive note as the Wolfpack coach in the ACC wars against Duke.

"The very first time I played against a Coach K Duke team was at Reynolds Coliseum in January of 1991. I didn't know it at the time, but we were playing that year's national champion. We upset them at our place. But I knew that Mike had something special that year.

"And when we went over to Durham a few weeks later, we had a real shot at sweeping Duke. My players were up for that game, as well," Les remembers.

Something unusual happened in Durham. It could have been quite a distraction.

"Bissell Graves and my daughter Kelly had not been married that long. Bissell loved going to the games, and I would always try to get him a good seat whenever he could make it. He was a great fan. We were able to get him seated behind the team bench over at Cameron when we played Duke my first year at State. The Duke administration made that possible. He sat right behind my bench near the half-court area.

"The guy sitting next to Bissell was maybe the most legendary fan in NC State's sports history, Frank Weedon."

Frank Weedon began his career at NC State as part of the athletic administration. He served many years as the publicity director for NC State sports. Weedon even represented the university at Springfield, Massachusetts, when Coach Everett Case was posthumously inducted into the Basketball Hall of Fame.

"Everybody knew Frank at State. He was a great guy," Les intimated. "But he was also sometimes out-of-control when he came to the events. He'd get very excited and vocal. He was kicked out of many basketball games over his career, including a few times he was escorted out at the ACC tournament. He was even kicked out of a wrestling match one year when I was the AD. It really got comical. Frank Weedon may have been kicked out of more sporting events than anyone in history!"

The Wolfpack team was in a close contest against the 1990-91 Duke basketball team. This Bobby Hurley-Christian Laettner-Grant Hill Duke team went on to win the 1991 NCAA Basketball Championship, beating UNLV and Kansas in the Final Four just six weeks later. But what happened at this game could have turned out to be embarrassing to the ACC office.

Les set up the incident.

"Since we had beaten Duke three weeks earlier in Reynolds Coliseum, I knew this game was going to be a hard-fought back-and-forth show for the fans. It was loud, as always in Cameron. I played there 30 years earlier and remembered how loud it could be. The Cameron Crazies were out. We had that rare chance to beat Coach K twice in the same season. And when that game started, it was bedlam.We matched them point for point and knew we were in a tough game that would go down to the wire. We were playing very well. It was on national television—a late 9:00 start on ESPN.

"Bobby Hurley was guarding Chris Corchiani tightly right in front of where my coaching seat was positioned. I had heard Frank Weedon on the officials from the tipoff on—as was always the case with him. Suddenly, everyone was puzzled when the game official blew his whistle and stopped the action. He then pointed at the guy in the red-checkered shirt and told the security police to remove him from the game. I looked back, figuring Frank had gotten kicked out, but they were escorting Bissell, my son-in-law, out of the gym. The officials resumed play. What really happened is that they were pointing to Frank Weedon to be removed, who was sitting next to Bissell. The security guard got the wrong signal. Barbara was there and leaned over to me at the bench when it happened. She said, 'You know they're taking out the wrong person.' Bissell knew it too."

"Well, of course I realized it, but there was no way I could straighten out that incident in the field of battle. But somehow, the security people figured it out a few minutes later. But when they realized it, it was too late. Bissell was outside of Cameron by then.

"Bissell later told me that they offered to take him back in to his seat. But Bissell knew that he was already identified by 8,800 screaming Duke fans as a big troublemaker. He told the security people, 'I'm not stupid.' He knew he would not get back in without a lot of names called to him and maybe things thrown as well. So, he got to see the rest of the game by monitor in the ESPN truck.Duke won at the end, 72-65. And Bissell had a story to tell his friends.

"Now Mike Krzyzewski found out what happened later and apologized that my son-in-law was carted out of the gym. Mike cared about families.

"Years later, I took the family up to one of the tournament sites to see a few games. Duke was one of the four teams. Since I was on the committee, I got Bissell a good seat at the site to see Duke play. When Duke came out on the floor, you could hear cheers and boos, as usual. It was a funny thing about Duke. You loved 'em or you hated 'em. Personally, I've played and coached against Duke, and I think that Mike has always done a superb job recruiting and teaching. He's a class act.

"But before the game started, I had gone over to the head of security for the tournament site. I pointed out Bissell to him and asked for a favor. Sure enough, the guy followed through. Just when the crowd noise rose with Duke's entrance, a uniformed guard came over to Bissell—and with a straight face—said, 'Sir, you will need to come with me.' Bissell looked shocked for a second. Then, he smiled and asked the policeman, 'Did Coach Robinson happen to send you?' We all broke out laughing."

Les stayed within the coaching circle of the ACC, trying to accommodate events that the other coaches sponsored for various causes.

"I always played in Mike's charity events. Mike was much like me. He preferred to play tennis. When the others were playing golf, Mike, Bobby, and I would usually play in a celebrity doubles tennis match. Over the years we played with others like Dave Odom, Charles Barkley, and Dick Vitale," Les recalled. "Mike was a super competitor, even in those charitable events. But, despite those hard-fought basketball games of the ACC, we have remained as great friends.

"Now Mike has won more games than any coach—male or female—in the history of the NCAA. He did so because he had a great combination of talents. He brought his players to a top national institution that had a fine academic reputation before he arrived. Yet he built that reputation even higher. He had an eye for talent that fit—not just talent. If he needed a rebounder, a ball handler, or a defensive specialist, he could find the raw material and refine it with his coaching ability. He was like Dean Smith in that way. He could change game momentum with defensive pressure like no one else in the business. And he was able to transfer his competitive edge to his players. He got them to believe in each other and in him as a coach. Keep in mind that he arose to the top in a league that is—year in and year out—the toughest in America. You have to play hard every night."

In what would be considered an odd circumstance of Les's coaching era at NC State, he noted that Coach K found friendships with he and Bobby Cremins—two staunch opponents each year. Coach Dean Smith had a similar relationship with Les and Bobby.

"Yet the media and fans clamored for the heat in Coach K's battles with Dean," Les observes. "In the end the word 'respect' finds a home. Mike respected Dean and vice versa. They became close friends over a career. And the guys like Gary Williams, Bobby, Pat Kennedy, Dave Odom, and myself found the same common ground. Others did as well. Coaching in the ACC requires patience, confidence, and respect. Coach K has an abundance of these qualities. That's why he has achieved above anyone in the business."

Les goes over strategies in The Citadel's locker room 1981.

CHAPTER 26
COACHES HAVE MOMENTS

Coaching at the D-1 level of college basketball requires much attention to the earnest pursuit of wins. The next contract requires them, if there is to be a next contract. Most NCAA coaches are hired on a four-year cycle. Every April, there are multiple openings with top conference programs. The cycle is a given.

But beyond contracts and wins, job searches and losses—life happens. But it happens around, in spite of, and because of basketball. Its variables are more immense and more important than moving the ball against the zone or blocking out fundamentals for defensive rebounds. As much as he followed his coaching passion, Les made it his priority to always keep the game in proper perspective.

The Citadel team that went to Los Angeles in 1972 to challenge UCLA's Bill Walton in his first college game had Les as their assistant coach. Another cross-country jaunt back to LA occurred soon after Les had assumed the reigns as head coach at the military college.

"A dozen or so years later, I returned to Los Angeles with a team that was developing. We had a few good wins early and were playing in a tournament out at Shrine Auditorium in Los Angeles. Duke University with Mike Krzyzewski was also in the tournament.Remembering Jerry West's advice about where to stay in LA years earlier, I booked the team into the same hotel, the Sheraton Miramar across from this very nice city park.

"We were set to play in late December of 1984.My close friend, Keith Hamilton and I went out first and I scouted Southern Cal in a tournament. Keith administered the scoring desk at basketball games and was also the

Citadel's head track coach. Our families joined us two days later on the 23rd. We spent Christmas there in the Miramar Hotel. Keith and I jogged every day in that park. He was a big workout nut, too. We ran every day. He had fully recovered from some freak heart attack ten years before. He had been given the green light on everything. He told me could buy life insurance and he was 100% back healthy again.

"On the last day, it's the tournament finale on the night of December 30th. Duke and Southern Cal played in the championship game. We had played in the consolation game against UAB (Alabama-Birmingham). The Southern Cal coach had made a special point to ask all three visiting coaches to have a little meeting.

"Normally, tournaments have something much more formal like a media dinner. But because of time constraints, there was no formal coach's meeting prior to the start of the tournament. At the short informal meeting, we were given all the tournament gifts and the sweat suits for the players. We did meet briefly—all four coaches. The Southern Cal AD made it a point to ask us to come to a private reception after the championship game. We agreed to come, knowing it would be late that night.

"The championship game ended late as we expected on the last day—at nearly 11:30 p.m. The Southern Cal reception we had agreed to attend is the opposite direction of the Miramar Hotel.

"Barbara and I had a rental car there. The team went back on the bus after our early game. Keith and Jean Hamilton also had a rental car and we had the four girls, their two and our two.

"Well, the four teenage girls want to get Jay Bilas' sweatband. This is Jay Bilas before he became Jay Bilas! He was a Duke player, but the girl's thought he was the handsomest guy in the world, and all that. He was a probably a junior at Duke.

"The game had just ended and Mike's still emotional. The officials had made a couple of bad calls near the end. But Duke won anyway. He said, 'Did you see that crap?' I nodded. He was getting hosed at the end and he knew it.

"After the win I asked Mike what he thought because it was pretty late. Krzyzewski had settled down some and replied, 'Yes we should go, let's go to the reception. That would be best.' I said, 'Okay.' So, it worked out because I wanted to speak with Mike anyway.

"Keith and Jean Hamilton and Barbara are standing there with the four girls at the entrance to the dressing room waiting on me. The teenage girls are content to wait on a chance to meet Jay Bilas. Keith Hamilton speaks up after the girls go to try and get Jay Bilas' wristband, and says, 'We'll take the girls back, Les.'

"And I said, 'Are you sure you don't mind?' He said, 'No, no. Cause it's late, and they wanna get back and I didn't really wanna go to the reception that badly.'

"Knowing that Keith and I were set to jog the park in the morning I said, 'Hey, don't call me in the morning, I'm not running in the park tomorrow, cause I'm not getting in the bed until three o' clock.'"

Les and Mike Krzyzewski headed to the reception as they had promised. They rode together in Krzyzewski's rental car.

"I go back to when we picked up the post-tournament stuff they give to the players. Mike hadn't been at Duke that long. We're carrying the tournament gifts to the car and it's a little misty rain. We're carrying all these boxes and everything and we had to make two trips with no assistants or anybody there to help us.

"Mike said, 'Well, at least we know we've made it to the big time.' It was in the wee hours of the morning and we're carrying boxes to his trunk. We just laughed it off."

"We're putting all this stuff in the car to take back to the players. We didn't know why they did that in that manner. We headed back to the Miramar Hotel. It was at about three o'clock that I got in the bed after the reception.

"The next morning about 7:00 or 7:30, I get a call, it started, 'Mr. Robinson?'

"'Yes.' I answered. 'This is so and so from the Santa Monica Police Department, you better get down here to Santa Monica Hospital. Your friend, a Mr. Hamilton, has had a heart attack. He might not make it.' I was immediately stunned.

"Barb and I jump up, get dressed quickly and ride down there. It's not even a mile away from the hotel. Keith and his wife Jean had gone to the park together that morning. Their daughters were still not up. Keith had run that morning. Jean walked, and they were going to meet at a certain point in the park, Jean told me later. They had been down there every day. We all had. She gets to the place to meet, and he's not there. So, thirty yards away, she sees a lot of commotion. There's EMS, so she walks down there. It's Keith. He's had a heart attack.So, she goes with Keith to the hospital in the ambulance.

"When I got the call, we hustled to get there. I go down there with Barbara. I run in there. The doctor and nurse say, 'Get the daughters, he's not gonna' make it.' I run to get them. Barbara goes on in with Jean. They call the hotel. Their two daughters are waiting on me in the lobby, Julie and Joanie. They already know that he's had a heart attack, but they don't know how severe. I take them back there. All of us were in a waiting room, Barbara and Jean and the two daughters. I'm in there with the nurse and the doctor and—and—he died while they were in the waiting room before they got them in. They did everything they could to try and save him. But the heart attack was fatal. I was devastated. Keith and I had become the very best of friends.

"Now the doctor was asking me some questions, personal things about medication, habits, this and that. I had been with him several days and they asked, 'Did he take heart medication?' I said, 'Yes, he took it every day.'

"The nurse spoke up and said, 'No he wasn't, his wife told me, I had already quizzed her on that. That was allergy medicine you saw him taking. He quit taking heart medication back in September.'She said that they cleared him and said that was ok.

"This doctor, for some reason, he gave the nurse and myself a lesson in heart condition 101.

"He spoke up, 'The three of us are all gonna die.' He repeated, 'We're all gonna die.' And he pointed at the nurse and he said, 'But let's say you've had a heart attack and he and I hadn't and we're all the same age we are now.' He said, 'The odds are greater that you're gonna die of a heart attack than he and I. We're gonna die. We could die of one thing or another. But if you've had a heart attack, you don't ever quit taking your medicine. You take it forever.'

"Keith had the first heart attack in 1975. So, it might have been his doctor that let him stop taking his meds after nine, ten years. He might have seen him in top physical condition and said, 'You're fine.'

"Seeing my best friend die and trying to handle the arrangements for his family left me reeling back then. It was an incredibly sad time," Les relates.

"The year before, Bill Foster, the South Carolina and Duke coach had a heart attack. He missed part of the season. He was still coaching at South Carolina.

"In that spring of 1984, he was still recuperating. This is nine months before Keith's fatal heart attack in Los Angeles. His assistant, Steve Steinwedel, tells me, 'Bill's having problems with the heart thing and is cautious. I'm worried about him.'

"Steinwedel asked, 'Didn't you tell me that your friend down there, the track coach, had a heart attack ten years ago?'

"I said, 'Oh yeah.' I was proud that Keith took such great care of himself.

"He asked, 'I wonder if he'd talk to Coach Foster?'

"I said, 'Sure. I'll ask him to call him. Knowing Keith, he'd be glad to assist.'

"He said, 'Well, he's gonna be down there in a month for a clinic or something, doing something down there.' They were doing a camp in July.

"He persisted, 'Could we set it up for them to have lunch?'

"July came. We had lunch at what's now the Marriot. It was Sheraton then. It was strictly for Keith to talk to Bill Foster about taking care of himself. Now, Keith was a workout tiger. Nobody took care of himself like Keith.

"Keith starts out, 'Hey Coach, I'm fully recovered, I'm running four miles every day. I watch what I eat. I take it one day at a time. Take your medicine.'

"But in just two months, September, Keith stops taking the medicine. In late December, he has a massive heart attack.

"I stay out there with them—with Jean and the girls because you can't just leave the body. The team flew back that same day of the tragedy. The flight was at about one o'clock that afternoon. I stayed for two more days. We were playing back home in Charleston on January 2nd. We have a scheduled double-header with Foster's South Carolina team in McAlister Field House.

"The irony is, the games are on the same day as Keith Hamilton's funeral. And the funeral is done on campus. I'm at the funeral, of course. USC's shoot around on our floor is during the funeral. I tell the manager, 'Don't tell Coach Foster where I am.' I've decided, because of what Steve Steinwedel told me months earlier, not to tell Coach Foster about Keith. I thought it best to not throw him into a depression. I remembered that Steinwedel told me that after Keith met Coach Foster at the lunch, he was completely over the heart-attack paranoia."

The doubleheader Les set up was The Citadel against Erskine in the early game and South Carolina against Wofford in the nightcap.

"Well, that funeral was nearly over when Foster arrived on campus. They came by the Summerall Chapel, and he stopped and asked a cop or somebody about it. Somehow, he found out that it was Keith Hamilton's funeral. And I gave explicit orders to shield him from that information. I was still upset, personally devastated, about Keith's passing and especially after the funeral.

"I walked over into their practice after the funeral. They're out there. Coach Foster runs to me. He takes me to the dressing room. He said, 'Is that true? Is that your friend?'

"I'm still thinking that he couldn't have known. I thought that I'd covered all the bases. As if he already knew, he asked, 'Who died?' The cop had told him already that it was our track coach. He told me that.

"'It was who you thought Bill—our track coach, Keith Hamilton,' I answered solemnly. I was still reeling from it.

"I said, 'Yes he did die, Bill, but let me tell you something.'

"I told him the doctor's advice story from the Emergency Room in LA. I said, 'Keith had quit taking his medicine. I guess what I'm saying to you is, you never quit taking it. You're taking the medicine right now, right?'

"He shook his head and said, 'Yeah.'

"I advised what I knew, 'You never stop taking that medicine, according to this heart doctor at Santa Monica City Hospital who sounded like he knew what he was talking about.'

"Coach Foster got really uncomfortable talking about the guy he met who gave him advice on his health. He liked Keith Hamilton. Who wouldn't? Keith was a stand-up guy.

"We had a 6:00 and 9:30 doubleheader that night. Even at our gym, the fans were not coming out until the second half of our game against Erskine. They wanted to see South Carolina play. I had to coach the game at 6:00 when I'd rather spend time with my family after the Keith Hamilton funeral. Our families were very close. It was a tough day for me. But I knew that Keith would be disappointed in me if I didn't coach the game on the day of his funeral.

"We had a good team and dispatched Erskine easily that evening. The game was a blur, I suppose because I was still reeling from Keith's sudden passing. It was the first game our team played without Keith at the scorer's desk.

"Months earlier, I gave South Carolina a choice of opponents. It really didn't matter to me who they played, or who we played.My deal was to get in the gate with USC coming in. I had done that with Coach Frank McGuire. Now I'm doing that with Bill Foster. It's good because I, in effect, was providing them an opponent for what should be an easy win on the road.

"Coach Foster asked me which team he should play back during the summer. I didn't know much about Erskine but knew that we had beaten

Wofford the year before by 30. I answered, 'They're both NAIA's and neither one of them is that good. I would suggest because they have football and have a little better name in the state, that USC would gain a better benefit by playing Wofford. But you decide. I'll play who you don't play.'

"Wofford gets off to their best start ever that season. They're like 10 or 11 and 0. And I was the one who suggested Wofford to Coach Foster. We beat Erskine by 35 in the first game. With a minute to go, Wofford's ahead of South Carolina in the nightcap. It was just one of those freak deals. And South Carolina probably wasn't as good that year as they usually were. They ended the season at 13-13.

"I'm sitting over there, and I've never sweated a game that I wasn't coaching. I was sweating that damn game. The Gamecocks got a whistle or two at the end. And they win. I don't want to see Bill Foster that night. I go to the dressing room after he went up to do his post-game radio show. I thanked Steiny. And I was gonna hide from Foster.

"So, I go to the other side to the visiting restroom. Steiny is standing over by the other basket, right there, the entrance where the restroom is. Steve Steinwedel was a big 6'9" guy. He played at Duke. He was an assistant at Duke with Foster. He later became the head coach at Delaware. Foster's radio show took a commercial when I was next to 'Steiny' down on the floor, well away from Coach Foster.

"But Foster hollers down, 'Steiny!' He shouts it loud so the whole gym could hear.

"He said, 'Don't ever take a call from this guy. For anything!'

"When I'd see Coach Foster over many years at the Final Fours, he'd bellow out to someone near that 'Les Robinson is the King Schedule Maker. He'll beat someone by 30 and set you up to fight for your life!'"

Coach Foster became a person most diligent about taking care of himself. He coached four college programs that each experienced at least one twenty-win season—at Utah, Rutgers, Duke and South Carolina. He made it the NCAA National Championship game in 1978 with a team led by Mike Gminski, Gene Banks, and Jim Spanarkel, but lost to a Kentucky team that featured Jack Givens who scored more than any player ever in the final game, 46 points.

Bill Foster died on January 7th, 2016, at the age of 86, more than 30 years after his heart attack. He had become a senior statesman in the game and had stayed friends with Les over many years. When The Citadel football team traveled to College Station, Texas in 2006 to play the Aggies of Texas A & M, Les was serving as The Citadel AD. He invited Foster to his visiting team suite. Foster enjoyed the reunion and even called Les the 'Master Scheduler' to the enjoyment of those who knew the story. The respect was mutual.

"Bill Foster knew how to coach. He was a master of game strategies and always seemed to get the most out of his teams. What I knew was that his players were most complimentary. He had demonstrated over a great career that he was a winner," Les summarized.

When Foster was still at Duke University, he promoted the 'One-Two Basketball Clinic' in Charleston in 1978. His team was runner up for the national championship to Kentucky in a close game played in St. Louis. He and Joe B. Hall came to Charleston to co-manage this most unique basketball clinic at The Citadel's McAlister Field House. Kentucky's Joe B. Hall enjoyed his visit to Charleston and mostly enjoyed the stories Les told him about Pistol Pete Maravich, Everett Case, and Jerry West.

Les recalled the timing.

"That Charleston clinic that Bill Foster set up ultimately led to me being offered the top assistant's job at Kentucky four years later. It sounds crazy now, but I turned it down. I went up there and changed my mind to sign up, then came home and turned it down again.

"I began by turning it down in a soul-searching conversation with Joe B. Hall on the phone. It was within twenty-four hours of the offer.

"I said, 'Coach, I am so honored. But this is just about the timing; my daughters are in school; my home is here and everything. It's just a bad time. When they heard Barbara and me talking about it, Kelly and Barbara Ann started crying. So, I knew I couldn't pull them out of Charleston to go to Lexington.

"Hall did not accept the answer. He said, at first, that he completely understood. He then suggested that I take some more time and visit Lexington

"He suggested, 'Why don't you just ride up for the day and spend the night?'

"Instead, I flew. He and Sam Bowie picked me up at the airport. Bowie was drafted ahead of Michael Jordan. I'm like a 12-year-old going to Disney World and thinking 'Ride every ride you want and eat anything you want. Whatever.'

"I mean that's Kentucky basketball. Even when UCLA was winning big, they didn't have the fan base that Kentucky did. The State of Kentucky was basketball crazy when I was growing up—and I grew up 39 miles from the state line. There used to be a saying. When a mother gave birth to a boy in Kentucky, she had two dreams for that son. First, he was to get a basketball scholarship to Kentucky. If he could not do that, he should try to be President of the United States. That's how big basketball is in Kentucky.

"Couples got divorces and would not give up their tickets. They still sat together. There are stories that they sat together 25 years or more after the divorce because the tickets were golden. They sell out every game. It's bigger than Duke, North Carolina, or NC State basketball in terms of the passion. It's the entire state. There, they have the basketball season and the time before the next basketball season. It's the Big Blue.

"Joe B. Hall takes me into Rupp Arena. He shows me the basketball floor and the weight room, the training room, the offices, everything. There are banners hanging everywhere. It's Dan Issel, Pat Riley, Jack Givens, and Cliff Hagan.

"I realized that Hall was right. Seeing the place was a game-changer. This is way ahead of where I was. It was too much to pass up. The money was also considerably more. I started thinking about how I could coach guys that were sure to make it into the NBA. Now I needed to convince Barbara and the girls.

"Just as soon as I got on the plane, I began thinking about the advantages of staying in Charleston or coming to Kentucky. I began to feel like I shouldn't go to Kentucky again. The further I got away from Lexington, the more I became settled with Charleston and our home on the island."

The attraction of moving to one of the top national programs was difficult to pass, but the Robinsons were first a family and secondly a basketball family.

"I made one more stab at the prospect of moving to Kentucky with Barbara that night. I wanted to know for sure that she wanted to go or to stay. Barbara had always been dedicated to my career and where it might lead—from St. Albans to Raleigh to Cedar Key to Cullowhee to Charleston. I knew that she was willing to make whatever sacrifice or adjustment was in store for the family, especially getting the 'buy in' from the four kids. What I heard from her was much like the way I felt. It wasn't about the money, the bigger stage, or the opening of other opportunities as much as it was about family. In the end, I decided to call Joe B. Hall and decline the offer. I can't say that I never looked back, but I can say that I did not dwell on it once I closed that door."

Les with Coach Norm Sloan. Photo courtesy Robinson family archives.

CHAPTER 27

CIRCULARITY

His preponderance of associations across the sports world for a lifetime has meant that Les has gained lasting friendships and indelible memories. His story-that-leads-to-another-story reflections merit a catalogue. Les's details of the intersections with those he knew could best be reflected upon by selecting a name and letting this consummate storyteller furnish the episode.

Les liked Al McGuire's street sense and ability to recruit.
Photo courtesy Robinson family archives.

ON AL MCGUIRE

Al McGuire made his name known across America by being both unpredictable and original. As a player at St. John's University, a professional player in the NBA, a top college coach, and as a broadcaster, McGuire was unique. He rode his motorcycle out on the open road well before Coach Phil Jackson had the urge to do the same. He passed up an NCAA bid to win the NIT Tournament in 1970. He said it was because he wanted to visit his mother in New York.

McGuire Marquette University team won the NCAA National Championship over the University of North Carolina in 1977 and he promptly retired. He coined phrases and basketball terminology over a colorful second career in the broadcasting field, where he retired again suddenly in 1992.

His quirks included removing blankets and pillows from hotel beds to sleep on the floor. His player recruiting practices were legendary, as well.

"My rule was I wouldn't recruit a kid if he had grass in front of his house," McGuire stated in 1997. "That's not my world. My world was a cracked sidewalk." He took pride in scouting inner city players to fill his roster.

Les first met Al McGuire as he walked into the arena in Greensboro, North Carolina in 1974. He was about to play the thrilling NC State Wolfpack with the great David Thompson. His opposing coach was Norm Sloan. He was fifteen minutes away from playing for the NCAA National Championship.

Les recalled the incident. "Some of the other young assistants were with me near the entrance when I saw him approaching. He was one of my all-time favorites, and I really liked his coaching style. I started to introduce myself, but he interrupted me when he saw my Citadel logo. He stopped and came over. It made me, just an assistant then at a small college, feel pretty special next to the other coaches. He said to me 'I know The Citadel very well. In fact the last time I matched up against Norm Sloan was when I was at Belmont Abbey and Norm was at The Citadel. It was the late 1950's.'

"Incredibly, the cameras were just beyond the tunnel where we were talking, waiting for him to come out, but he continued telling me the story," Les recalled. "The players were warming up. The bands were playing. The NC State team had beaten mighty Johnny Wooden's defending champion UCLA two nights earlier."

The NC State win over UCLA broke a streak of seven straight NCAA Championships for the Bruins. The Maurice Lucas–led Marquette Warriors had beaten Kansas, 64-51, in the other semi-final game.

"He went on to tell me the details. He said, 'We were coming all the way down from Gastonia. I had made a deal and took our players in rented funeral cars, a black limousine and a hearse. We came down Highway 52 through Goose Creek, but there was an accident. The hearse was sideswiped. We didn't cause it, but by the time the cops came we were charged. It was a hometown cop protecting the local. Then we went into Charleston to play Coach Sloan and that great bunch of cadets he had down there with Art Musselman. They won, but we gave them a heckuva game.' It was incredible how Coach McGuire remembered those details. And only he would think of renting a fleet of funeral cars to transport his team two hundred miles to Charleston."

The Citadel star and all-time leading scorer at the time, Art Musselman was on NC State's bench that evening as Norm Sloan's assistant coach. The Wolfpack won their first National Title just hours later, 74-60.

"Al McGuire spoke to me as if he had nothing else to do that night. After telling me about his Belmont Abbey experience, he walked on into the Greensboro Coliseum. Those guys around me must've thought that I was somebody important. I just happened to be someone that jogged his memory of a story," Les summarized. "I enjoyed the exchange more than anybody."

Les would see Al McGuire again under similar circumstances.

"Move forward three years [1977]. I'm now the head coach of The Citadel Bulldogs. All coaches are guests of the NCAA at the tournament, and I liked to go to catch up with friends in the profession. We're in Atlanta at the Omni. Marquette and Al McGuire are back again. He had guys like Butch Lee and Jerome Whitehead on that team. I'm there and planning on taking off after the game to drive back to Charleston. He beats Dean Smith's North Carolina Tar Heels in the championship. I see him sitting on the bench with his head in his hands when the Marquette team was jumping for joy. It's his final game. He announced his retirement between the semi-final and the championship game."

Les noted that McGuire had not run out on the floor like most coaches, or even grabbed his players in the excitement. He just sat and buried his head into his hands.

"I left after a few moments and went back to the hotel adjoining the arena. I got my bags, then chatted with a few others I knew there for a few moments. My car was ready out front and I was ready to head on back to Charleston. As I got down the road a bit, I pulled over to get gas and went into this small out-of-the-way diner to get a coke. Who's sitting over by himself drinking a beer? Al McGuire. The man had just won a National Championship an hour or so ago. He likely did a postgame interview and got in his car and left. I went over to re-introduce myself. I figured he didn't want to be disturbed, and I wasn't staying.

"He says hello and smiles. He told me that he needed to get back home. He was going on a bike trip. I knew he had peculiar habits. But here he was in a nothing place—he had just retired about an hour ago, coached his last game, won it all, and was likely the interview that every sports journalist in America was looking to score. Instead of relishing the moment in the lights of fame, he was drinking a beer outside of Atlanta in a hole-in-the wall place just off the interstate. It was too weird for words, but it was his way. I think that's what I liked about him.

"I saw him many more times over the years, especially when I was coaching at NC State. but I could never seem to get that image of him alone and in his thoughts after he had finally won it all," Les concluded. "He became the most colorful basketball announcer around later on simply because he could relate to the common folks like me and others. He would do the hard things because he knew that they would pay off. There will never be another like Al McGuire."

Al McGuire died in 2003 after a battle with leukemia.

Coach Steve Spurrier's minister-father is the reason Les grew up in the Episcopal church. Photo by author.

ON STEVE SPURRIER

Les's mother, Mary Trowbridge Robinson was most responsible for Les's admirable ability for remembering the smallest details. She rarely forgot names. The gene pool is verdant.

"The state of Florida was a great place to coach in high school because the colleges were the best at keeping up with in-state talent. We were 57 miles from Gainesville, Florida, when I was head basketball coach at Cedar Key High School in 1966 and 1967. The University of Florida Athletic Department sent every coach four tickets to their games—football and basketball. I used the basketball tickets to scout SEC teams for Coach Maravich when he was at LSU. I used the football tickets because I liked going and they had a Heisman Trophy candidate playing then, Steve Spurrier," Les recalled.

Steve Spurrier won the Heisman Trophy—emblematic as college football's best player in 1966.He was a consensus All American and the SEC Player of the Year.The 9-2 Gators beat Georgia Tech in the Orange Bowl to cap off an amazing season.

"When I'd call home, because of the long-distance expense, I'd talk in a hurry and my parents would listen in on two phones back in St. Albans. I remember telling Dad about how good the quarterback at Florida was, Steve Spurrier. Mom interrupted, asking if he was related to Reverend Spurrier who pastored the Presbyterian Church two blocks from our house. Dad and I both cut her off, knowing we weren't going to waste precious long-distance time trying to figure that out. We figured that it was a preposterous thought. Besides Mom would try to relate every last name she ever heard to someone she may have known forty years before," Les related. "So, she let it lie."

"The back story to this is that we went to the Presbyterian Church just down the street when I was a toddler, but Mom insisted that we leave that congregation because the Reverend Spurrier she talked about was too strict, especially about what women should wear. So she looked for another church and found the Episcopal Church six blocks away. That's why I grew up as an Episcopalian.

"Many years later I had the opportunity to see Coach Spurrier at an NCAA function out in Arizona. I noted to him that I remembered the Florida football program listing when I saw him play at all of his home games back in 1966. He was impressed that I came to see him play. I remembered that the University of Florida had only one or two players on their roster then who were not from Florida. I remembered that he was from Johnson City, Tennessee," Les continued. "I knew most of his story because of my time seeing him play in Gainesville and his coaching career I followed when I was at ETSU, located in Johnson City. Some older people in Johnson City seemed to know his family and remembered him from high school.

"When I mentioned that he was from Johnson City, he took the time to tell me that the program was actually wrong. He said, 'I was in fact born in Florida. My Dad was a church pastor down in Florida at the time but moved on to Johnson City after I was born.' As soon as he said it, I remembered that my mother left the Presbyterian Church next to us because of a

Reverend Spurrier being too strict. I immediately asked him if his father had ever preached in West Virginia. He responded that his father pastored a church in St. Albans outside of Charleston. He had no idea of the significance of that fact," Les confided.

"I told him, not being funny, 'Steve, it's because of how strict your father was that I have been a member of the Episcopal Church all these years. Once I explained it to him, we both laughed about it. Mom knew what she was talking about back in 1966.'"

*Al Davis coached at The Citadel. Les met Davis to reconnect his career back to Charleston.
Photo courtesy of the Oakland Raiders.*

ON AL DAVIS

The current owner of the Oakland Raiders, Mark Davis, was born in Charleston when his father was the head recruiter for The Citadel's football team during the 1955 and 1956 seasons. Mark Clark Davis was named for then-Citadel President Mark W. Clark, a World War II commanding general whose burial marker is on The Citadel's military campus. Mark Clark Davis is the only child of Carol and Al Davis.

When Les began to champion the need for a new football stadium at The Citadel in 2003 while serving as the college's Director of Athletics, he made a list of potential donors. Oakland Raiders owner Al Davis was on it. Davis was an innovator. He was also a master at producing winning football teams. His 'Just Win Baby' philosophy vaulted the Raiders to Super Bowl XI, XV and XVIII championships. He was the first to hire an African American head coach in the NFL, Art Shell—also from Charleston. His work in pressuring the NFL led to their merger with the AFL in 1966.

Les called Davis from The Citadel to solicit a financial commitment from Davis. It was in April that Les made the call.

"Since there was a summer NCAA meeting scheduled in San Francisco, I asked, 'Al, could I come on this date in early August? He laughed out loud. He said, 'Les I don't make appointments four days in advance, much less four months.' But he did invite me to come to the Raider's pre-season camp. We decided that I'd wait until I got there in San Francisco, and then call him. For that reason, Barbara and I went out a day early. I called, and he gave me the appointment. He said, 'Tomorrow at 11:00 works.' That morning he called back to me at 10:00 and I thought he was cancelling the meeting already.He called to tell me not to wear a tie. He said he only wears sweat suits. So, I wore a sweat suit, too. I went to his office.

"I didn't do my homework. I talked about General Mark Clark because everyone told me that Davis admired the former World War II general who was the president of The Citadel when Davis was there. Plus, I knew that his son—his only child—was named Mark Clark Davis. I asked for money to name the media room at the new stadium as the General Mark W. Clark Press Room. I figured that he'd like that. But he said, 'Let me think about it.'

"Looking back, I think he was being courteous because he knew things that I did not know. When I got back to Charleston, I asked around about Al Davis with people there that knew him. One of the Citadel graduates he recruited there told me to read his book, *Slick*. I got the book, figuring it would help me with Davis when I called back to ask about the General Mark W. Clark

Press Room idea. The book quoted an article from the Charleston paper when Coach John Sauer stepped down [1957]. A reporter asked General Clark about the possibility of replacing Coach Sauer with Al Davis. Unfortunately for me, General Clark responded, 'I wanna win, but I don't wanna win that damn bad!'"

Davis took an assistant's job at Southern Cal after seeing that he had no future at The Citadel. He took several talented football players with him, including Angelo Coia. The episode of transferring many of The Citadel's top players and paying athletes put Southern Cal on NCAA probation the following year. But they won games.

Davis attempted to lure The Citadel's other prized recruit, Paul Maguire. But Maguire's father was adamant that the young and talented linebacker-receiver-punter should remain at The Citadel. Maguire became one of the best to ever play in the American Football League as a starter for all ten seasons that the league existed. His career as a football color analyst made Maguire a household name in the sport.

"I really should have done my homework," Les lamented. "I think he would have done something, but Al Davis was not likely to name a feature of the stadium after General Clark. But I think he might have honored Paul Maguire or someone else here he recruited. But I didn't know that at the time."

Al Davis died on October 8, 2011, in Oakland. He was 82.

Former Raider lineman Mickey Marvin worked as a scout for the Raiders during the Medal of Honor Bowl All-Star Game in Charleston in 2014. Les suggested that Marvin take a photo of the apartment building that his owner, Al Davis, occupied during his Citadel stay. It was where young Mark Davis was a toddler. Marvin took the photo and sent it to the Raider's owner, Mark Davis. Les took the photo knowing that The Citadel had plans to tear down the old apartment structure. They did so soon after the photo was secured.

"Had Mark Davis come to see the stadium or the old apartment building, he might have honored his dad in some way. Al Davis's time in Charleston is a fact that old-timers cite often. I'd bet his son Mark wouldn't have known how popular his dad was here," Les retold.

Gary Williams and Les just missed each other as player-opponents in the ACC.
Photo courtesy Maryland Sports.

ON GARY WILLIAMS

"I have always gotten along with the other head coaches. We had one thing in common. We wanted to beat each other's brains in," Les conceded. "But that didn't automatically mean that these weren't good guys. Most of the coaches were great friends. I built friendships with Terry Holland going back to his days at Davidson. I knew Cremins from back when he coached App State and I was at The Citadel. I knew Gary Williams from back during his days coaching at Boston College. I remember when he played guard at Maryland. He was just behind my years at NC State."

He smiled in anticipation to tell a good story he knew about Williams.

"It was no secret with anyone in the business that Gary Williams was not fond of his athletic director at Maryland, Debbie Yow. They couldn't be in the same room," Les retold. "He knew it. Yow knew it. Everyone in the

ACC knew it because Gary wouldn't pull punches. You knew exactly where you stood with Gary. His ability to turn a phrase with a few colorful words always caught the other coaches off-guard."

Les related to the event.

"In the summer of 2011, sadly, Fred Barakat passed away. Fred was once a head basketball coach at Fairfield College. He was with the ACC for twenty-six years. He was the assistant commissioner and in charge of the game officials. Fred caught a lot of grief from all of the coaches, year in and year out, but was much respected. He had a tough job, and he performed it probably better than anyone.

"Fred's funeral was up in Greensboro, where the league office is located. At the time, his daughter (Nancy Barakat Vaughan) was involved in politics and was later elected mayor of Greensboro in a landslide. The Barakats were good people.

"All of the coaches went. Gary and I arrived around the same time at the visitation the night before. The day that Fred died suddenly in surgery just happened to be the same day that Gary's nemesis, Debbie Yow, left Maryland to take the AD job at NC State. Gary was elated with that news, to say the least.

"We end up together in line at the visitation for Fred Barakat. Gary was in front of me. When he got to the open casket, he looked like he stopped to say a prayer. But instead he says out loud, "Fred, why did you have to die on what would have been the happiest day of my life!" Others heard it. It was Gary's way. He wasn't being funny as much as he was being honest. It seems that the story got around."

Les continued with the postscript. "Me, Gary Williams, Dave Odom, and Bobby Cremins attended the service together the next day at a church in Greensboro. They sat together with coats and ties and were leaving the church after the service ended together.

"The family was outside the church and was receiving a few people who were not at the visitation. Fred's wife stopped Gary outside and asked him to repeat the story about his lament at the casket that she'd already heard by the next day. He did! Her daughter that became mayor was there, as well. She found the story to be endearing at her time of personal grief," Les observed. "They knew that Gary Williams was sincere in his appreciation of Fred Barakat."

Les recounted another Gary Williams highlight. It was the year that Williams won the NCAA National Championship in Atlanta in 2002.

"I was serving on the NCAA Selection Committee and had access to the floor. Gary and I were good friends, and his team had just beaten Indiana by a dozen to win it all," Les recalled. "I was over by the scorer's table and looked for Gary to congratulate him after he did the ceremonious things, the TV stuff, and the floor interviews. Of course, his AD was Debbie Yow and I looked for how he would handle that situation in the chaos. She was there, but not near Gary. I noticed it. When time was right, I walked over to shake his hand, but instead of saying what he expected, I said, 'Gary, it's traditional that when you win it all, you go and give your boss, the AD, a big warm hug. I haven't seen you hug Debbie yet.'

"Gary didn't even hesitate to answer me. He said, 'You blankety-blank SOB, I'll hug that blankety-blank so-and-so when hell freezes over.' I guess Maryland's first ever men's basketball national championship did nothing to help that relationship."

Gary Williams retired as Maryland's head basketball coach a month before Fred Barakat's passing but returned to serve in the Terrapins Athletic Department the following season—after Debbie Yow left—as special assistant to the Athletic Director. Williams retired as the coach with the third highest victory total in the history of the ACC, behind Mike Krzyzewski and Dean Smith.

Les recruited Richard Johnson as a player, and then as a coach.
Photo courtesy Wofford College.

ON RICHARD JOHNSON

"I never worried that Richard Johnson wouldn't be a good fit for our program," Les recalled. "In fact, he got his degree in business in four years and a nine-year degree in basketball after that. He's the first assistant coach I ever hired with no coaching experience. He was a great choice."

Richard agreed. "I had my undergraduate business degree back at The Citadel, and I shared my (career) thoughts with Les Robinson; and he said, 'Have you ever thought about coaching?' He was the one who got me thinking about a grad assistantship. Well, it didn't get funded, but it turns out one of his assistants left and he took the chance and hired me full time. I was able to get my MBA. But, of course, once I started coaching I loved it and wanted to stay in it."

After nine years as Les's assistant, Richard was selected by Wofford College as their next head basketball coach. Wofford was an NAIA program at the time, but the administration and Athletic Director Danny Morrison wanted to move them into Division 1 to advance the program, even though Wofford had only 1300 students. Richard was a key supporter of the transition. He coached the small Spartanburg private college to an upset win at Clemson during his last season. It was his 200th career win. He then moved to the AD position and hired his assistant, Mike Young, to become Wofford's second D-1 basketball coach. Young has taken Wofford to four NCAA tournament births and remained as head coach into the 2017-18 season.

As a player, the 6'8" Johnson hailed from Blue Island, Illinois—near Chicago. He once scored 33 points playing against the nation's leading scorer, Bob McCurdy of Richmond University.

"The rest of the story is that I held him down to 38!" Johnson retold.

Les loves to retell his favorite story about his protégé.

"Clemson University's basketball team came to Charleston with Coach Tates Locke and their seven-foot center, Wayne 'Tree' Rollins. McAlister Field House was packed with Clemson fans. We lost the game (81-68) and my starting center (Richard Johnson) was not even dressed out. He was in The Citadel Infirmary with the flu. After our postgame chat with the players in the locker room, I had a radio broadcast that I had to attend and comment for the game's wrap-up. The announcer, George Norwig, asked me why Richard Johnson was not dressed out or even in the gym. He had no idea that Richard was sick. I simply stated that he was not feeling well and was resting over in the infirmary. But George followed up, 'Coach, what does he have?' I couldn't resist the chance for humor and answered, 'George, he came down with a bad case of Tree-itis.' [a reference to the assignment of covering Clemson's Tree Rollins]"

Les and Richard have remained close over their careers. Richard was appointed to the Football Championship Series (FCS) selection committee, eventually serving as its chairman in 2017.

Les named Chuck Amato as Head Football Coach at NC State.
Photo courtesy NC State University.

ON CHUCK AMATO

"It was during the most turbulent political debate ever that I hired Chuck Amato away from Bobby Bowden's Florida State Seminoles. Tallahassee had the world press there at every street corner it seemed—trying to determine who was going to be the next United States President. On the same day that Amato was hired at State—January 6, 2000—Congress certified George W. Bush as the forty-third United States President.

"Chuck Amato was a former Wolfpack player, so the fit was there with the media and the fans," Les recalled. "I just needed to make sure we could do the things he needed to advance our football program."

Amato came into Raleigh with a fine reputation as Bobby Bowden's offensive coordinator. After several discussions, Les decided to act upon Amato's first request to raise private funds to pay upper level salaries to Amato's new coaching staff assistants. He spent seven seasons at NC State compiling a 49-37 record.

Together with Les's unique fundraising abilities, the Wolfpack faithful were able to raise nearly $100,000,000 to enhance the athletic facilities at

NC State. Those dividends are still being paid in Raleigh. After the 2007 season, Amato returned to Florida State University as Bowden's Offensive Coordinator.

"As an aside, I knew that I had a great situation at State to hire a premium quality football coach. I knew that we had some alumni that were willing to make a large investment into the program.

"I made preliminary telephone inquiries to Pittsburgh Steelers coach Bill Cowher, a Wolfpack grad, and Stanford's Tyrone Willingham. Coach Willingham was negotiating a new contract out at Palo Alto at the time. When I called their Director of Athletics to talk to him, it raised the stakes for him, I'd bet. I don't doubt that he would have been a fine coach anywhere. And I knew it would be difficult for Coach Cowher to leave the NFL for his alma mater. But I had to ask if he was interested," Les explained.

Coach Chuck Amato was Robinson's last major hire while serving as Athletic Director at NC State (1996 – 2000). An Easton, Pennsylvania native, Amato had been a fine football player and wrestler at N. C. State before serving nine years there as an assistant football coach. After a short stint at Arizona, Amato spent 18 seasons under the tutelage of Bobby Bowden, the *winningest* coach in the history of NCAA D-1 Football at the time of his retirement. Amato coached at NC State for seven years with a modicum of success (49-37) before returning—full circle—to Florida State University in Tallahassee as Associate Head Coach under Bowden. A contemporary of Les's during his college playing days at NC State, Amato became another sphere that entered into the circle. He was not unlike the myriad others along the periphery or into the center of it all.

"My point in hiring Chuck Amato and interviewing others at the top of their careers was that it seemed to be the catalyst to raise awareness of the needs of our Department of Athletics. I learned a lot in the process. The transition time between head coaches is an excellent time to speak with donors and get input while informing them of the tools necessary to compete at the higher levels."

Les first met Hot Rod Hunley as a sixth-grader in St. Albans.
Photo courtesy Robinson family archives.

ON HOT ROD HUNDLEY

Les saw Rod Hundley play ball many times in college and at his dad's tournament.

"Hot Rod Hundley had the right nickname. He was a showboat, but he could back it up. He came to my dad's tournament one year and taught me how to spin a basketball on my index finger while we were in the hotel lobby. He was the best basketball player that the University of West Virginia ever had by the time he graduated in 1957; but three years later, that changed when Jerry West came along.

"Many wouldn't believe that Hundley grew up on the streets. He had a very rough childhood. He lived for a time in the YMCA. It made Hundley a tough self-sufficient person. But it was easy for Hundley to make friends, and most around him in awe of his basketball skills. He knew my dad well and that relationship helped both of them.

"One year Hundley convinced the Lakers to come to Charleston to practice and play an exhibition game. The Lakers had the NBA Player-of-the-Year, Elgin Baylor. In those days, the hotels were segregated, and Hundley couldn't get Baylor into the main hotel, the Daniel Boone. So, Hundley canceled the whole Laker team at that hotel and took Baylor and the rest to a second-rate roadside hotel just outside of town instead. The Lakers went there in support of Elgin Baylor.

"Ironically, the proceeds of the event were going to the YMCA—who helped Hundley and so many others who were homeless. The Laker team was there to support the whole area.

"Neither Hundley nor my dad were happy with the management at the Daniel Boone Hotel. Three years later, Hundley asked my dad to get Elgin Baylor into the Sportsman's Tournament. This was a really big deal. Dad was also able to get Bill Russell through Jerry West. By then, the Daniel Boone Hotel changed and accepted all players. But Elgin Baylor remembered the situation from before. He came to the tournament but stayed with a local friend instead of checking in at the Daniel Boone. The situation reversed. It was the hotel manager's dumb move from before and it cost them. Everybody in Charleston wanted to meet Elgin Baylor."

Before Hundley enjoyed a six-year NBA career, he averaged 24.5 points per game at the University of West Virginia. The flashy guard was the NBA's first pick of the 1957 draft with the Cincinnati Royals, but was traded immediately to the Minneapolis Lakers.

When Rodney Clark Hundley passed away at the age of 80 in late March of 2015, Jerry West issued a statement.

"I am saddened by the news of the passing of my longtime friend, Rod Hundley. I first met Rod when I was 18 and he encouraged be to attend West Virginia University. We were Laker teammates and never lost contact."

The personable Hundley spent another thirty years as a broadcaster for NBA teams, mostly with the Utah Jazz.

Retaining quarterback Philip Rivers while trying to hire a coach was a balancing act for AD Les Robinson.
Photo courtesy NC State University.

ON PHILIP RIVERS

The transition between football coaches ushered an unusual situation for Les as the NC State Athletic Director. Between the time that Mike O'Cain left State in late November of 1999 and Coach Chuck Amato was hired in early January of 2000, Les requested and received permission from the NCAA to administer duties as the interim football coach. It was a brilliant move that had rarely been requested by an Athletic Director.

His reason for the request was to keep the current players from transferring to other schools and to solidify the verbal commitments that the departing Mike O'Cain had already achieved. The most important of those verbal commitments was that of an Alabama high school quarterback, Philip Rivers. Rivers had committed to the Wolfpack because there was a logjam at that position at both Auburn and Alabama. He had also applied to early admittance into NC State because he had completed his high school core curriculum. But his attendance at NC State was in jeopardy without a head coach in place. Les wanted to avert losing Philip Rivers to other high-powered programs seeking his services.

"I received interim coach status permission from the NCAA and contacted all football recruits, especially Philip Rivers. My job was to keep him in our program until I could get a top-level head coach," Les recalled. "He had to be thinking about why the former head basketball coach was calling him. But I explained the situation and Rivers was receptive. He still wanted to be in Raleigh."

"I'd say that Rivers responded to a difficult well, though he was concerned at the announcement that Mike O'Cain was not going to coach at NC State when he arrived. Quarterbacks and other skill position players want to know what type of offense the team will install. Not having a head coach leaves that up in the air.

Rivers had reservations as any 18-year-old would.

"I remember being in the car, driving to my grandmother's house, about two hours away and I remember hearing 'Mike O'Cain fired' on the radio," Rivers said. "I can remember thinking, 'What in the world am I going to do now?' "

Les's six weeks as interim head football coach was successful.

"I never lost a game as interim coach!I was able to keep our recruits in the loop until I hired Coach Amato and he could sign the 2000 class in early February. Chuck Amato would not say this, but he owes me a steak dinner for keeping Philip Rivers in school. Rivers showed up the week I hired Amato and started taking classes at NC State."

Rivers set season and career records at NC State for touchdowns (95) and passing yards (13,484).Through the 2017 NFL season, Rivers had thrown for over 50,000 career passing yards. Rivers ranks ninth all-time in NFL passing statistics—ahead of Joe Montana, Johnny Unitas, and Fran Tarkenton.

Mike Krzyzewski, Les, Charles Barkley, and Dick Vitale ready for a charity doubles match. Photo courtesy Duke University.

CHAPTER 28
FIXING THE NCAA

In 2005, Les proposed a way to fix the controversial NCAA football national championship in a column written in the *Los Angeles Times*. He did so as a fictional linebacker at a fictional university. What he proposed was not in the public consciousness of the sport. There was not a Power 5 football delineation of football conferences. He was just proposing common sense.

"I suggested that the biggest argument at the end of the college football season was about which college was ranked #3. It was because the #1 and #2 would play in the National Championship game at that time," Les recalls. "Yet every other sport in the NCAA played off for a champion in a tournament format of conference champions and top-ranked teams. There were 81 other NCAA sports playing it out on the fields and courts to determine a true champion. FBS football was the only NCAA sport that did not play it out. At that time, Division 1-AA [now FCS] college football played out with sixteen teams over four weeks to get a champion.

"The argument that the NCAA made concerning a playoff format was that such a plan would take the students out of the classroom too often. Yet they were already doing that in every other sport. College baseball can play nearly thirty games away each year without even advancing to a playoff. NCAA Baseball has a 56-game schedule. Basketball plays at least 30 games—and then a team can play as many as six more in the tournament. The argument for missing classes had no merit whatsoever.

"My sense is that the whole football world was upset when the #3 team was eliminated from winning the NCAA football title all too often. Several times the #3 team was undefeated. I proposed that there would be only one small group that could be upset if they did it right and selected the best sixteen college football teams. Only the fans of the #17 team would care. That team would not draw a mountain of discussion because that it would likely have lost three games over the course of the season.

"The revenue could be astounding. The college football fans would get a showcase close to the NCAA March Madness for basketball. At the end of the season, teams with two losses would keep playing hard just to get into the playoff system. Plus, it opens the format up for the non-Power 5 conferences. Central Florida won thirteen games without a blemish in 2017 but could not play for a National Championship. The sixteen-team format creates a path for the Cinderella story to occur.

"This plan would also fix the sagging attendance at bowl games over the last few years. The playoffs would prop up the top fifteen bowl sites because every game means something. A #16 seed plays a #1, a #15 plays a #2, etc. You could still rotate the National Championship game to the traditionally major sites in Miami, Atlanta, Phoenix, LA, and others. When those bowl games send losers home and the winners advance, watch the TV package go up as well."

Eventually the NCAA saw the tremendous benefit of more meaning and announced an expansion to a four–team FBS Football Playoff System. It was eight years after Les suggested a real playoff system. But they did not embrace the entire concept.

"It's better now—but they didn't go far enough. I suspect they'll go to eight teams soon because it works, and it has brought interest way up," Les contends.

Les has street instincts about the intercollegiate sports world. He currently suggests that the NCAA has been its own worst enemy. But that opinion is not related to playoff systems, but rather to the governing body's ineffective policies. There are never-ending stories of corruption, greed, and an imbalance of punishments meted out.

"Would I say that the NCAA has too much authority? Maybe they don't have enough oversight in some areas and too much in others," Les theorizes. "But if you look at it, the whole pie is worth billions of dollars in revenue every year, but the NCAA directs crumbs back to the most deserving colleges and large slices to those household names that defy them most often. But, with some common sense, the NCAA can be fixed.

"The NCAA is screwed up, and they have people running it who have no business running it," Les points out. "Look, it's like having me run Westvaco or Ford Motors. I know nothing about what they do to be successful. So, I would be lost in either job. In the same way the NCAA finds people who are good at law, or politics, or scientific formulas—and they place them in charge of the largest sports organization in the world. They are not equipped to deal with managing college athletics, Title IX, television, or sports marketing. They don't know what issues Nick Saban or Mike Krzyzewski or Dawn Staley face. They dole out restrictions and sanctions that make little sense. They make rules for one sport that breaks rules for others. They just don't get it.

"In today's NCAA, sports agents might be the biggest issue. Gambling influences are still a concern, as well. You can look back at every major scandal and you'll find one or the other—illegal payments to buy players or point-shaving schemes to pay players to skewer an outcome.

"Early in my career I travelled to Salt Lake City for a Final Four [1979]. I was coaching at The Citadel. With some other coaches we flew into Las Vegas for a couple of days. I had never been there. I went into Caesar's Palace—eyes wide open—not to gamble but just to see what everyone was talking about. I passed outside the big sports betting area and saw from a window a final list on a big board. The Citadel was ranked #4. I was immediately curious. So, I went in and asked why The Citadel was on the board. The guy at the counter told me that The Citadel was the 4th best basketball program in the country that year at covering the spread. In other words, if you had bet on The Citadel that year at whatever point difference the odds professionals had calculated, you would have made a lot of money. I took that as a compliment!

"I had even thought about using that information to negotiate a pay raise," Les grins, "but my AD [Eddie Teague] would've probably docked my pay or fired me just for telling him I was in Las Vegas."

"At NC State, I was interviewed by the FBI in 1961. Why? They had been tailing a varsity player who was part of that awful 1961 point-shaving scandal. They made 37 arrests of players from 22 colleges, including Stan Niewierowski. Stan had free tickets to a movie in Raleigh and asked me and others to go. So, I did. Evidently, the FBI followed us to the movie.

"When they called me in to tell them what I knew, I was dumbfounded and very naïve. My first reaction, thinking Coach Case would get the information, was to tell them that I had not had a beer. But the guy said, 'We don't give a damn about drinking beer. We want to know if you have ever met or seen this guy or that guy, or if Stan had given you money.' They wanted to see if I was being set up to throw games the next year.

"Stan and Anton Muehlbauer always had money. I didn't know at the time that they were getting it from fixing games. As a matter of fact, I told my dad that Christmas that I was going to work hard on my game because Stan and Anton were getting paid to be that good. I didn't even understand what was happening right under my nose."

"That 1961 scandal was the one that made the University of Iowa's Connie Hawkins ineligible to play in the NBA. He was probably among the top five players in college then," Les recalls. "So, it ruined players' careers and set colleges back."

In early 2018, a widespread NCAA Basketball scandal was again being monitored by the FBI. This time it was the other major "no-no" for college athletics—paying for players. A player's family, his high school coach, or his AAU coach employed these shadowy agents to move the player to a top college program on the way to the NBA. The pay-for-play deal would be to obtain a much larger professional contract. There were deceptions used to separate the basketball recruiters from the finances required to land the blue-chip players—many who were bought on a one-and-done rental basis.

Similar incidents have happened for many years in both NCAA basketball and football. Over the last twenty years Reggie Bush [Southern Cal] had to give back the Heisman Trophy in 2005 because he was paid to play for the Trojans. Yet, Auburn's Cam Newton was able to keep his Heisman Trophy after a verified $180,000 payment was made to his father from his previous college choice, Mississippi State. In 2010, five football players at North Carolina were suspended for taking payments from agents. That same year, five players from Ohio State sold their conference championship rings on eBay as well as accepting discounts from vendors. They were suspended for five games the following season.

Les saw some of the underside of recruiting top players first-hand back in the 1990s.

"Me and Buzz Peterson were talking with this kid in 1991 and his 'so-called-agent'," Les recalls. "They didn't call them agents back then, but that's what he was, the guy we had to go through to get the kid. It could have been an AAU coach, a neighbor, or a drug dealer. They called themselves agents, but they were there just to get in on a piece of the action. Normally, they had no financial or legal background. We backed off. But not everyone backed off. Others were willing to pay.

"Five years later, I recognized a photo of a man in a *Sports Illustrated* article about buying players in college basketball. It was the same agent from years before, and he was in prison. The point is, this stuff has been going on for a long time. It's from different factions now, but people have been buying players for a long time."

When the FBI broke the latest 2018 scandal of pay-for-play at top programs across America, Les was glad that the FBI had cracked the schemes open.

"It's about time. I'm glad it's happening; I want it cleaned up," Les insisted. "My goal when I graduated from N.C. State in 1966 was to coach at the highest level in America. Today, knowing everything I know now, the highest level I'd want to coach at is Davidson or The Citadel or Wofford, or maybe a Division II program. At that level, you don't have to deal with that stuff. Maybe this will clean it up, but it will be ugly. There are a lot of bad stories out there."

Les saw several of these stories developing when he was in on a player, but it became obvious that the player expected money to sign.

"I was coaching at The Citadel in the 1970s when a local star turned down offers from big-time schools N.C. State, South Carolina, and Louisville, as well as The Citadel. He signed with a mid-major school in-state. The coach that got him already had a reputation for this kind of activity and everybody knew it. They bought the player," Les states. "I didn't know it for sure at the time, but highly suspected it. The verification came to me by accident two years later. Our trustee board chair was a law partner with the gentleman that supplied payments to the player to facilitate this behavior. But kids make mistakes and this player made a big one that revealed the scheme. He showed up at the law office one late Friday afternoon after the other lawyer had already left. Our board chair—his law partner—was still there. He asked if the other lawyer had left his usual cash payment in an envelope at their law office. My instincts were confirmed."

He explained why the player and player's family are readily complicit. "A guy, maybe in a big city, goes to a player's mother," he explains. "She's got seven kids, is working two or three jobs. The street agent buys her a car and takes care of her. He's not doing it for any particular school. He's setting the player up for a bid for himself. And he sends him to the school that he thinks can get him to the NBA the quickest. That's another payoff for the agent a year later."

Some of the details of the 2018 FBI probe uncovered that there are legitimate sports agents involved as well.

Les opines, "It won't be easy to clean up the mess. The one-and-done rule, which requires players to be 19-years-old or one year removed from high school to be eligible for the NBA Draft, makes the timing critical for the agent, the player, and the accepting basketball program. Top programs have been more-than-willing to accept a one-year superstar. It's all about getting wins. Those W's turn into money for getting into the NCAA Tournament. The coaches get bonuses for NCAA qualification. And the coaches and sign these incredible contracts for winning. It's okay for agents to get money, too. But that should only happen after the player has met and agreed-upon amateur status minimum rule—I suggest three years—or expended all eligibility. I like three years because a player can go to summer sessions and earn a degree in three years.

"The one-and-done or even two-and-done—the only way forward is for schools to quit taking them," Les suggests. "And nobody is going to do that. It's a very complicated problem. The NCAA has rules, but obviously people are getting around them. And then the NCAA hands out punishments that show an obvious bias for one program, and a disdain for the other. Fans see that and do not trust the NCAA.

"Over the next couple of years, the TV ratings are not going to be the same. The NCAA has got to have the guts to do what it preaches across the board. There will need to be several rule changes regarding eligibility, agents, family connections, and oversight. The one-and-done rule is simple to fix. But the NCAA needs to coordinate that plan with the NBA like NCAA Football has done with the NFL. Payments? There needs to be a realistic discussion on what constitutes amateur status. And finally, the NCAA will need to be prepared to dole out sanctions and restrictions equally."

In the end, there is too much money at stake to not fix the problems. It's tournament money for the NCAA, turnstile money for the colleges, and turn-around investment money for NBA franchises.

Les and Bobby Cremins, both retired, enjoy a laugh at breakfast.
Photo by author.

CHAPTER 29
HIRING, FIRING, & RETIRING

"I had been around not as many bad coaches as I had good coaches. Bad coaches were usually good people in the wrong profession. In time, and with experience, you learn to separate the two—ability and personality." Les explained the process of finding good coaches, not only as assistants, but also sometimes in his role as an athletic director, to head up the entire football program or women's athletics.

"There are hard choices," Les intimated. "And sometimes you are in danger of losing friends."

Les continued. "You can look at all aspects of the functions that head coaches perform. There is a wide requirement of abilities. We could start with the most essential: recruiting. If you can out-recruit other coaches, your job is much easier. One of the best recruiters when I was coming along was Frank McGuire. He was a very good one. He was a slick sales-man when he tried to recruit me to play at North Carolina.

My own college coach, according to Rod Hundley, was one of the best ever. I heard Hundley speak at a banquet when he referred to Everett Case, the coach I signed with to play at NC State.

"Hundley stated, 'People just think Uncle Sam can recruit—but this guy right here, Everett Case, is the best recruiter there ever was.' Hundley said that back in 1962. He was right. Coach Case made recruiting into a science, much like everything else he did as an innovator." Les remembers.

"In the more recent times, John Wooden was obviously a great recruit-er. Add Dean Smith. And Bobby Cremins was one of the best ever. Bobby, my goodness, I mean, look at the players that went to the NBA. He was a great extension of Frank McGuire. Like McGuire, he could convince the moms. He was always exceedingly polite. And the kids took to his personality. McGuire was a great mentor for Cremins to learn the trade.

"McGuire had a guy on the bench that everybody says was terrific, Buck Freeman," Les continued. "He was another really good assistant for many years.

"When McGuire first got to Columbia, the University of South Carolina was a football school. Early on, they went into Chapel Hill to play North Carolina and were getting killed every time. They couldn't get the ball up the court. The story goes that Buck Freeman pleaded with Coach McGuire to call a timeout for some X's and O's to beat the press. McGuire takes a timeout and Freeman is concerned and asks McGuire, 'What are we going to tell them? How are we going to get the ball up the court?' McGuire calmly answered Freeman, 'Don't worry, Buck, I'm going up to New York tomorrow. We're gonna get some guards and we're gonna get the ball up the court.' And he goes up to New York. Over the next few years he comes back with Skip Harlicka, Jack Thompson, John Roche, Bobby Cremins, Mike Dunleavy and Kevin Joyce.He recruited them all out of that very strong New York City Parochial League. He pretty much had the inside on the Irish Catholics there. As the story goes, he didn't need to teach X's and O's as much as he needed to bring in talent. McGuire saw it early and changed South Carolina to a basketball school overnight.

"When I hired or fired a coach as an athletic director, there may have been a few that had great abilities in one area but not in another. The coaching profession is so demanding. You have to recruit, manage, train, condition, install, scout, and handle pressure. You have to handle the media, the parents—and these days, even the AAU coaches.Most importantly, you have to gain the respect of your players," Les detailed.

"I get calls all the time about a coach to fit one program or another. I have even gotten calls about football coaches. And in general, I can usually either help or hinder the coach in question by being honest in my assessment. And sometimes, I'll want to recommend a coach I think highly of but may not be a good fit with a particular institution or may need another year or two as an assistant. Now, I do not do any of this as a consultant. I do it to respect the person that calls and asks.

"I've hired my share of football coaches, baseball coaches, women's volleyball, tennis, basketball, you name it. They all have one thing in common. They have to love the sport and the institution that hires them. They have to demonstrate a willingness to do what it takes to succeed. And like I remind them all—recruiting is the ticket.

"In my own personal case, I began coaching while I was still in college. It was in my blood. I loved it. But I completely retired from coaching at the age of 53. That's too young to step away. But I did it only after I had assessed everything. I had worked to bring three programs back to the top in spite of various degrees of adversity. They were situations not of my making. I had found a high level of success at each. And I knew that I had given each place 100% of what I had to give. So there were few regrets."

Les alluded to his most troubling experience.

"One episode that I recall upset both Barbara and me. It was Coach Mike O'Cain's last game at NC State. The 'Pack lost a close one, 10-6, in Raleigh. That ended a 6-6 season, and our fans were rightfully angry that we had lost the season-ending football game to North Carolina for seven consecutive years.

"I waited after the game for the drinking tailgaters to clear out so that they would not shout things that I already knew. And as much as I liked Mike O'Cain, I knew that a change would have to be made. What happened next changed my attitude about working with administrators who know nothing or very little. Our NC State Chancellor, Marye Anne Fox, was new. Her background was in science. She wanted me to walk her back to her car. It was about 45 minutes after the game ended. I just knew that this was a disaster situation. She had no idea how difficult angry fans could be.

"Predictably, we were inundated by a few colorful remarks from the Wolfpack faithful. They hated losing to North Carolina. But the chancellor took it all-too-personally. She bristled. When we got to her car, she said, 'You are going to fire the coach, Les.' Well, she didn't realize that there are civil procedures in place. I intimated that we have a one-on-one meeting the first thing every Monday to discuss the season after its last game. We would talk about contract issues, recruiting, and whatever. But in Coach O'Cain's case, I knew that it was time. He was a fine man with a great family. So, these issues needed to be handled properly. I explained that clearly to Marye Anne Fox. She seemed fine with it when she left Saturday night.

"But the chancellor started receiving terse messages and demanding calls at her home. I received as many or more than she did. It didn't change my Monday plans with Coach O'Cain, who likely already knew that he had coached his last game at State. But it did change Fox's plans. She panicked in the heat of battle.

"I get a phone call on Sunday morning from her just after 6:00 a.m. It was like a fire drill or something. Barbara and I were barely awake. Marye Anne Fox demanded that I head on over to Mike O'Cain's place and fire him then and there. I listened to her rant for a while and figured that I couldn't calm her down. She had over-reacted to the pressure of the alumni and the press. She wanted to come by and pick me up to go, like she thought I might forget.

"Coach Mike O'Cain's firing did not make it to Monday because of Marye Anne Fox's impatience along with her insistence on exerting her authority. She caved in to the odd timing because of the alumni.

"It made me see that she was not the right person to work under for me. Seeing what she did made me realize that I had other options. It's a lesson for college presidents and chancellors everywhere. If you hire someone to do a job, then let him or her do it! Marye Anne Fox acted as the Athletic Director when she should have trusted that she had has the proper person in that role already. In time, I left because I knew that I could move back to

Sullivans Island and accept the AD's opening back at The Citadel. It was the best move for me, money notwithstanding. But Barbara and I were never about money, anyway," Les recalled.

A similar situation occurred when Les stepped down as head basketball coach at NC State. He could continue coaching basketball or move his career into another direction.

Marshall University and several other programs immediately sought Les to be their coach after he stepped down at NC State. Les had made up his mind about his career after nine excruciating losses in the 1995-96 season by a sum total of 15 points. He decided to plan more time with Barbara, and divert to another path in the sports world. The athletic administration role had promise. Within a month of Les's resignation, Todd Turner, the NC State Athletic Director, accepted a similar position at Vanderbilt University. Les was named as the interim AD, then asked to replace Turner as AD within weeks.

"So to step away as I did was difficult. But fate stepped in. I immediately became an associate AD, interim athletic director, then the AD. I was invited to join the NCAA Selection Committee. Then I came back home to Sullivan's Island with the AD's job at The Citadel. It was a job I was offered by General Grimsley back in 1985.

"I went to work for the NIT. In essence, I stayed in basketball, but at levels I never dreamed of achieving. So, my new career started at 53. I was never really out of basketball, even to this day."

Division I Men's Basketball Committee

Administrators and Supervisors of NCAA Division I Men's Basketball Championship

The National Collegiate Division I Men's Basketball Championship is administered and supervised by the 10-person NCAA Division I Men's Basketball Committee. The committee is appointed by the NCAA Division I Championship/Competition Cabinet.

Chair of the committee is **Craig Thompson**, commissioner of the Mountain West Conference.

Other members of the committee include **Doug Elgin**, commissioner of the Missouri Valley Conference; **Lee Fowler**, director of athletics at Middle Tennessee State University; **Jack Kvancz**, director of athletics at George Washington University; **Jim Livengood**, director of athletics at the University of Arizona; **Les Robinson**, director of athletics at North Carolina State University; **Judy Rose**, director of athletics at the University of North Carolina, Charlotte; **Gene Smith**, director of athletics at Iowa State University; **Mike Tranghese**, commissioner of the Big East Conference; and **Carroll Williams**, director of athletics at Santa Clara University.

Administrative assistance is provided by **Tom Jernstedt**, NCAA senior vice-president; **Bill Hancock**, NCAA director of the Division I Men's Basketball Championship, Administration; **Jim Marchiony**, NCAA director of the Division I Men's Basketball Championship, Media; **Bernard Muir**, NCAA director of the Division I Men's Basketball Championship, Operations; and **Kendyl Baugh**, NCAA assistant director of the Division I Men's Basketball Championship.

Craig Thompson
Mountain West
Conference

Doug Elgin
Missouri Valley
Conference

Lee Fowler
Middle Tennessee
State

Jack Kvancz
George Washington

Jim Livengood
Arizona

Les Robinson
North Carolina State

Judy Rose
North Carolina-
Charlotte

Gene Smith
Iowa State

Mike Tranghese
Big East Conference

Carroll Williams
Santa Clara

Tom Jernstedt
NCAA

Bill Hancock
NCAA

Jim Marchiony
NCAA

Bernard Muir
NCAA

Kendyl Baugh
NCAA

The NCAA Mens' Basketball Selection Committee is scrutinized by fans and universities. The Big Dance brings big bucks to the NCAA. Courtesy NCAA.

CHAPTER 30
SELECTION COMMITTEES AND FINAL FOURS

As the new Athletic Director at NC State, Les received a phone call from the NCAA headquarters in Indianapolis. Usually, these kinds of calls are taken hesitantly.

There exists the dreaded thought that a wrestling performer may have taken an illegal substance or that a football recruit was offered illegal inducements. Les had worked much harder than most ADs, given the historical record of previous regimes at State, to make certain the program remained impeccable. He had also overseen the most demanding academic standards of any school in the ACC including Duke, Virginia, Georgia Tech, and North Carolina. His tenure as basketball coach and then Athletic Director attained the #1 goal of the Board of Trustees—a return to academic prominence.

Les supported the academic shift. "The university had been awarded a chapter of Phi Beta Kappa, the elite national academic achievement society. That designation was a high priority with the academic side. Re-instituting the student performance in the basketball program had much to do with that achievement."

Les had become the new sheriff in town, and the previous mindset had vanished. NC State was back. Les had been largely responsible for the university's enhanced academic reputation in athletics.

However, any phone call from the NCAA for even a potential minor infraction could change all that. Les had spent countless hours altering the culture, instructing coaches, filing reports, and overseeing results.

A call did come from the NCAA Headquarters in Indianapolis [1999]. He took the call, questioning the purpose.

This call would prove to be propitious. On the other end of the line was Tom Jernstedt, the Executive Director of the NCAA Basketball Tournament. Les's leadership, reputation, and character did matter. It mattered more beyond campus. This was one of the great calls to get from the NCAA.

"I had taken the call wondering what may have happened beyond my control that would cost us, and instead it was what the NCAA had decided, without my knowledge, that had honored us," Les reflects. "I was being asked to join the very elite team of ten selectors for the NCAA men's basketball tournament. He asked me if I wanted to think about it. I told him that I would think about a lot after I got off of the phone, but that I didn't have to think about the answer. It was an enthusiastic YES!"

Les would serve as an observer in the room as the selections were made in March of 1998. During that first year, he had voice, but did not have a vote. For the next five March Selection Sundays, 1999 to 2003, he would have both. Importantly, a Selection Committee member becomes an Emeritus Member (2004 and after) and is invited back each year and credentialed for each Final Four.

"It's like nothing you've ever seen. There's a big board in the room and placards of all the teams are moved around, taken off, and placed back on. Discussions of schedules, key player injuries, placement sites, and even religion are within the framework of the decisions.

"Why religion? Brigham Young University is a Mormon-dominated college that cannot play on Sundays. That's not a problem if they're in and they reach the Final Four. Those games are always Saturday-Monday.

"But in the first two weekends, you can't put BYU on the Friday-Sunday rotation," Les explains.

"There are so many other factors and so much is riding on the decisions. We feel like we do the best job we can, but there is so much room for the debate of fairness after the selections are divulged at 6:00 (eastern time) that Sunday. We realized that every sportswriter, office worker, and college president is going to take a shot at us afterwards. But, if you're in that room, you'd understand the thinking, the ranking, and the site placements better. And, yes, we have never claimed to be perfect in our choices. But we're always trying to be as fair and as free-thinking as possible.

"In a way, I know this impact better than most. I coached a 16th seed to a 1-point loss to a #1 seed. Had we won, I'm sure that the committee would have been red-faced. But there will be a day when a #16 will beat a #1. The committee will still have done its job well. Anything can happen in college basketball. I've seen it my entire career," Les observes.

Most fans would be unaware of the other duties ascribed to the selectors after the brackets and teams are announced.

"Each of the ten voting members has other pre-selection responsibilities. They each are assigned multiple leagues to study—from the big boys to the mid-majors and to the smaller conferences. They review potential sites and test likely Final Four sites by selecting them as regional sites in the lead-in years," Les divulges.

The NCAA tries to bring all of America into your living rooms—from Seattle to Miami, Albuquerque to Minneapolis. The tournament is for fans, advertisers, athletic department budgets, players, pep bands, and vendors. The list is long.Many share the profits.

Les gave an overview.

"Ninety-nine percent of the funding that the NCAA receives each year is from the NCAA Men's Basketball Tournament. Most of that money goes back into the NCAA member institutions, most notably to the teams that didn't make the tournament," Les intimates.

"So, when a smaller school like Davidson with Stephen Curry made a run a few years ago to the Elite Eight, the entire Southern Conference field of teams received extra NCAA tournament money for three years. Success breeds success. The more these teams win, the more the affiliated conference schools benefit."

During Les's first year as a voting member (1999), the NCAA negotiated a $6.2 billion-dollar ten-year television contract for the NCAA tournament. The latest extension of that contract with Turner-CBS is much higher, paying out over a billion dollars a year to the NCAA.

Even the game officials are scrutinized for the tournament. Every detail at the tournament sites is orchestrated with a very competent and capable NCAA staff augmented with the authoritative selection committee personnel. There are other special factors in the administration of the games that had not even been contemplated—the unforeseen contingencies—that had to be resolved.

"I was in charge of a site that had Duke one year, and the game had to be delayed because the networks and the NCAA were trying to finish a prior game that went into overtime," Les recalled. "You have to be able to adjust. And we did.

"There was a game being played at another site that went into overtime, just as the game at my site in Atlanta was about to start. I'm carrying two phones. One is a direct line only to the NCAA. I get a call from the tournament director, Tom Jernstedt, as the overtime occurs. There's seven minutes counting down on our clock in Atlanta to begin. Jernstedt tells me that our game will be delayed. Our Atlanta crowd was expecting a tipoff in minutes, but millions of viewers across America wanted to see who would win the overtime game. So I immediately turned off the clock. It went off without a hitch. Jernstedt loved that I handled it that way," Les recalled.

There were even some odd circumstances that Les encountered immediately after the team selections were finalized.

"I was returning from the selection committee and had gotten to the airport in time to catch a flight back to Charleston. Oddly, we were able to finish up earlier than normal before the telecast came on at 6:00 p.m. Eastern Time. The timing was such that I was actually in the airport when the CBS Selection Show began to air. The bars were crowded, as everyone wanted to know if their team made it or where their team was placed. I happened to be early enough to see the start of the bracket pairings next to an excited bunch of young men from the University of Michigan. They had a good team and I remembered where we had them in the tournament.

"They were standing next to me and suggesting the options when I answered one of them saying, 'Nah, that team won't go there. The committee probably will place them in this other region instead. If it were my call, I'd have 'em playing so-and-so.' As the first bracket was announced, they saw that I had it right. They were amazed at my predictions.

"I followed by telling them who I thought ought to be the #1 seeds. Of course, my memory isn't bad enough not to remember who they were. Again, as the #1's were announced, I had 'em right. One of them brought up a bubble team, and I said that they'd probably be in the NIT. Another asked about a certain conference tournament upset winner, and I said that I'd probably move them to sixth in the Mid-West Regional. Everything was dead on. Those kids had no idea that I was on the committee. After a few minutes I headed to my gate. A couple of them walked with me asking me if I'd come out to Vegas and pick some teams and point spreads for them," Les recounted with a smile. "I told Barbara about it when I got home to Sullivans Island. She just shook her head knowing that I had made a bunch of kids think I was actually smart!"

The NCAA Selection Committee has a set of their own 'inside' rules. Les detailed the issue.

"This is our event—and the television network pays a fortune. The sponsors pay heavily to get this airtime. Everyone in America, it seems, has a bracket picked for an office pool or something even more substantial," Les intimated. "That's why we carry two cell phones. You may be in charge of a site or just sitting at the end of a team's bench in practice. You're always working. Once I got a call from the NCAA during a timeout to move a Gatorade bottle on the scorer's desk closer to the head coach's seat with the label turned towards the cameras. Gatorade was paying a lot of money for exposure. That's a rule. Promote the sponsors.

"Another rule is to never go to a press conference of a team that lost a close game because you're likely to get an ear full. For example, one time I was monitoring a site with a game ending in controversy. Iowa State lost a close game in the final minute with a few tough calls. Coach Larry Eustachy was livid.And I would have been, too. But my job was to not let the result contribute to a poor press moment or embarrassment to the colleges involved. In the heat of battle, that can happen. So, I caught the coach before he went in to see the reporters. He had a few choice things to say. I told him that he needed to get it out of his system before he went in and fed the reporters because they would turn every phrase into something that Athletic Directors, school presidents, and Iowa State Fans would scrutinize. 'Besides,' I added, 'You're going to be out on the road next week seeing some recruits you have signed and some that you hope to sign next year. Do you want them to see you at your very worst?It's an opportunity to go in there and show class and poise. It won't change the result, but it will change your standing and effectiveness.' I advised."

"Eustachy did just that. In doing so, he elevated the university."

The committee members had to be familiar with all rules. Les told about a rule that a committee member would hope never to act upon.

"Another rule had to do with altercations. The site representative is totally in charge, though there are many steps to be made and paperwork to be filed. The site rep does the post-game interviews. I only had one altercation happen—and it was so unlikely and unexpected that I know every detail because of that quirk.

"Matt Christianson was this brilliant student whose father was a professor at Harvard. I knew him and his family because I tried to recruit him to NC State. Matt was 6'10" and a Mormon who signed with Duke. He had six years to play four, owing to his religious affiliation and the LDS church's mission work. He was truly an exceptional young man from an outstanding family.

"As a substitute on Duke's 2001-2002 team, they were favored to reach the Final Four that year. But in the Sweet Sixteen, Duke was upset by Indiana,

74-73. There were some tight calls at the end of that game that did not go Coach Mike Krzyzewski's way. It was frustrating for him and their team. Unfortunately, an altercation broke out at the end and Matt Christianson was in the middle of it all. One game referee was confronted as he left the floor by Christianson, and Coach K nearly tackled his player to save the referee from being harmed. I was there and assumed it to be over. It wasn't.

"After the game the NCAA sent video of the entire incident to me with instructions to get interviews from all involved, including the police, and security guards.I had to interview and write a report from the player, the ref, the coaches, even the assistants and any bystanders there that may have been identified. One of the first interviews I did was with the game official involved. I went into the referee's locker room and asked the guy if he was okay. He just smiled and said, 'It was nothing.' He said that it was a non-incident in his mind and that he would not be pursuing anything from whatever was on the film.It was easy to conclude that out of every basketball official in America, this was the one guy that would be the most nonchalant about altercations. He'd had his share. This particular official, Bruce Benedict, spent his previous career catching fastballs and blocking home plate for 12 years with the Atlanta Braves (1978-1989). He's been in plenty of bench-clearing incidents over his career.

"After all interviews were taken, the Duke team received a fine because of the young man's momentary indiscretion; and the player would have received a suspension as well, but he was a senior. The shame of it was that, in my opinion, this was one of the truly admirable players in college basketball," Les retells. "It was just the heat of the moment."

There were other experiences that accompanied this most visible sporting showcase. Celebrities came to the Final Four regularly. Many of the country's top sports figures are there each year, along with several Hollywood stars. The Final Four is easily among the best ticket in the world of sports.

"I had met the great Dodger pitcher Sandy Koufax before, but didn't really know him," Les informs. "He was a regular at ACC games. I knew that he loved college basketball. I had a staffer knock on my door one time before a game in Raleigh and he told me a man was outside that wanted to meet me. When I went out to see who it was, I was stunned to see one of my childhood heroes, Sandy Koufax. Koufax had gone to games at Chapel Hill, Durham, Winston-Salem, and Raleigh. He did so pretty often. He loved the atmosphere. Years later I did get to know him, and it was an occasion I will never forget."

The city of Seattle hosted the Final Four in 1995 with the game being played inside the famous Kingdome. This was the setting for the only NCAA Basketball Championship ever won by a UCLA team not coached by John Wooden. A friend from Les's West Virginia childhood was UCLA's winning coach: Jimmy Harrick.

Harrick, a fine coach and friend to the Robinsons, was born in Charleston, West Virginia, and played at Morris Harvey College (now known as the University of Charleston). He had taken over the Bruins' fortunes in 1988 after a successful run at Pepperdine University. Les was hoping one of his friends, Dean Smith or Jim Harrick, could win the championship.

"During the April 1st semifinals on Saturday, I sat in front of New York Yankees owner George Steinbrenner. I acknowledged him. He was over-the-top and at one point told his buddies he had a bet on the game. He asked me about what I thought about his bet and the point spread in front of his friends. Being a NCAA coach and on the selection committee, this was very poor judgment on his behalf. Of course, I had to be almost rude in my reply. I said, 'That is not anything I can tolerate or discuss with you or anyone because its illegal and unethical for any NCAA coach, and especially any member of the NCAA Basketball Selection Committee.' And I turned back around. I didn't smile or treat the comment as anything but an affront. I'm sure Steinbrenner got the message."

They enjoyed watching two good match-ups. UCLA topped Oklahoma State 74-61 and defending 1994 Champion Arkansas beat Dean Smith's North Carolina team, 75-68. Steinbrenner had a running conversation with those around him, mentioning a few sports' stars he had encountered at the event. The Final Four has a reputation for bringing together major sports stars well outside of basketball, as well as actors, singers, and media celebrities. During one break in the action, the Yankees owner mentioned an interchange with Sandy Koufax, the great Dodger lefthander, whom he said he spoke with earlier. Koufax, famously reserved and insular, avoided the cameras, but enjoyed all avenues of sport, nonetheless. Les overheard Steinbrenner namedropping the Baseball Hall-of-Famer as if they had just conversed at some length. Les had great admiration for the spectacular career of Sandy Koufax. He remembered thinking about how he hoped to meet the famous Dodger southpaw one day.

UCLA, with Tyus Edney and tournament MVP Ed O'Bannon, earned the hard-fought championship trophy the following Monday evening. Les retired to his hotel with plans to leave early the next day to fly back to Raleigh. As part of the NCAA tournament committee, his flight was booked out of the NCAA offices. His ticket was First Class. Once he boarded, Les noticed that the passenger next to him in First Class was the subject of Saturday's Steinbrenner conversation, Sandy Koufax. He remembered the Steinbrenner boast and conversation.

"I knew right away it was Koufax," Les recalled. "What he didn't know was that I was either going to talk or listen all the way to Raleigh. I preferred to listen. Once I sat down, I introduced myself by referring to the Steinbrenner conversation that went on behind my seat. I figured that he would have talked to Steinbrenner, who was sitting right behind me. It was a reference I used to get Koufax talking."

"I began by saying, 'Small world. George Steinbrenner sat behind me on Saturday and was talking about chatting with you during the tournament somewhere.' I started."

"Koufax looked at me as if I were a bit crazy. He responded, 'I know who George Steinbrenner is, but I don't think I've ever met him and I know I've never spoken to him. He must've talked to someone who he thought was me.'

"That exchange aside, I began wondering why a guy like Steinbrenner thought he needed to impress someone by namedropping Sandy Koufax. It made no sense to me. He must've been mistaken," Les recalled.

"After we settled in, I did start by asking him where he played college baseball. I knew part of his story from growing up as a baseball fan, but not all of it," Les related. "I had no idea of the extreme circumstances that got Sandy Koufax to the front pages of the sports section."

Les decided it was a great time to listen. Koufax was talking—something he does privately with friends, but rarely with anyone else. It was like being a reporter at the most exclusive interview ever—and Raleigh was more than four hours away. He had lucked upon the youngest player in the history of the major leagues (at age 36) to be inducted into the Baseball Hall of Fame. Surely, there would be some tidbits Koufax would tell Les that were never intended for authors and books.

He told him the inside stories, stage by stage, with each insight included.

Sandy Koufax gave Les the inside story of his path to the major leagues.
Photo courtesy Robinson family archives.

Sandy Koufax was born in Brooklyn, New York. He emerged as a fine basketball athlete.

"He told me that he walked onto the Cincinnati basketball team before earning a partial scholarship at the university. He had maintained his love of baseball but was enrolled at Cincinnati as a basketball player. Fatefully, his Cincinnati roommate played on the Bearcats baseball team. It was the roommate who convinced Koufax to join the baseball team because of a scheduled multi-team bus ride to Tulane in the spring of 1953. He said, 'the baseball team would be on a bus with the tennis team and the golf team.'

"The tennis coach had made the arrangement with the Cincinnati athletic director by booking one bus for the three teams. Koufax said he'd never been to New Orleans and consented to walking onto the baseball team after his basketball season was over that year. But his motivation was the upcoming free trip to New Orleans. He also said that he would love to try baseball again. He said he was a left-handed catcher and outfielder during his teen years. He smiled when he told me that he pitched very little," Les recalls.

The post-Cincinnati Bearcat left arm vaulted the Koufax name into several baseball front offices. One Pittsburgh Pirate scout said that Koufax was the best pitching talent he had ever seen. Oddly, the Pirates' organization lost the report and Koufax signed for $6000 with his hometown team, the Brooklyn Dodgers. In 1956, he was the last pitcher to take the mound in the bottom of the 9th inning at old Ebbets Field. Ebbets Field was torn down after the season, and the Dodgers moved to Los Angeles. By 1972, Sandy Koufax was in the Baseball Hall of Fame in Cooperstown, New York.

In between, Koufax was the top pitcher in an era full of top pitchers like Juan Marichal, Bob Gibson, and his teammate, Don Drysdale. He set records for strikeouts in a game and in a season by a lefthander. He won three Cy Young awards and pitched four no-hitters, including one perfect game. But an arthritic arm forced him to retire after the 1966 season when he was only 31.

Les knew enough about baseball and about the very private Koufax to simply segway to other players and managers to keep Koufax talking about his career. He learned about Koufax's double-holdout with Don Drysdale prior to the 1966 season. It was Drysdale's wife who suggested that they hold out together to get Dodger General Manager Buzzie Bavasi to pay them their value. Eventually, Bavasi came to terms with this incredible pitching duo.

"By the time the plane landed in Raleigh, I had spoken less than I had ever done on a flight of any length and had gotten the introverted Koufax to talk more than his reputation would have predicted. We parted as newfound friends. And it was partially because of George Steinbrenner," Les grinned.

"I look back and realize that one of the greatest benefits of serving on the Selection Committee and attending so many Final Fours over my career was an unplanned happenstance. It was meeting and talking with Sandy Koufax. I guess you could say that a listener talked, and a talker listened."

As a Selection Committee member, Les learned to distinguish degrees of success from the foibles of failure by comparative reasoning. It is in these areas of his life that he excelled. The common sense of commonalities is what he best understands. Common opponents, common circumstances, common advantages, different results. The committee taught him that.

"My friends at Chapel Hill wouldn't believe me when I tell the story, but I was a key supporter for the Tar Heels to get in the tournament one year when they were on the bubble. It wasn't that I was favoring them at all. It was all about getting the best teams in; and I had to convince the others that their record late in the year was better than the others we were considering, especially against top opponents. They were 18-13 at season's end, and most of the media thought they were headed to the NIT. I must've been convincing because the committee came around and they squeked in. What happened in the tournament over the next two weeks supported everything I said in the committee room. Coach Bill Guthridge used the momentum to take what was a mediocre North Carolina team all the way to the Final Four," Les recalled. "I truly believed that they belonged."

Les stood up for what he thought was a proper choice for the right reasons. It wasn't about making friends. It was about making well-conceived suggestions to others in the decision-making process. The University of North Carolina benefitted because they had a pragmatic voice in the room.

"Besides, the rest of the committee knew that I would likely be the last person supporting North Carolina for a spot. But they all knew that I had no agenda other than to place the best teams in the tournament based on their performance and common sense. I truly believe that Coach Guthridge and the Tar Heels had earned their inclusion," Les states. "And their performance in that tournament proved me right. I wasn't there to make friends, but to do the job to the best of my abilities."

Les was never short of friends, anyway. His fellow West Virginian., Jim Harrick, detailed his view of Les's career.

"I can truly say that I have met only one man in my profession that every other coach I met liked: Les Robinson." noted Harrick. "And he'll out-coach you and kick your butt! What that tells you is that he likes people and people like him. I suspect that he has gone his entire life without the uncomfortable circumstance of dealing with people that may dislike him. Disliking Les is almost impossible."

Les and Barbara's fiftieth wedding anniversary was celebrated at the NIT fianls.
Photo courtesy Robinson family archives.

CHAPTER 31

GOLDEN ANNIVERSARY IN THE GARDEN

There are venues in American sports that awe and inspire. Fans coddle them as "bucket list" checkmarks. The Brickyard, Augusta National, the Rose Bowl, Fenway Park, and Madison Square Garden would be at the top of nearly every listing.

The National Invitation Tournament Championship game of 2013 in Madison Square Garden was not as close as had been anticipated. The Baylor Bears had thumped the Iowa Hawkeyes by 20 points. The Baylor team would enjoy a fine celebration at game's end.

The celebration that mattered most to Les and Barbara Robinson was flashed upon the center-hung video scoreboard at halftime of the Baylor-Iowa game. It was April of 2013. Fifty years prior, Les and Barbara were married by a preacher they never saw again. The elopement ceremony was in a church they never saw again until weeks before Barbara passed away in 2017. On the scoreboard of one of the most iconic venues in sports, the loving couple was featured and applauded. A video of them sitting together was a surprise to both. It was simultaneously streamed onto television screens into millions of homes across America.

By the standard of which couples remain as couples, it was most appropriate.

"That was done at halftime unbeknownst to either me or Barbara," Les smiles at the remembrance. "And just after that, one of the game referees came over to congratulate Barbara only—for hanging in there with me for all of those years. After he smirked at me and went on, a second ref came over. You would think this was planned, but it wasn't. The second ref did the exact same thing. He got Barbara's attention and avoided looking at me. He gestured to her that she had achieved something nobody else could do. Then he winked at me and went on. I guess I should have a complex!"

The Robinson marriage is an amazing story of devotion.

There have been couples who have filtered through history with fame, but not with game. There's JFK and Jackie. Well, okay, there were some problems we didn't know about. There's Joe DiMaggio and Marilyn Monroe. Oops. There was also Marilyn and Norman Mailer, not to mention her tryst with JFK. How about Bonnie Parker and Clyde Barrow? You can't shoot holes in that one, can you? Well, yes you can. They weren't married. Prince Charles and Lady Diana… never mind. How about the first family? No, not that one. The real first family–Adam and Eve. But leave the apple out of it. Elizabeth Taylor and Richard Burton? Which time? Don't cry for me, Eva and Juan Peron. Pocahontas and John Smith? The penultimate Native American actually married someone else. Franklin and Eleanor. Oh? Other problems existed there as well. Elvis and Priscilla? They broke up like a karate chop through balsa wood. Antony and Cleopatra? Poison. Newlywed Eva Braun and hubbie Adolf Hitler? It didn't last a day. Napoleon and Josephine. *C'est bon* apart. John and Yoko? Oh no! These were popular pairings, but none of them made it to fifty years.

Barbara and Les. Les and Barbara. The story of their first fifty years married becomes even better when further enhanced by the decade before they married. They met in the 6th grade. Their humble beginnings would never have predicted the moment they were enjoying on the big screen in Madison Square Garden.

A simple marriage prevailed. It was just Les and Barbara, the preacher, the preacher's wife, and a spirit of devotion. The late evening nuptials in Tazewell, Virginia, were complete with vows they kept past a half-century. They did so without ever contemplating the spotlight of an anniversary enjoyed in Madison Square Garden.

CHAPTER 32
REMEMBRANCES OF OTHER PLAYERS

Les described memories of his former players with details that many others may have forgotten. They are stories about individuals that left a lasting impression upon their coach. Les's unusual ability of recall startles those he entertains with his attention to the details. Yet, one could name a former player outside of those he cites herein and get a full story of interest heretofore untold.

CRAIG BARDO

"Craig Bardo left Indiana University and Coach Bobby Knight," Les retells. "He was one of the purest shooters to come out of the Illinois high school system and was selected as a first team all-state player. He joined the Navy after the 1980-1981 NCAA Championship season at Indiana. His father worked in the Department of Athletics at Southern Illinois University. His mother was a teacher. He was an excellent student from Carbondale, Illinois. Both Craig Bardo and his brother Stephen are members of the Illinois Basketball Hall of Fame." [They were inducted on the same evening.]

Craig Bardo knew what he wanted in life at a young age.

"It was the craziest thing that I recruited Craig Bardo from the U.S. Navy. He was stationed in San Diego. Things just didn't add up." Les recalled. "Here was this focused young man from a great family with a basketball pedigree. He was Indiana-good. Bobby Knight fought the recruiting wars to get him, and Craig was on an NCAA National Championship Team as a freshman. I found out that he left Indiana because of his grades. That made even less sense. Craig Bardo was a straight-A student in high school, and I knew he was an articulate young man. The grade reason for leaving Indiana made me suspect something else entirely.

"In any circumstance, he was completing a two-year Navy commitment and was interested in playing at The Citadel. It was like looking at a gift and questioning why we were receiving it instead of being happy about the outcome," Les said.

"He came in and was an impact player right away. We won 18 games, and Bardo was an immediate outside threat. He averaged ten a game, but more importantly, he wasn't lost on defense and knew how to protect the ball. His presence helped us to have a banner season. We finished third in the Southern Conference at 11-5. By season's end, I felt that I was ready to ask him what happened at Indiana. It was such an unusual story.

"As a top student and a major recruit for Bobby Knight's Hoosiers, Bardo just couldn't seem to fit in with the loaded team. He was behind some great players—and all were just sophomores. He was behind Isaiah Thomas, Randy Wittman, Tony Brown, Jim Thomas, and Chuck Franz. There was no room for playing time. Bardo got into four games only as a first-year player. He tried to get his parents to help him transfer to a place where there was room for a 6'4" shooting guard. But the family was opposed to the transfer. So Bardo, because he was smart enough to predict a result, intentionally failed his courses at Indiana. It was his only way out of the Indiana program.

"It was a crazy way to solve a problem, and I had no comeback to him. I figured that he knew exactly what he was doing. He was—intellectually— well ahead of most college kids. Now he came back to college and enrolled into our business department which has a reputation for being tough, and he was getting straight A's," Les noted. "I left the next year for ETSU, but Bardo got even better, leading The Citadel team in scoring the next season."

Craig Bardo eventually became an investment banker. His expertise in market strategies has made millions for both individuals and non-profits. As Senior Director for Investor Relations for BroadRiver Asset Management, his office is halfway up the Empire State Building in New York.

Les made an impact upon the life of many players—none more than Patrick Elmore.
Photo by author.

PATRICK ELMORE

Patrick Elmore came to The Citadel because Les Robinson saw something special in him. The 6'6" forward was thin, but he had a nice touch. Les knew that they could build his endurance at The Citadel. In time, Elmore would mature and have monster games against tough competition. He had 36 points and 20 rebounds against Davidson. He scored 26 and pulled down 16 rebounds against Furman.

"Patrick Elmore was my best mentorship story ever. And it came back to haunt me!" Les retold the circumstance.

"It was just after the 1984 season. Elmore had made an impact as a sophomore. He was averaging double figures and looked to be the best player on the roster after the conference Player of the Year, Regan Truesdale. But Patrick had some growing up pains that made me realize I had to take action," Les recounted.

"He hadn't been going to class and had miserable grades because of it. He began to slide and, frankly, gave up on his academics. By the time the late spring came around, he was playing pick-up games with players over at the College of Charleston who had talked him into transferring there. I doubted that they knew about his grades. With the situation as it was, I received a call from the College of Charleston's head coach John Kresse. Of course, I told him that I would release Patrick if that were what he wanted to do. The college was an NAIA school at the time and Patrick could play right away if he could academically qualify. Kresse was concerned and didn't want to damage our coaching relationship. I assured him that I wanted to do what was best for the player and would convince our AD, Eddie Teague, to sign the NCAA release. I was deeply disappointed in Patrick's classroom effort. As an afterthought I called over to another friend at the college, Fred Daniels, and made sure he knew that Patrick would have a difficult time meeting the eligibility requirement due to his grades. I just didn't want there to be a misunderstanding.

Les continued. "After the school year ended and his transcript showed that Patrick had not done the classwork at The Citadel, the College of Charleston had no ability to qualify him.

"As I parked my car to go into the gym one morning, I see Patrick sitting outside of the gym on the curb. His head was down into his hands. He's waiting for me. He starts out telling me that he changed his mind and that he wanted to stay. I listened to him for a moment, knowing he would not be eligible at the College of Charleston or at The Citadel—even with Summer School. He doesn't know how badly I wanted him to be eligible to play. He was a fantastic player for us. And he really was a good kid, but he needed to get his life together and take the academic side seriously. It would have been easy to say, 'Patrick, I'm sorry but we don't have a roster spot' and give up on him. But that was not in his best interest. I wanted to use the situation to teach a life lesson. I felt I owed him that. My master's degree in guidance counseling triggered my heartfelt and sound response to Patrick. So, I was quite cordial, but asked him to follow me to the basketball office. I thought about what I was going to say."

Les took the young Elmore into his basketball office and closed the door. Both sat. Patrick Elmore was at a crossroads.

"Here he was lost in life with no direction and coming back to cross a bridge he had burned—by not doing his work in the classroom and by leaving his teammates high and dry. He realized his error, and he was contrite. But I knew it was too late. I quit being a coach and took the role of being a stern father.

"At first I raised my voice for emphasis to let him know he had ample opportunity to get the job done in the classroom. I let him know that no matter how good he was as a basketball player, he was not mature enough to meet life's challenges and accept responsibility for himself. I told him that no team in America could take a chance on him. I also knew that somewhere in Patrick was the right stuff to become someone exceptional. So I suggested that he put a plan together immediately to change the course his life would take. My first suggestion was that he should consider joining the military. If he could sign up, get his act together, and earn the respect of others, I'd be happy to take him back at The Citadel. I was sincere about the promise. I told him that he had my word that I would give him back his scholarship once he had completed a stint in military service."

"He left. His body language was evident. He was deflated and upset with blowing an opportunity for a college degree. He meekly thanked me for the time. I didn't know what he'd do or what would become of him.

"Two years later, I'm at East Tennessee State trying to rebuild a team that had faltered over the past few years. I scheduled an exhibition game with a traveling team out of an Air Force base in Texas. I notice someone familiar in the warm-ups. It's Patrick Elmore. His thin 6'6" frame had filled out. He looked much stronger. When the game started, he displayed skills well beyond what I had coached in 1984. Though we beat that team in an exhibition, the best player on the floor that day was probably Patrick Elmore. We talked after the game.

"Patrick said he'd be out soon and wanted to come to Johnson City to join our team the following year. That was unbelievably tempting since he was a very skilled player, but I reverted to my guidance counseling again. I said, 'Patrick, you don't know how great it would be for me to coach you again, and especially how good it would be to have your leadership and skill set on this team, but you owe it to The Citadel to look into going back. They have your transcript and Coach Nesbit can walk you through the process. The Citadel would be your best fit as a military veteran," I emphasized. "I called Randy Nesbit so that he could follow up. Randy was on my staff there when Patrick played at The Citadel earlier, so he already knew Patrick."

The mentorship had come the full way back around to the mentor. Patrick Elmore sparked a Citadel win over the University of South Carolina, 88-87, with a 34-point effort. The Brent Price-led Gamecocks could do nothing to stop Elmore that evening on South Carolina's home floor. South Carolina made it into the NCAA tournament a few weeks later—their only loss in their last eight games was to Elmore and The Citadel.

"Where it really came around was when one of my best teams at ETSU came to The Citadel in 1988. We made the NCAAs that year. Patrick Elmore scored 41 points and pulled down fifteen rebounds. He became the only player to score 40 or more points against any team I had ever coached in my career. It was his night. The Citadel beat us in that game, 78-75. Patrick Elmore had taken my advice and grown up. I hadn't anticipated that my own selflessness and heartfelt advice would come back to haunt me!"

Patrick graduated from The Citadel. Les had not seen him in nearly twenty years. Meanwhile, Les' career had progressed to NC State for a decade and then back to The Citadel as Athletic Director when Elmore showed up again.

"Patrick was married, had children, and had come back to play in an alumni basketball game twenty years after his graduation. I was the alumni player's team coach—so I was selected to coach Patrick again for the exhibition. After the game, he brought his wife up to see me in my office. It was what he said that made it all so memorable," Les recalled.

"He started out by introducing me. Then he said, 'This is the coach who gave me the advice to join the military. It's the best advice I could have received. Had he not told me to do that, I would never have had the opportunity to finish college and probably would not have met you. Coach Rob changed my life.'

"I was stunned. I did not expect the compliment. It was a moment I'll never forget. I then told his wife that Patrick had grown up around the experience and learned how to rely on himself. He had become a great example to every young player struggling to make it in college athletics," Les stated. "He earned everyone's respect, especially mine.

"And now I still tell that story to illustrate that most any situation can have a great outcome," Les concluded. "Patrick Elmore became my best story ever in the area of advice.

"His career with UPS moved him into middle management, then further up—and eventually into their corporate headquarters. I had no idea that I had impacted his future so much just by doing what I was trained to do in my master's guidance field."

BRYANT FEGGINS

Bryant Feggins had an unusual NCAA career. He was able to utilize six years to compete in four. The NCAA rule dictates a maximum of five years. Feggins became an exception.

"He was the one player who would always try to 'slick' me. Bryant Feggins. He was a monster talent out of Winston Salem. He was the state's high school Player of the Year in 1989—North Carolina's Mr. Basketball. But he always had an angle. There was always something extra-curricular that you knew better than to ask," Les retold.

"He could play. He was burly and was the type of player, undersized at 6'6", who could dominate the inside game. He started for us until he tore his knee cartilage as a sophomore. His freshman year was under Jimmy Valvano. He was likeable, but you just knew that he always had an angle."

The one allowable "redshirt year" came as a result of the aforementioned torn knee ligament. His additional year was granted after he was shot in the upper right shoulder. He had been in a quarrel with someone at the North Carolina A&T campus in Greensboro. The gunshot nicked an artery and was for a time, life-threatening. Feggins was lucky to survive the incident.

"I went to the hospital in the middle of the night. His mother was already there. Bryant was in a lot of discomfort. He wasn't sure he'd be able to play again because some of his fingers went numb. But in a few days, he was fine, but really rattled," Les recalled.

"Bryant had been counseled—as I did with all of my players—that they are athletes and, therefore, they sometimes become targets in public. People want autographs, insights to the program, dates, and even foul play. Bryant had heard this lecture from me many times. He knew that he was not where he was supposed to be, and he paid the consequence. Now he had back-to-back rehab assignments. He had the knee and now the shoulder. He was right-handed, so getting his shoulder healed was key.

"Basketball is a very aggressive sport. But off the floor, players have to be different—and they have to learn to walk away. I knew this as a life lesson from Coach Case."

After about 36 hours and much medication, Les was able to step in and see Feggins for the first time. Feggins was sheepish. He knew that he had let the coach down.

"I remember when I went in. The timing for a conversation about using common sense was not meant for a hospital setting. It could wait. I was just there for support and to make sure that Bryant was okay," Les recalled. "There was another day that I could work with him about decisions. The hospital was not the right stage.

"As he healed, and we applied for other eligibility to get him a highly-unlikely sixth year, I kept my eye on him. What he didn't know was that I was a street kind of kid who knew the angles growing up. I figured that there was more to the story. In time, I called him into my office to get to the bottom of it and to chastise him for his decision-making. He listened. He had heard the lectures, but he was still a little stubborn about the message. I had to assert myself—which I did. After that, Bryant played well and helped us to become a better team. The big players at North Carolina like Rasheed Wallace and Eric Montross had fits trying to keep Bryant off the offensive glass. He could be very forceful.

"When I asked Bryant exactly what happened at the shooting in Greensboro, he danced around it. He had given the Greensboro police no lead to investigate. After pressing him, he said, 'Coach, it was a fight. I may have caused it, but I can't remember. I don't know the guy who shot me. Let bygones be bygones. I'm good with it.' That told me that—more than likely—Bryant didn't want the police to arrest the shooter. I can speculate a dozen reasons why, but it came down to Bryant's assessment in the end. He didn't want to pursue it. I realized that he was probably more like me growing up. He got in trouble but wanted to leave it at that and learn from it.

"Had he not suffered the knee injury and the shooting in Greensboro, Bryant would have had quite a career at State. As it was, his college career off the floor was just as memorable."

CHEROKEE PARKS

The ACC selected Les to coach a team of young all-stars to play a schedule in Europe during the summer of 1992. The tour had a basketball purpose combined with a cultural tour. The cultural portion was mandatory for the players.

The team was comprised of underclassmen from teams across the ACC. Each ACC coach selected a player. For this reason, the ACC all-star roster was top heavy with post players. They included Cherokee Parks of Duke,

Sharonne Wright of Clemson, Kevin Salvadore of North Carolina, Andre Reid of Florida State, Ted Jeffries of Virginia and Evers Burns from Maryland.

The guards selected were Travis Best from Georgia Tech, Mark Davis and Curtis Marshall from NC State and David Rasmussen of Wake Forest.

They played seven games in Holland and Germany, winning all of them handily. Les recalled a few of the details as notable experiences.

"Early in the trip I had explained to the team that the trip was meant to incorporate ACC basketball with a wide cultural experience. I explained that our schedule would take us into museums, churches, historical sites and the like. I also told them that when the bus left for these places, everyone had to be on it – no exceptions." Les retold. "Now wouldn't you know that we got into Amsterdam early in the trip and the first guys that tested the cultural requirements were Cherokee Parks and Sharonne Wright. They must've stayed out half the night. Barbara and I were having breakfast when they came by begging to be left at the hotel.

"I could see that they had overdone it, so I accommodated them by responding forcefully, 'Not only are you not going, you're not getting a per diem today – which was $60 – and you're heading to your room and you will not leave it today. You are embarrassing the ACC, your university, and the USA. Now get your asses up to the room and you better hope that I don't decide to put you on the next plane back.' I suspect they got the message when I didn't allow the per diem the next day either."

The very next day, the team of ten headed to a cathedral. The reverend spoke perfect English, so Les asked him where he was from originally.

"I'm from the U.K.," he replied.

"Not missing a beat, I responded, 'Oh, the U.K. You guys lost a close one to Duke on that last second shot by Laettner.'

"The reverend, of course, didn't get it. Worse yet, the whole team figured that I really thought he was talking about the University of Kentucky when he said 'the U.K.' They were not used to me trying to be funny. Years later, they might read about this and laugh. But it was dead air when I said it.

"We also had a big 7'0" player, Andre Reid, from FSU. He was not having a good trip. He had a miserable first few games. After the first three games he came to me and said he didn't want to play anymore. I was intrigued.

"I didn't know whether Reid wanted to quit basketball altogether, or if he was frustrated with his performance. Or maybe he was upset with his teammates. So I asked him if he needed to catch a flight back home. He declined, saying that he wanted to stay on and act as the team manager. He just didn't feel like playing. That was a little weird. We went the rest of the trip with a 7'0" team manager. We had a game in Germany and his brother-in-law was stationed there and coming to the game. Reid arranged to get him tickets. I asked him if he wanted to suit up and get in, but again he declined. When I got back I spoke to Coach Pat Kennedy at Florida State about the situation. Reid had played on a team with Sam Cassell, Bob Sura and Charlie Ward. He'd played a good bit off of their bench and could block some shots.I followed his progress with FSU. He was injured during the next season and played out his career afterwards. Still today, I remain intrigued about Andre Reid and why he suddenly quit.

"The loss of Reid put more pressure on Wright and Parks—who were in the doghouse—and Kevin Salvadore. They worked their way back into good graces and we were a dominant inside team for the duration of the tournament. Parks, especially, played well."

Years later, Les saw Cherokee Parks at an NCAA event. Parks brought up the European trip. He apologized for the Amsterdam incident.

"He told me that he and Sharonne Wright decided to test my control in Amsterdam. He remembered my stern response. But then he told me, 'Coach, we were in the wildest city in the world for a 20-year-old American.' I thought about it and agreed with him. I thought to myself that if I had I been a young basketball team in that crazy city, I might have gotten in trouble for being out all night, as well. We both laughed about it.

"That trip was for nine days in August of 1992. I was able to coach my two young guards—Mark Davis and Curtis Marshall. They stepped it up and got the ball into the post well. That paid off for us with the big guys we rotated in at NC State the next few seasons—Todd Fuller, Bryant Feggins, and Kevin Thompson.

"But Cherokee Parks, despite our clash over his staying out in Amsterdam, turned out to be a fine person with a perspective of life that was much like my own. I am glad I had the opportunity to coach him."

CALVIN TALFORD

"We were able to land Calvin out of Southwest Virginia in 1988. That area was not a heavily recruited part of the basketball world, but Calvin Talford was a great reason to go to Castlewood," Les recalled.

"We had a small recruiting advantage because his family wanted to see him play, and Johnson City was only an hour and a half away. Castlewood is in coal country. I drove there in a newer courtesy car issued to the coaches. When I got near Castlewood, I saw Highway Patrol cars everywhere. There was a coal strike. Tensions were rising. I had no idea how intense the area had gotten. When I drove past the Holiday Inn near to highway, a sign said, 'Highway Patrolmen Not Welcome.' They didn't want to house the law there to keep the peace. The coal strike had everyone on edge.

"When I got to the high school to talk to Calvin about coming to ETSU, I was interrupted by the Castlewood High principal. He wanted to know about the car I had parked outside. When I told him it was mine, he strongly suggested that I leave because the miners would mistake a new shiny car like that as one belonging to a lawyer or one of the coal mine owners. He thought that it could be shot at or that I could be harmed.

"He was serious enough that I only spent about an hour and a half selling East Tennessee State to Calvin before leaving cautiously. I have made good sales presentations before, but this is the first time I had to make a good and fast sales presentation. We signed him."

Les continued.

"He was the youngest in a family of nine. And the film we had assured us that he could play. He was rough around the edges, but his athleticism was as good or better than any player I had ever recruited. His favorite shot was a one-handed power dunk and his second favorite was a two-handed reverse dunk," Les laughed.

"He was a fine baseball player who was drafted by the Major Leagues out of high school. He passed that up because he wanted to play basketball. And he was outstanding in track and football, too. He made the Virginia all-state first team in four sports. So, he could have played anywhere on scholarship in any sport he chose. Luckily for us, he liked basketball above the others.

During Talford's senior season at Castlewood High School, he scored five touchdowns in a state playoff game and 59 points in a basketball game. Talford set the state high jump record at 7'0', the triple jump record at 49 feet 8 ¼ inches and the long jump record at 23 feet 11 ¼ inches.

His teammate Greg Dennis saw what Les saw in Talford.

"After a couple of minutes of seeing him play, you just got a feel of what kind of athlete he was," said Dennis. "You knew pretty quick after seeing him how special he was. I got a chance to play a little bit professionally after finishing school…and played with a lot of different guys, but by far he's one of the greatest athletes I've ever seen."

Talford's #24 jersey was retired by ETSU and hangs in their new arena. He was the main attraction over those four years—even on a team that featured 5'7" Keith "Mister" Jennings and 6'11' Greg Dennis. Talford played on four consecutive NCAA qualifying teams at East Tennessee. They went 99-30 over those four years [1989-1993].

After his senior season, he was signed by the Chicago Bulls—who already had a famous #23 on their roster. The Michael Jordan-like comparisons of Talford's physical abilities compelled the Bulls to sign him. At 6'3", Talford would find it difficult in the NBA as he had never played consistently in the ball handling positions. His explosiveness was best utilized near the basket where he was too undersized to make up the difference by athleticism since most NBA small forwards were 6'7" to 6'10". As a result, he found better opportunities playing in professional leagues overseas.

"Back then, the NCAA Final Four featured a college dunk competition. I saw Calvin Talford win the 1992 NCAA dunk contest on national television. I was proud of him, Les recalled. "And he brought the gym down when he went up and hung in the air like Michael Jordan or David Thompson."

Les recalled the impact of Talford's athleticism at the ETSU ticket office.

"People were lined up to come into the mini-dome to see a show when Calvin was playing. They would have lined up to see Mister and Greg, but when Calvin started showing his abilities, it became a whole other level. Everyone, including me on the bench, anticipated a move or a float that ended in a thunderous dunk. He was incredible," Les detailed. "And it seemed like defenders on the court were nervous, too. They didn't want to be dunked on and the photo ending up in their hometown newspapers."

TODD FULLER

Les found Todd Fuller at Charlotte Christian School in 1992. He was stellar student with both an academic mission and a desire to play basketball at the highest level his abilities could take him.

"Todd Fuller was the most unusual student-athlete combination in college basketball since Bill Bradley played for Princeton in the early 1960s," Les opined.

Bill Bradley was the NCAA Player-of-the-Year in 1965. He graduated from Princeton University and accepted his Rhodes scholarship, returning to resume his basketball career with the New York Knicks in 1967. Bradley eventually rose in political circles as a United States Senator from New Jersey. He ran for president in 2000.

By comparison, Fuller was a first-team ACC selection, the league's top scorer and field goal percentage leader. He became an NBA lottery pick. In the classroom, he was studying advanced courses in applied mathematics. As if that wasn't enough, he completed his career at NC State with only one blemish to his academic record. He had all A's and one B+.

"When he got the B+, he was devastated. Our assistant, Buzz Peterson, clued me in. He said that Todd was really depressed by getting the B. He said, 'Les, you gotta talk to him.' I knew why. He had never gotten less than an A in any year of his academic work from the first grade on. He had a perfect record. So, I called him into my office to talk about it. Based on my counseling experience and coursework for my master's, I wanted to put things into perspective for him and decimate the importance. I told him that when I graduated from NC State in 1965 I also finished with just one B. He was totally shocked to know that. It made him feel better right away.

"Todd assumed that I had made all A's at State just like he did. I didn't tell him until after the season that I got that B in my junior year and it was the highest grade I ever got at State. In my case, all of the other grades were lower than a B! Todd broke out laughing."

Fuller's career was compelling. He was offered a rare Rhodes scholarship to study at the University of Oxford in Cambridge, England. He turned down the opportunity to pursue an NBA career. He was the eleventh player taken in the first round by the San Francisco Warriors. At 6'10" and 250 pounds, Fuller could weather the demands of an 82-game NBA season. He followed exercise routines to remain in excellent physical condition.

"What is not in his athletic or academic record is something coaches rave about when they see it in a player. Todd was a great teammate. The guys playing around him liked that he was on the floor. If anything, he was just too nice. Yet he could go out and dominate the best post players in the league. He was also a very dedicated Christian. He was true to his faith, and he never wavered from always doing what was the right thing. It was an honor to recruit, mentor and coach Todd Fuller."

After Fuller's NBA career he returned to the Charlotte area. He became a certified pilot and has worked in missions as a volunteer around the world. He still sponsors a statewide mathematics competition in his home state each year. He is a high school math teacher. He returned to NC State to earn his master's degree in Analytics. He continues to assist others through his church.

Tom Gugliotta went on to a twelve-year NBA career.
Photo courtesy NC State University.

TOM GUGLIOTTA

Les's sports agent Richard Howell intimated, "Tom Gugliotta had several people that he could have leaned on including his own family for advice about sports agents. But he listened to Les. That's how I signed him and how we built a great trust for his career. It was because of Les.

"I asked him once why he chose me after he had so many knocking down his door. He said, 'Coach Robinson said you would be a solid choice. I could tell that Coach Rob was more concerned about my welfare than his own. I trusted him in that regard because I knew that he could read people especially well.'"

Indeed, Tom Gugliotta was not a professional basketball prospect in his first few years at NC State. He played his first two years for Jim Valvano—his last two for Les Robinson. Even Valvano later admitted that he hesitated to even recruit Gugliotta, but was pressured to do so by his father, who was a Valvano friend. He played sparingly. Fortuitously, he grew nearly four inches after enrolling.

"I felt that he was a tough kid and worked hard to be better every day," Les reflected upon the emerging star. "He had a nose for the boards and could score in so many ways that he was too tough to defend. He had an attitude that he would not settle upon just being good. He wanted to be the best."

Gugliotta averaged 15.4 points and 9.3 rebounds per game as a junior. The Wolfpack made the NCAA's and won twenty games. Les would depend upon him even more as a senior. As ordered, Gugliotta stepped up. He averaged 22.5 points and 9.8 rebounds, showing the nation his skills when he poured in 36 points while defeating #1 ranked North Carolina 99-88 in January of 1992. The ESPN game was televised into 90 million homes. At 6'10" Gugliotta hit eight three-pointers. He had arrived.

Tom Gugliotta, nicknamed 'Googs,' became the sixth overall player taken in the first round of the NBA Draft. During his eleven-year NBA career, he scored more points than any other player that came out of NC State with the exception of David Thompson. He made more than $80 million playing NBA basketball after his two years with Les.

"He showed a deep desire to maximize his talent and had a willingness to do what it took—hard work. I felt that I always gave him the best advice. The work ethic came from Gugliotta. He made himself great," Les said. "He did not settle for being average."

DAVE HANNERS

Dave Hanners was well respected throughout the basketball world. He was hired by Les and coached at ETSU for four years.

"Many years after Dave Hanners was my assistant coach I ran into Coach Larry Brown. Dave worked in the pros for years with Larry. Larry Brown played in my dad's tournament many years ago, so we knew each other from back then. I asked him how Dave was doing. Now Larry Brown had won NBA championships, the NCAA championship, the NIT, and was considered among the best head coaches ever. His opinion mattered.

"Larry answered, 'Dave was the best assistant coach I ever had.' Now that tells you a lot. Dave was out of Ohio and could recruit with anyone. He came to North Carolina in the early 1970s and played for Dean Smith. Dave worked hard; he was articulate, and he made every coach he worked for a better coach.

"I remember a story Larry Brown told when Dave was with him at Kansas. Dave didn't drink. But when he signed a particular blue-chip kid to come to Kansas, a couple of glasses were poured. The kid he scouted was an excellent player and a must-get player for the Kansas program. When Larry Brown signed the 6'11" Danny Manning, a toast was in order. Dave Hanners, Larry Brown and the blue chipper's father had the toast together—despite Dave's aversion to anything alcoholic. The 6'11" recruit that they toasted that evening would become the main player in Kansas' run to win the NCAA Basketball Championship four years later.

"Dave had dozens of Dean Smith stories. He was another one who owed his career to Dean. And Dean helped me to get Dave on my staff. Every coach who Dave Hanners assisted were bettered by his work ethic and ability. Hanners was a great one."

KEITH 'MISTER' JENNINGS

Keith "Mister" Jennings was a high school player without a future in Culpepper, Virginia. Nobody wanted him. Coaches came to see him but passed on the opportunity.

Jennings tells the story of how he kept an unusual nickname.

"It happened growing up. I was playing football when I was 7 years old and my dad was ready to go. He was yelling, 'Keith, let's go.' I kind of was ignoring him and all of a sudden, we heard this booming voice, "Mister Jennings, get over here!" It kind of stuck after that. Meeting teammates for the first time in college and the pros, they didn't want to call me Mister at first, but after they saw me play and we played together a little bit, it became kind of easy for them to call me that."

Les knew about Jennings through several sources and was looking for a point guard. He knew that he was not in competition with other schools because most colleges had already passed on the diminutive guard.

"I went to see him out of curiosity. Everyone said he couldn't play at the college level because he was too small at 5'7". I might have been the only coach in America that would take a little guy like Mister. It was because I had a lot of success at The Citadel with small guards—Randy Nesbit, Eddie Paone, and Greer Huguley. They were fine players who helped us to win. None of them were over 5'9". So, I wasn't afraid to take a small point guard if he could play."

Les recalled the recruiting story.

"My brother Mark lived near Culpepper and I asked him to go with me. Mark knew more about basketball than most anybody without ever being involved in the sport. He knew talent as well as I did. I wanted his opinion.

"Mister was playing a fine floor game that night. He had made very few mistakes and had a bunch of assists from penetration into the lane. I saw the same things that inspired me to bring Randy Nesbit to The Citadel—another player nobody wanted because of his size who could get after it.

Mister could play, and I knew it. I found out that VMI and a few other schools in the northern Virginia area turned him down, including James Madison. He had zero offers. That would make some coaches stay away, knowing that other coaches have already passed on him. But I had a different view of small guards than anyone. I liked him, and I knew right away he could fit in at East Tennessee. We needed his quickness and his ball skills.

"Once the game was over, my brother Mark asked me what I thought. He assumed that I was not going to offer a scholarship like everyone else. Mark saw him as others did—good, but too small. He said he'd be a defensive liability. But instead of discussing it further, I was direct. I told Mark, 'I'm taking him.' Mark was surprised. "He started laughing like I was joking with him. He said, 'Really? You're taking that little guy?' I told him that I thought he'd be a starter for us. Mark was shocked."

Les detailed Jennings' impact in an incredible game that he still mulls over from time to time. It's because he didn't have Mister Jennings in at the end.

"When we played the NCAA first round game in Nashville against the number one team in the land, Oklahoma, we had them beat. It was the closest that a #16 seed came to beat a #1 seed in the NCAA tournament until the UMBC upset of Virginia in 2018 thirty years later. We lost by one point.

"We were up by 15 early in the second half and by 6 in the last four minutes when the call that changed the game happened in the lane. Oklahoma—with Stacy King and Mookie Blalock—could not force turnovers with Mister running the show. Mister controlled the action. But he had four fouls. On a play in the lane, Mister draws an obvious charge. But the outside official called a reach. There was no reach. It's on film. His feet were set. He executed a perfectly positioned charge situation. I've seen that film a dozen times. It was an awful call by the ref that changed everything. I was livid. But I kept my head. We were still in the lead. But without Mister on the floor to run things, our offense suffered, and Oklahoma's defense was more effective. That poor call by the official gave us four minutes to still pull the upset without our best ball handler. We fell one short. The kid nobody wanted was that important.

"Mister shot 59% from the three-point line in his senior season, leading all of the NCAA with that statistic. He set the Southern Conference record for assists. Mister started the first forty games of his NBA career for the Golden State Warriors before he was sidelined by injury. He played there for three full seasons. He only had one scholarship offer, but he was starting in the NBA. I love telling people about finding Mister Jennings and offering a scholarship that same evening. I had that experience with the little guys and did not discount the height, as would other coaches. I just didn't think it was a long-shot gamble."

There were coaches across America that saw Jennings as a prep player and didn't see what Les saw. Four years later he was a consensus 2nd Team All-American.

CHAPTER 33

IN THE END THERE IS A BEGINNING

Things happen within unbroken circles. Les had the map to the trail to the road to the highway. His compass never failed. He pointed the right direction to others. Along the way, he gathered fiends and memories. A composite of his experience remains.

IN MEMORIAM

Coach **Everett Case** recruited Les from St. Alban's High School in 1960. The experience of playing for one of that era's legends is a point of pride for Les. At his passing in 1965, Case left Les a small share from his estate.

Coach **Bill Foster** died on January 12, 2016. Foster lived to be 86. He and Les remained friends and Les visited Foster in Texas in 2007. The "other" Coach Bill Foster left The Citadel to start a new basketball program at UNC-Charlotte. His departure opened a position on The Citadel's staff and began Les's college coaching career.

Coach **George Hill** changed his middle initial and fell away into the mist of the nether land of his own volition. Hill died in December of 2009. His quirkiness merited stories that could fill a separate book. Les appreciates those three years coaching under Hill because they provided 43 years of stories—and counting.

Pistol Pete Maravich died from an enlarged heart condition while playing in a pick-up basketball game in 1988. It was just nine months after his father died. Les saw the Pistol's magical talents mature while playing pick-up games with the high school upstart while Les was serving his first assistant coaching job under Pete's father, Press.

Coach **Press Maravich** died in 1987 when Les was the head coach at East Tennessee State University. Les holds a profound reverence for his coaching mentor. He even scouted teams for him when Press served as head coach at LSU.

Coach **Al McGuire** exhibited the personable traits that Les emulated for a career. As the years passed, he became more impressed by McGuire's anecdotal humor and quirky habits. He died in January of 2001.

Coach **Dean Smith** spent the end of his career, including his retirement from 1997, in Chapel Hill—passing away in 2014. He was among the best-loved figures in college basketball. He had a special affinity for his rivals—Les and his good friend Bobby Cremins. His record for career Men's NCAA D1 basketball wins was broken by Duke's Mike Krzyzewski.

Coach **Eddie Teague** passed away in 1987. Teague was a pre-war student at North Carolina and a post-war graduate of NC State University. He exhibited impeccable ethics as a head football coach and athletic director at The Citadel. He awarded Les for his loyalty, providing him with his first Division 1 head coaching opportunity.

Coach **Jim Valvano** passed away in April of 1993. His legacy at NC State was to take an underdog team all the way to the National Championship in 1983. Les accepted the head-coaching job at NC State following Valvano and exhibited class in his defense of Valvano's Wolfpack legacy. They were friends.

OTHERS IN THE CIRCLE

Frank Beamer built a legendary career at Virginia Tech and retired in the fall of 2015. He began his coaching career at The Citadel in 1973.

Greg Blatt served as Les's assistant before becoming head basketball coach at Western Carolina and Presbyterian College. Blatt was a tireless recruiter.

Chip Carey was Les's play-by-play broadcast partner for ACC basketball in 2000. Carey has earned his advancement in the broadcasting industry by being among the very best in the game.

Ed Conroy served as head basketball coach at Francis Marion University, The Citadel, and Tulane. As of 2018, he serves as an assistant coach at the University of Minnesota. The Davenport, Iowa, native was Les's last basketball recruit at The Citadel.

Al Daniel remained in coaching as a major recruiter at several top collegiate programs. The Furman graduate served as an assistant with Les at NC State. He is currently the coordinator of student development at the University of South Carolina.

Fisher DeBerry retired from the United States Air Force Academy football program as their legendary head coach after the 2006 season. The Cheraw, SC, native resides on the Isle of Palms along with UNC basketball Coach **Roy Williams**, former American League Baseball President **Gene Budig**, former Maryland head football coach **Ralph Friedgen**, and former VMI head coach **Cal McCombs**. The retired coaching fraternity grows like sweetgrass in the dunes at the Isle of Palms.

Marye Anne Fox became chancellor at NC State before moving on to the University of San Diego in 2004. She does not have the Robinson phone number and will not be waking the family on a Sunday morning at 6 a.m. ever again.

Ralph Friedgen's career took him to a National Championship at Georgia Tech and to the Super Bowl as Bobby Ross's Offensive Coordinator. As head coach at Maryland, he brought the Terrapins back to national prominence. He and his wife Gloria retired to their Isle of Palms, SC, home that he bought shortly after they were married.

Al Gore shared a win for the Nobel Peace Prize in 2007. He is an entrepreneur, but was not elected president, possibly because of hanging chads. Les had a beer with him in 1985 and never forgot the experience.

Tom Gugliotta retired from the NBA Atlanta Hawks in 2005. 'Googs' had a stellar NBA career. He is always mentioned as one of the great people Les coached that could also play basketball.

Jim Harrick retired after his last coaching stint at the University of Georgia. His team won the NCAA National Championship at UCLA in 1995. His instructions to Les to switch assignments and cover Jerry West in the 1960 Sportsman's Club Tournament proved his acumen as a coach.

Les and Terry Holland first met as college players.
Photo by author.

Terry Holland and his wife Ann often visited Sullivan's Island to spend time with the Robinsons. In addition to his coaching, Holland has been Athletic Director at three Division 1 NCAA programs (Davidson, Virginia, and East Carolina).

Tom Izzo continues to make Michigan State University synonymous with winning basketball. He is much admired within the college basketball fraternity. He and Les are long-term friends.

Bobby Johnson is an NCAA Football Selection Committee member and resides at with his wife Catherine at his new home on Johns Island, S.C. He says the house's best feature is the dock at the tidal creek. He and Less meet for breakfast often.

Richard Johnson began his coaching career with Les at The Citadel before becoming head basketball coach at Wofford College in Spartanburg, SC. He currently serves as the Wofford Athletic Director and on the NCAA FCS Selection Committee.

Bobby Knight: The coaching fraternity transcends sports and time.
Photo courtesy Robinson family archives.

Bobby Knight played in Inky Robinson's Sportsman's Club Tournament with John Havlicek and Jerry Lucas in 1961. Knights career took him from West Point to Indiana to Texas Tech. He retired. He revisited Les in Charleston in 2017.

Sandy Koufax lived in the Los Angeles area before moving to Vero Beach, Florida.He is notoriously private, but never had that opportunity for his preference around Les Robinson.

Cal McCombs coached under Red Parker and Bobby Ross at The Citadel and Fisher DeBerry at the US Air Force Academy. He served as a professional scout for the Denver Broncos for five seasons and as the head football coach at Virginia Military Academy. He has known Les since 1969.

Mike Montgomery has coached two of the top programs on the west coast— Stanford University and the University of California. He was able to develop his career far past the disaster of being an assistant coach under The Citadel's George Hill. He and Les see each other annually at the NCAA Final Four.

Gene Moore was the mayor of Boynton Beach, FL, and was **Ted Williams**' lawyer. He began writing a book about his deceased friend and baseball legend. He became the first million-dollar donor to assist Les in the rebuilding of Johnson Hagood Stadium. He wears a ball cap when he travels that simply reads, "Free Ted Williams."

Les recruited Randy Nesbit and then hired him as an assistant. Nesbit is nearing 500 career wins.
Photo courtesy Roane State College.

Randy Nesbit is Head Coach and Athletic Director at Roane State Community College in Rockwood, Tennessee, where he has won 377 games through the 2017-18 season. With his 75 wins at The Citadel, he has won 452 games as a head coach and is a sure bet to win 500 over his career.

Tom O'Brien graduated from the U.S. Naval Academy and served in the Marine Corps before coaching football at Boston College and NC State. He and his wife Jenny live at Daniel Island, SC. He does color commentary for Navy Football.

Buzz Peterson was the North Carolina's High School Player-of-the-Year coming out of Ashville. Les retold, "What made that even more significant is that there was a fine player from Wilmington that he beat out. Michael Jordan became Buzz's college roommate at Chapel Hill. Buzz coached with me at NC State until he got another job at Vanderbilt. He was an excellent coach, but I convinced him to take the opportunity because when we were going badly at State, they unfairly blamed him instead of me."

Bobby Ross retired from coaching at West Point in 2007. He remains one of the class people in all of college football. He lives near Richmond, Virginia. He and Les were next-door neighbors at The Citadel from 1973 to 1977.

Regan Truesdale manages a mill near Rock Hill, South Carolina. His reputation was as the nicest and best dispositioned player Les ever coached. Les explains, "His natural humility prevented him from realizing what a great player he was." Truesdale expressed a deep devotion to the man he called Coach Rob by stating, "He gave me confidence and believed in me from the day I stepped on campus."

Jerry West retired from basketball—having seen it from nearly every level as a player and front office executive, lastly with the world champion San Francisco Warriors. He'll forever be the NBA logo. He and Les have stayed in contact for a lifetime.

Gary Williams retired as the fiery head basketball coach of the Maryland Terrapins in 2011. His coaching fraternity awaits his first full English sentence not interspersed with colorful and rollicking invectives. He and Les share a few laughs often.

V.O.C.A.L.

A group of old friends that has a strong attachment to athletics meets for breakfast every other Thursday in a local Charleston area restaurant. The group includes the "winning-est" tennis coach in NCAA history, **Paul Scarpa**, the wrestling coach from West Point, **Ed Steers**, and an ESPN color analyst, **Debbie Antonelli**, and various others—some who come regularly, and some who have visited (**Dave Odom, Larry Conley, Roy Williams, Joe DeLamielleure, Denny McLain, Coach John McKissick, Art Baker, Dr. Harvey Schiller, Willie Jeffries, Ted Valentine, Drew Meyer** and **Mike Veeck**). They call themselves by the acronym **VOCAL** – "Venerable Old Coaches Association, Loitering." The "regulars" include area residents **Fisher DeBerry, Cal McCombs, Ralph Friedgen, Bobby Johnson, Tom O'Brien, Bobby Cremins, Dan Carnevale, Rusty Hamilton, Andy Solomon** and, of course, **Les Robinson**. The author of this work regularly attends to better understand the pulse and tenacity of American sport.

And so it goes for all of us.

Electing to enjoy the meaningful areas of his life, Les Robinson returned to Charleston as Athletic Director of The Citadel—where he had raised his family while coaching basketball from 1969 to 1985.He retired from the position in June of 2008.

Off and on, he had spent 24 years at The Citadel. Like both sides of a transparent clock, there are twenty-four markings. One goes forward, the other backwards at the same pace. Perhaps it's in balance. Or maybe it's in defiance of time.

It's Les Robinson's circle. He has defined the circumference and the diameter. Though it has touched so many of us, it is still his sphere. Our circles are bigger or smaller and define us as they whir through space and time. In the end one is still in a singular place at the beginning of something else—at peace with oneself and caught within the circle that has been moved around to get there.

The earth is a spinning sphere.It tilts slightly and embraces the changing seasons. Its orbit is vast.And Les Robinson is at the center of it all.

Les didn't change basketball or invent new strategies.
He fixed failing programs and elevated the ethics of the sport.
In doing so he developed friendships and built careers for others.
Photo by author.

CHAPTER 34

NET RESULTS

Andy Solomon, the long-term Assistant Director of Athletics at The Citadel compiled Les's career achievement for a "retirement roast" at The Citadel's McAlister Field House in May of 2008. The career record and statistics were distributed at the dinner.

The Solomon compilation [reprinted with his permission] serves as a terrific summary.

Les Robinson remains the only figure in NCAA history to serve as head basketball coach and director of athletics at three different Division I institutions. He served as head basketball coach and later director of athletics at The Citadel, East Tennessee State and North Carolina State.

On June 30, 2008, he concluded his coaching and administrative career, which once began as a basketball player at North Carolina State University in 1960. He remained involved with the NCAA and NIT as a consultant and committee member to choose deserving NCAA teams for those respective season-ending tournaments.

"It has been a wonderful time and a tremendous amount of fun. I have often pinched myself because I have lived a life that many dream about, but the best part of this ride has been the genuine and personable people I've met along the way," he noted at his retirement ceremony.

His last college president, Lieutenant General John W. Rosa of The Citadel, remarked upon the occasion.

"As one of the most highly respected people in college athletics today, Les has consistently championed the highest ideals in college athletics and

brought out the best in our student-athletes, our coaches, and all others he has mentored. The Citadel is lucky to be the place where he will finish his outstanding career and it has been my privilege to have Les on my team."

Les Robinson's TIMELINE:

Born in 1942, Les Robinson grew up in St. Albans, West Virginia, a very small town with less than 4-square miles and less than 12,000 residents today. This is where he met Ms. Barbara Simon, in the 6th grade. She became Mrs. Barbara Robinson some years later [1963].

As an undergraduate at NC State, Robinson served as team captain and led the Wolfpack freshman basketball squad in scoring in 1961 while playing for legendary coach Everett Case. He earned two varsity letters with the Wolfpack in 1963 and 1964, spent the 1965 season as a student assistant coach and was promoted to graduate assistant status in 1966. The previous year, Robinson graduated in 1965 with a bachelor's degree in parks and recreation and physical education.

He departed NC State after the 1966 season to coach at Cedar Key High School in Cedar Key, Fla. where he went 41-9 in two seasons. Robinson then made a one-season assistant coaching stop at Western Carolina where he earned his master's degree before joining The Citadel's coaching staff prior to the 1969-70 campaign.

Robinson served five years as a Bulldog assistant coach under Dick Campbell and George Hill, and eventually spent 11 seasons as The Citadel's head basketball coach from 1974-85. He directed the 1978-79 and 1984-85 teams to 20 and 18 victories, respectively, marking the two most successful seasons in Citadel basketball history. Another highlight of his coaching career came when the Cadets won 23 consecutive home games. For those efforts, Robinson was named the Southern Conference Coach of the Year in 1979 and was tabbed South Carolina's Coach of the Year in 1979 and 1985.

Following his tenure at The Citadel, Robinson became the head basketball coach at East Tennessee State, where he coached the Buccaneers for five years increasing their win total (7-14-20-27) each of his final years. He resurrected the ETSU program that won just seven games in 1987 to its finest run of basketball success in school history. He guided the Buccaneers to two NCAA Tournament appearances (1989 and 1990), a pair of Southern Conference Tournament championships (1989 and 1990) and was named Southern Conference and Tennessee Coach of the Year following the 1990 campaign. The Buccaneers also produced record levels of departmental revenue while he served the dual role of head basketball coach and athletics director.

Robinson returned to Raleigh and his alma mater prior to the 1990-91 basketball campaign to coach the Wolfpack. He replaced Coach Jim Valvano. Robinson promptly guided NC State to a 20-11 record and a NCAA Tournament appearance while earning the NABC's District Coach of the Year honor in his first season atop the Wolfpack program.

His Wolfpack teams also enjoyed commendable academic success during the decade while graduation rates and grade point averages increased, and the academic qualifications of incoming freshmen improved. Robinson recruited and coached a Phi Beta Kappa player (Todd Fuller) who later became a NBA lottery pick. He also posted the best career winning percentage against Dean Smith and the University of North Carolina of any ACC coach during his tenure.

Robinson was appointed as NC State's athletic director from 1996-2000. There he oversaw a department with an operating budget of $25 million and sent 11 teams to post-season play. During his final year, the department earned a $1.1 million surplus.

In addition, the cumulative grade point average of athletes at the ACC institution exceeded that of the general student body. Robinson and the N.C State family also witnessed the opening of the Entertainment and Sports Arena, a 19,700-seat facility that serves as the home of the Wolfpack men's basketball program and the Carolina Hurricanes of the National Hockey League.

After serving The Citadel Bulldogs' basketball coach from 1974-85, and spending five prior seasons as an assistant coach, Les Robinson became The Citadel's Athletic Director on September 1, 2000.

During his tenure as director of athletics at The Citadel, the school witnessed the opening of the Altman Athletic Center at Johnson Hagood Stadium, the Inouye Marksmanship Center, the Maybank Triplets Football Practice Field at Willson Field Complex and a facilities addition to McAlister Field House for women's athletics. He hired the school's first senior woman administrator, took measures to revamp the college's weight training facility, led the college into a 10-year marketing relationship with Daktronics, and made significant contributions to the revitalization of Johnson Hagood Stadium, which opened the West Side Grandstands in 2006.

Robinson donated $100,000 for the facilities project, marking the college's single largest donation ever by an employee. He also issued a challenge for others to match his donation resulting in nearly a million dollars for the stadium. During the renovations – and owing to his considerable intercollegiate relationships – Robinson brought in more than $5 million in guarantees for playing games against teams from the Football Bowl Subdivision.

The Citadel, under Robinson's guidance, has hosted the SoCon's cross-country championships, the first two rounds of the women's basketball championships, the men and women's tennis championships and the Southern Conference baseball tournament. The Robinsons have maintained a home on Sullivan's Island since his time as assistant basketball coach at The Citadel. They have four children and eight grandchildren.

Other Noteworthy Accomplishments:
- *In 2006, ETSU inducted him into their Athletic Hall of Fame after receiving an honorary alumnus citation in 1997.*
- *Robinson remains the only coach in Southern Conference men's basketball history to earn league coach of the year honors at two different schools, and he ranks fifth on the conference's list of basketball wins.*
- *He became the first coach in the history of the ACC to win 20 regular-season games, one game in the ACC Tournament and one game in the NCAA Tournament in their first season.*

- *Robinson spent six years serving on the prestigious NCAA Division I Men's Basketball Committee, one of the NCAA's most influential committees. The committee is responsible for site selection for each round of the NCAA Division I men's basketball championships. Additionally, it chooses the at-large teams that compete in the field and makes many important decisions regarding the NCAA Basketball Tournament. He was involved with the NCAA's contract with CBS that paid $6 billion for the rights to televise "March Madness."*

- *As a coach, Robinson also served a pair of stints with USA Basketball as head coach of the South squad in the 1995 Olympic Festival in San Antonio, Texas, and as an assistant coach to Bobby Cremins at the 1989 World Qualifying Games in Mexico City. He also guided an Atlantic Coast Conference (ACC) All-Star Team on a European Tour in 1993.*

- *He has accumulated a lengthy list of former basketball assistants and administrators who have become head coaches and directors of athletics.*

- *In 2007, Robinson was recognized as the AstroTurf Southeast Region's Director of Athletics-of-the-Year at the annual NACDA (National Association of Collegiate Directors of Athletics) Convention in Orlando, Florida. The previous year he was recognized with a "Lifetime Honorary Alumnus" citation from The Citadel Alumni Association.*

LES ROBINSON
Year-By-Year

Year	School	Position
1960-61	NC State	Freshman Basketball Player
1961-62	NC State	Varsity Basketball Player
1962-63	NC State	Varsity Basketball Player
1963-64	NC State	Varsity Basketball Player
1964-65	NC State	Assistant Basketball Coach
1965-66	NC State	Assistant Basketball Coach
1966-67	Cedar Key (FL) HS	Head Basketball Coach
1967-68	Cedar Key (FL) HS	Head Basketball Coach
1968-69	Western Carolina	Graduate Assistant Basketball Coach
1969-70	The Citadel	Assistant Basketball Coach
1970-71	The Citadel	Assistant Basketball Coach
1971-72	The Citadel	Assistant Basketball Coach
1972-73	The Citadel	Assistant Basketball Coach
1973-74	The Citadel	Assistant Basketball Coach
1974-75	The Citadel	Head Basketball Coach
1975-76	The Citadel	Head Basketball Coach
1976-77	The Citadel	Head Basketball Coach
1977-78	The Citadel	Head Basketball Coach
1978-79	The Citadel	Head Basketball Coach
1979-80	The Citadel	Head Basketball Coach
1980-81	The Citadel	Head Basketball Coach
1981-82	The Citadel	Head Basketball Coach
1982-83	The Citadel	Head Basketball Coach
1983-84	The Citadel	Head Basketball Coach
1984-85	The Citadel	Head Basketball Coach
1985-86	East Tennessee State	Head Basketball Coach

1986-87	East Tennessee State	Director of Athletics & Head Basketball Coach
1987-88	East Tennessee State	Director of Athletics & Head Basketball Coach
1988-89	East Tennessee State	Director of Athletics & Head Basketball Coach
1989-90	East Tennessee State	Director of Athletics & Head Basketball Coach
1990-91	NC State	Head Basketball Coach
1991-92	NC State	Head Basketball Coach
1992-93	NC State	Head Basketball Coach
1993-94	NC State	Head Basketball Coach
1994-95	NC State	Head Basketball Coach
1995-96	NC State	Head Basketball Coach
1996-97	NC State	Director of Athletics
1997-98	NC State	Director of Athletics
1998-99	NC State	Director of Athletics
1999-00	NC State	Director of Athletics
2000-01	The Citadel	Director of Athletics
2001-02	The Citadel	Director of Athletics
2002-03	The Citadel	Director of Athletics
2003-04	The Citadel	Director of Athletics
2004-05	The Citadel	Director of Athletics
2005-06	The Citadel	Director of Athletics
2006-07	The Citadel	Director of Athletics
2007-08	The Citadel	Director of Athletics

Former Assistant Basketball Coaches Under Robinson
Who Became Head Coaches

- Eddie Biedenbach (Davidson & UNC Asheville)
- Greg Blatt (Presbyterian & Western Carolina)
- Ed Conroy (Francis Marion, The Citadel, Tulane)
- Butch Estes (Presbyterian & Furman)
- Richard Johnson (Wofford)
- Brian Lane (Transylvania)
- Ben Ledbetter (Tennessee Tech)
- Alan LeForce (East Tennessee State & Coastal Carolina [women])
- Randy Nesbit (The Citadel & Roane State)
- Buzz Peterson (Appalachian State, Tulsa, Tennessee & Coastal Carolina)
- Barclay Radebaugh (Charleston Southern)
- John Shulman (Chattanooga)

Current Athletics Directors Who Worked Under/With Robinson

- Charlie Cobb (Appalachian State & Georgia State)
- Jeff Compher (Northern Illinois & Western Carolina)
- Joe Hull (College of Charleston)
- Eric Hyman (VMI, Miami [OH], TCU & South Carolina)
- Richard Johnson (Wofford)
- Mark LaBarbera (Valparaiso)
- Jim Miller (Richmond)
- Dave Mullins (East Tennessee State)

Former Athletics Directors Who Worked Under Robinson

- Dr. Janice Shelton (East Tennessee State)

Others, Including Ties to the NBA

- Chris Corchiani (NC State player)
- Greg Dennis (ETSU player)

- Todd Fuller (NC State player)
- Tom Gugliotta (NC State player)
- Dave Hanners (NY Knicks Assistant coach; Robinson assistant coach at ETSU)
- Keith "Mister" Jennings (ETSU player)
- Pete Maravich (Family friend and mentor)
- Rodney Monroe (NC State player)
- Mike Montgomery (coached with Robinson at The Citadel)
- Rick Swing (2nd Citadel player ever drafted by NBA after Gary Daniels)
- Calvin Talford (ETSU player)
- Kevin Thompson (NC State player)

Les assists other basketball interests in his retirement.
He is a much-in-demand speaker and a purveyor of "inside stories."
Photo courtesy Charleston Area Sports Commission.

CHAPTER 35
NO LAMENTS, NO REGRETS

There are never goodbyes as welcomed as hellos in the Robinson household—as long as their visitor returns. They love having company. It expands their circle even wider.

In the basketball world, Les did not win 500 games, invent a new offense, or set a new scoring record in a large arena. He did not win a national championship. The fans did not pay exorbitant prices to hear him speak at an event or to sign game programs. He was not a graduation speaker at Harvard or Vanderbilt. He was never invited to the White House.

He was set to go out quietly, in the full realization that he coached one high school and three colleges to the best of his abilities within the inherited circumstances.

It was a "goodbye" that best illustrated the respect he had earned over his career from those on the inside who knew the backstory. He had announced his retirement as Athletic Director at The Citadel in April of 2008. Without his knowledge, a local group formed to give him a proper send-off. It became the largest single catered event in the history of The Citadel.

The June evening boasted a Who's Who list of attendees and additional video messages—from South Carolina's then-Governor **Mark Sanford**, Coach **Mike Montgomery**, and Coach **Mike Krzyzewski**. Even his brother **Mark Robinson** sent his surprise wishes from a world summit on water that convened in Norway. Les had no idea of the breadth of respect his life's work had earned. Featured speakers included Coaches **Terry Holland**, **Bobby Cremins**, and **Roy Williams**. Former player **Xavier Starkes** gave a humorous insight to the locker room while former assistant **Richard**

Johnson 'piled it on.' Even former U.S. Olympic Executive Director **Harvey Schiller** brought his best stuff. **Dave Odom** drove in. **Eddie Fogler** was there. Former players came to Charleston from across the country. Even former opponent players came, most notably **Jerry Stackhouse**. Former assistants **Randy Nesbit**, **Ed Conroy**, **Greg Blatt**, and **Alan LeForce** were there. His wife Barbara was beaming. All four children attended along with his grandchildren. His sister and his brother-in-law came. His best friends hosted tables. They all came to honor a difference-maker who set admirable standards in the sport—Les Robinson.

There was a latent realization among the coaching fraternity, family, fans, and friends that Les had always done it the right way with no regrets. His coaching ability may have won more games when he was overmatched in talent than virtually anyone in the game. That talent chasm was part of the landscape he always seemed to inherit. Invariably, that college basketball landscape would be further impaired by nefarious acts that preceded his arrival. He fixed things that were broken.

A look back confirms the facts. He coached at the smallest public high school in the Florida system, and won. He coached at The Citadel, a small military college with other-than-athletic missions and was twice voted by his peers as Southern Conference Coach-of-the-Year. He inherited a heavily sanctioned program at East Tennessee State and lifted the program to 27 wins and a shot at the buzzer that would have meant a #16 seed beating the overall #1 seed of the NCAA tournament. That has still never happened. He took over his alma mater, NC State, when they were still in the afterglow of the 1983 Jim Valvano National Championship. He performed admirably under deep sanctions by the NCAA and deeper scrutiny from the university administration. He delivered the college basketball program, historically their flagship sport, to academic excellence while competing in the best league in America. It was what he was hired to do.

People who read sports journals and the morning box scores may not have cared about anything but who wins and who loses. Les witnessed this sentiment too often. Gary Hahn, a broadcaster and writer who traveled with the Wolfpack teams wrote about this dynamic. His wisdom and insight would develop the reason that Les Robinson would set an attendance record for a social event at his last stop, The Citadel. It was appreciation for a career well done. The overflow attendance at that event has never been topped.

A GOOD NIGHT'S SLEEP

(Reprinted)
By Gary Hahn
Wolfpack Sports Network

One of the darkest periods in NC State basketball came in the early 1990's after the firing of Coach Jim Valvano. Les Robinson, a former NC State player, replaced Valvano and after a successful 1990-91 campaign, the Wolfpack hit the skids and suffered through back-to-back 19-loss seasons.

I was the radio play-by-play announcer for State during those tough years and the job wasn't much fun, but Robinson's task was more difficult than anyone could imagine.

In January 1993, after a blow-out loss at Georgia Tech that dropped the Wolfpack to 0-6 in the Atlantic Coast Conference, the team returned to Raleigh immediately after the game. During the flight, I can remember looking over my shoulder. In the back of the plane was Robinson in a deep sleep in the last row of seats.

I'd never seen anything like that in the pressure-packed world of big time college basketball. A coach who wasn't a basket case after a loss? I'm not sure why, but for some reason, I was never able to forget that moment. I'm glad I didn't.

As I would learn a while later, Les Robinson's job involved a lot more than just coaching basketball. It was really about executing a very important two-fold mission. Les was given marching orders to improve the graduation rate of the NC State basketball program, which had dropped to an embarrassing level, and to repair severely damaged relations with the academic community on campus.

Standing in the way of success were some major challenges. NCAA sanctions restricted recruiting while the university imposed more stringent academic standards on the men's basketball program than on any of the school's other sports.

Robinson had little choice but to recruit student-athletes that were more students than athletes.

As the academic record improved, the basketball record took a tumble. Wolfpack fans became critical. The media piled on. Robinson became the butt of jokes. Talk radio hosts renamed the play-in game of the ACC Tournament the "Les Robinson Invitational."

Les never lost focus. He handled the situation with integrity, class, humor and tremendous humility. It was almost impossible not to like Les Robinson.

As my mind flashes back to that plane ride in January 1993, I realize now that Les could sleep on the ride home and was completely at peace because he knew he was doing exactly what he was ordered to do. He refused to get caught up in all the other stuff. Yes, the Wolfpack lost that night and the criticism hurt, but that wasn't the real issue.

Before resigning in 1996, Robinson successfully completed his mission and restored academic integrity to the Wolfpack men's basketball program, but he never coached again. In six seasons, his record at State was 78-98. Unfortunately, that record is the only thing a lot of people remember.

When I think of Les Robinson, I have a much different memory. I see a servant who focused on the mission, ignored adversity and persevered with class until the job was done.

That flight in 1993 taught me a life lesson. Rest and peace are by-products of obedience. Thanks Les, for showing me what a good night's sleep is really all about.

Les had friendships that flourished over a career. It may have been because he and Barbara never forgot others. They cared. It may have been because of his West Virginia roots where neighbors helped neighbors. It may have been because of his steady adherence to connecting others when he could—making a phone call to help get someone a job; meeting a parent for coffee, helping a student get into a university, or just sending a tee shirt to a youngster in an at-risk home environment.

In his career and personal life, Les has always prided himself on taking and returning all phone calls. He never screened calls to avoid disgruntled fans, sportswriters, or parents of players. He had confidence that he could cheerfully respond and—at the very least—agree to disagree. His attitude was always to confront adversity head-on. Crossing the line for Les was anyone who said anything about a family member or a friend. This was taboo. As such, he gained tremendous credibility as being genuine—as a father, a sibling, a coach, and a friend.

His greatest fan has always been the young lady he began dating as a junior in high school. Barbara Simon Robinson became among the most basketball-knowledgeable wives because she loved Les's career. He was doing what he planned to do since the fifth grade. She found great passion in the strategies Les employed to beat good teams with lesser teams. This was the case for most of his career. Barbara even 'TV-scouted' other teams when Les was away. She knew man-to-man presses and zone traps, motion offenses and out-of-bounds plays. And she knew the tendencies of every referee Les would encounter. Some were block-charge experts; some paid much attention to hand checking and push-offs, and some were rabbit-eared for criticisms that could lead to technical fouls. Barbara could have helped the Las Vegas handicappers with her knowledge of the game. She was that good.

Les retired to his 40-plus-year residency of Sullivan's Island, the profoundly residential barrier island town of only 1,900. He gets his mail at the post office because he likes going to the post office and chatting with others there he has known for many years.

He assesses conference teams each season for the prestigious and historical NIT Tournament, both pre-season and post-season. He served on the post-season NIT Committee for the NCAA for several years. His opinion, for selecting teams or hiring coaches, is considered among the best in the business.

Others might not define his routine as a retirement. He works out strenuously for an hour every day.He entertains many visitors—friends that may even stay at the Robinson home. He takes them on his golf cart for a tour of the island.

Visitors see Fort Moultrie, the Sullivans Island Lighthouse, and the southwest panoramic view of Charleston from across the harbor. It's best seen at sunset. The tour usually ends with a dinner at one of the old island restaurants, where Les arrives and may be greeted by more than a dozen friends and neighbors, the wait staff, bartenders, and often the owner of the establishment. He is Sullivan's Island's best-known and most-often-seen hometown celebrity. Steven Colbert lives two doors down.

Former Major League pitcher Denny McLain, the sport's last 30-game winner, described the experience. "The *Robinson Island Golf Cart Tour* is great for digestion, nice views, a lighthouse, an old fort—but is woefully short on details. He doesn't know any of the important history—just who lives here and there who nobody else knows but him."

McLain first met Les at a breakfast with Bobby Cremins in 2012. Because Bobby greeted Les that morning as "You asshole," from his loss of $20 in a card game the night before, McLain autographed his book *I told You I Wasn't Perfect* with a personalized inscription, "To Asshole." The breakfast crowd broke out in laughter.

On the island or elsewhere, Les could be coaxed to tell a story about an incident, a legendary coach, or a star player. The stories never change. Humor is likely. They are from a past that touched a thousand lives—or more.

The stories are remembrances of personalities like Everett Case, Pistol Pete Maravich, Jerry West, Mike Krzyzewski, Sandy Koufax, Rod Hundley, James Worthy, Bobby Cremins, Dean Smith, Al Davis, Bobby Knight, Frank McGuire, and David Thompson. Grab a beer. He talks about something every time someone comes a "round"—inviting everyone into his sphere. It is in this environment that one achieves the inner circle.

The life of a basketball wife is demanding because of its inherent commitment. Barbara Robinson passed away on August 21, 2017. She was truly loved. Photo courtesy of Robinson family.

EPILOGUE
A WIFE BELOVED

(Author's note: I had known Barbara since 1970 and visited her when she was able to see friends just days before her sad passing on Monday, August 21, 2017. She had no regrets. She intimated that she was lucky to have the great circumstance of her friends coming to see her for the last time. No one left without tears.)

Prior to this heartfelt loss, Les and Barbara Robinson sat down for a joint interview at their home on Sullivans Island. Les was assisting the National Invitation Tournament selection committee, and still sat in as an Emeritus Member of the NCAA Selection Committee in Indianapolis. He became a vital influence to athletic programs across the country looking for coaching recommendations—even for football. He seemed to know everyone in the sports world.

The interview was completed near the time that Barbara had begun feeling the effects of a rare lung condition with no cure. Much of what follows are her quotes related to basketball and her life with Les.

Barbara Simon had an inauspicious beginning. She had no silver spoon, no trust fund, and no one was planning for her debutante ball. Born in South Charleston, West Virginia, she and her older brother Bob moved to Clarksburg when she was only two to live with her paternal grandparents. It was during the war years and her parents had divorced.

She returned to St. Albans in the fourth grade, still with her grandparents. Her mother had remarried and moved to Miami. She and her brother remained in West Virginia. The Simon family was from stern stock. They were strict Baptists with the structure and demands set in stone to raise the young

Simon siblings. The austerity and disciplined environment helped Barbara to become an excellent student and handle much responsibility at an early age.

Her father died when she was only eight. Her grandfather died suddenly when Barbara was only ten. Her mother was a world away and never returned to reclaim her. It was just her, her brother Bob, and her strict grandmother, Esther Simon, to make it through the cruel West Virginia winters.

"We were both at St. Albans. Barbara knew I was the little smart-aleck kid that she just couldn't stand. I was a good bit shorter than her and was always a class clown," Les reminisced. "I knew she couldn't stand me. We were not anything alike and I just did things to spite her especially during that first year. I had no idea of the hardships she was handling at home."

The former Barbara Simon sets the backdrop.

Les and Barbara with their eight grandchildren. Photo courtesy Robinson family archives.

"I had come to live with my grandmother. There were some problems with my mother that resulted in the option to move and live with my granny," Barbara retold. "My mother was a classic alcoholic. But back then I really didn't know how serious her drinking addiction was. I loved my grandmother and came to Les's school wide-eyed. I was so young and really impressionable. My first interactions with Les were not positive.I guess girls grow up faster, and he seemed so immature to me. We were 12."

However, Les was not going to go away.

The beautiful sparkle that Barbara Simon had back then has remained. It was seen in her deep warm eyes, her square-jawed smile, and the sheer resonance of her down-home West Virginia accent.

"Barbara was a great student then and through college," Les recalled. "I was a screw-up that had decided the year before—when I was only eleven—that I would be a basketball coach. I wrote it in a paper for my fifth-grade teacher as part of an assignment of what we intended to be when we grew up. Some wrote about being a fireman, some wrote being a big-league baseball player, and others wrote about being a movie star. I had made up my mind to be a basketball coach. My father had to convince me to pay attention to my course work because I would have to obtain a college diploma to realize my dreams of becoming a coach. But I just did what I had to do to pass. Barbara, on the other hand, was a top student. She had nothing to do with me. I gave her good reason."

Les continued.

"My mother, Mary Trowbridge Robinson, was really the disciplinarian of our home. She didn't have to spend much time with Debbie, my sister, or my brother Mark. But she had to stay behind me. Studying for school was the last chore on my list every day. I procrastinated, and I skimmed by. As I got older, I became proficient at being barely efficient," Les joked. "My dad saw what I was doing, just getting by. In a way, he admired that. But my mother abhorred it. Years later, when Mark came along and made straight A's, Dad noticed that he did his homework without anyone's prodding. Mark took pride in his work. My father pulled me aside and asked me if I thought there was something wrong with Mark! He thought that schoolwork was meant to be a struggle. So being a little smart-alecky kid was what my dad assumed was normal. Resisting schoolwork was part of how he grew up, too. I came by it naturally. Barbara had no idea that, in a way, my dad was proud that I was how I was."

Barbara was not impressed.

Barbara added, "I was put off by how he was so little and cocky. He was the kid that would have been like the Eddie Haskell character on the old *Leave it to Beaver* television show. He was so courteous to everyone, but I saw him as a fraud. He just smiled like he'd gotten away with something every time I'd call him out. It really came to a head when they had a PTA meeting and Les was asked to be an escort to the classrooms by the principal. The parents had no idea what a devious kid he was."

Barbara smiled as Les told the story from his experience.

"Yeah, I went that evening to the school dressed up nicely and got to take all of the parents around from one classroom to another," Les remembered. "I'd take them to the lab or to the gym, over to the lunch room, and then to their child's homeroom. I was on my best behavior. I didn't know all of the parents, but I was not afraid to speak up and I'd always say 'yes, sir' or 'yes, ma'am.' I was snowing those parents over with every little bit of information. I'd say, 'here's where we do our experiments and lab work,' or 'here's where we eat lunch.' They had no idea that I was such an average student."

But Barbara knew—and Les could not snow Barbara. She told of the aftermath.

"My grandmother came home after the PTA meeting," Barbara recalled, "and told me that she had met the nicest young gentleman from my class, so courteous and cordial. When I asked her what his name was, she recalled it to be Leslie. I just about fell over. He had fooled my grandmother into thinking he was a goody two-shoes. I knew he was a little devil. But there was no way I could convince her of that. I thought, 'that little so and so has fooled everyone in that school but me.'

"I made a face and told my grandmother that she may have met Leslie, but she had no idea that he was this bratty kid who slid by on his homework and made the girls in class sick. We knew Les to be a troublemaker in the seventh grade, not a gentleman like my grandmother thought," Barbara retold. "It just made me even more guarded and skeptical about Les back then."

Les and Barbara's relationship was destined to change. By the ninth grade, Les's growth spurt had kicked in and he was taller than Barbara. By their junior year, they began dating. Les took her to the prom. Barbara helped Les with his homework. They talked openly about college plans and the life beyond, Les still certain that he was going to be a college basketball coach.

By graduation, Barbara, a merit scholar, had committed to Marshall University, just a short drive over the highway into Huntington, West Virginia, near the Kentucky-Ohio border.She was selected as a member of the first-ever class of nursing students at Marshall.

"I'm very proud of that fact. Marshall had just started the program and I was elated to be accepted," Barbara recalled. "It was a stringent course load and required a lot of study. But I was truly excited to be accepted there and to begin a new life as a college girl."

Les was being recruited for his athletic skills as a savvy backcourt player to major Division 1 universities. The aggressive ones were calling regularly. There was West Virginia, Marshall, North Carolina, and NC State.

In the end, the biggest coaching name in the upsurge of southern basketball had the inside track. Everett Case had offered Les a full scholarship to attend NC State in Raleigh. It was too good to pass up. Case was basketball's godfather in the area known as 'Tobacco Road.'

"My grandmother liked Les, and that was unusual in a way because she had a predisposition about people who were not of the Baptist faith. I would describe her as being a very puritanical person. But Les seemed to adapt to her well," Barbara recounted. "I guess that first impression in the seventh grade stuck!"

"I went to all of the high school basketball games, and even then I found myself studying the game stategy. I became a student of basketball way back then. I loved the sport and understood it better than my girl friends. I didn't like the girly chatter when the game was going on. I liked watching the action.

"Watching Les play in college was all the more exciting. These were the best teams playing in front of packed houses. It was so amazing to see those games against those really good teams in the ACC."

After dating around the long trips back and forth to St. Albans, the basketball practices and games in Raleigh, and the other rigors of college life, they decided to formalize their relationship. They both knew where Les's career was headed when they realized that they were going to be together for the duration. Both had not finished their academic careers as yet. They had no money.

Les's mother, Mary Trowbridge Robinson, loved Barbara and helped them to plan an elopement. As much as Barbara's grandmother favored Les, she would not likely support the idea of the elopement. The secretive event was at the end of the basketball season. Les and Barbara took off to Tazewell, Virginia, where they exchanged vows in a Methodist Church on Friday, March 8, 1963. It was at a time when Barbara's resourcefulness and Les's energetic approach to getting his career started would poduce great results. But they needed to be patiently determined.

Tracking fifty-four years forward, when Barbara knew that her lung disease made her passing imminent, she created a "bucket list" of activities. Prominent on the list was a return to the church in Tazewell where they were married. They had no photographs of the elopement wedding in 1963. Barbara wanted a photo of her and Les in the church. They made the trip and took photos. It was the first time they had been back. Barbara passed away three weeks later.

Her words of remembrance became especially meaningful at a time when Les wanted to hear her voice just once more. She spoke about the excitement of their secret wedding arrangements.

"It was a simple decision and a commitment that I had looked to that would change everything for me. Here I had Les, a most stabilizing influence in the midst of an upbringing that was anything but stable. I knew that if I married Les, it would be forever. I was determined not to be like the parents that abandoned me and my older brother. I wanted something better in life, and Les was there for me at every turn. We not only became a great team that supported each other, but like the old fashioned romances, we were firstly great friends. Even in our darkest times, Les has always been able to remain optimistic and reassuring. That's such a rare quality."

The new couple did not worry about finances. They had decided that they would work their plan to a goal of success. In that success, the needed finances would take care of itelf. The Robinsons had four childen in four years—Greg, Robby, Kelly, and Barbara Ann. With the many moves through a career, Barbara was able to endear herself to so many friends in the business.

"I have been blessed with great friends because of Les's career. Just from The Citadel experience I have remained friends all these years with the coaches wives from other sports—Lynne McCombs, Lee Shelton, Jean Hamilton, Alice Ross, and Carol Johnson. Even the opposing coaches have the wives that enjoy seeing each other— Shirley LeForce, Carolyn Cremins, Ann Holland, and Barbara Biedenbach. We stay close. We have a special bond. We always pull for one another. The wives all know each other and we share so much," Barbara said. "A coach's wife has a completely different family schedule than most spouses. For instance, we don't always have meals at a regular time. We travel on short notice. We entertain on short notice, as well. We look out for the players as much as we can. We cannot be routine, but rather always flexible with our schedules."

And there are competitive moments, too.

"One time at a game I saw the ACC game official, Ted Valentine, greet my dear friend Carolyn Cremins near the far sideline. We were playing Georgia Tech. He leaned over and gave her a kiss on the cheek. Well, don't you know that when I saw Ted later I mentioned that I'd seen it and snidely reminded him that kissing the coach's wife shows favoritism. He smiled big and told me that he would be happy to even the score by giving me a kiss, as well. Fair is fair!"

Every wife of an NCAA men's basketball coach becomes the team mother, to an extent. They are expected to provide the emergency needs of the players away from home—some for the first time.

"I did what I could to support the team. I was always there to help Les. We were especially close with the team at East Tennessee State and those boys really enjoyed coming over. They were a close bunch. I always had something for them like snacks and cookies. I remember giving The Citadel players haircuts from time to time on our back deck. Some of the freshmen were always looking for a place to rest or to get a bite to eat. They couldn't get back in time to get the haircuts on campus. Those Citadel boys were always so respectful, courteous, and appreciative.

"I remember a story from the early days when the managers always washed the uniforms for the team after practice. When school was out for Thanksgiving or Christmas, it was up to us to find food for the kids. There was no cafeteria or mess hall. We had The Citadel team over for Thanksgiving dinner. I had cooked two 25 pound turkeys. The team managers showed up later, but there was not one bite of meat left on either turkey. Those players had picked them both clean! The managers just got the rice and beans with dressing and gravy.

"Some of the great players we had at NC State were very protective of Les. With all that was going on, Les did not ever complain to anyone, including me. He was dealt a bad situation. The players read the paper. They knew that Les was hired to clean things up. Yet they saw him walk in to every practice and every game with a focus and strategy to win. They respected that and rallied many times to win games that, by injuries, the loss of scholarships, and the lack of bench depth, we had no right to be in the game. Les never let those issues get to him," Barbara noted. "That's what many of the coaches close to him knew. He would never throw in the towel. He wanted to teach kids and give them goals to make them better players—but more importantly—better people.

"Being a coach's wife, there were some tough times. There are coaches that get fired. There are players that quit or transfer. There are big wins and really tough losses. In his last year he had Duke beat in the last few seconds when a prayer 3-pointer by Chris Collins bounced high off the rim straight up, bounced five more times, and finally rolled in. That was a heart-wrenching loss after our boys had played so hard. I took that defeat a lot worse than Les did."

The stability of a marriage always plays a huge role. The ups cannot get too high or the downs too low.

"Les has always displayed the perfect temperament for a coach. He never internalized things like so many other coaches did. The little things didn't drive him crazy. He never worried about the officiating. He figured it would even out and that even officials make mistakes. He never got really angry over the various setbacks.

"Everywhere we went we faced some adversity. We had it at Cedar Key before we got to The Citadel. Imagine coaching in the smallest high school in the state at a remote fshing village setting sixty miles from anywhere. He never complained. In fact, we both hated to leave. Then, after his graduate degree at Western Carolina, we landed at The Citadel. There, the Vietnam War was an issue. There were people that just hated anything to do with the military. Les had to recruit during those hard times.

"We were all fooled into thinking things were clean at East Tennessee State. We had no idea that they were about to go on probation because of things done before we got there. Had Les known the real issues, he could have either stayed at The Citadel as head coach or moved to the Athletic Director position he was offered when Eddie Teague retired. We had no idea of what trouble ETSU was in before he accepted the head coaching job. He had to completely rebuild that program with his hands tied.

"And the NC State position was Les's dream come true. For heaven's sake, it was where he got his degree, where he had so many friends, and where he started his coaching career as the freshman team coach. But the Valvano years had a reaction from both the NCAA and the administration that meant Les would have to play with lesser tools than his opponents. He was going against the best in America—Dean Smith, Bobby Cremins, Mike Kryzyzewski, Dave Odom, and the others. It was—and still is—the best league in college basketball. He knew enough that the first few years would be a challenge. But he had not anticipated the wide range of restrictions the university would require. The university itself handcuffed Les beyond what the NCAA demanded. Les was there to clean it up like he did at East Tennessee. The insiders there knew that and appreciated what he did. But many of the fans were frustrated. That was really difficult for Les. But again, he never complained."

Barbara summarized his career in a retrospective.

"It seemed as though, as Les once said 'For some reason, the Lord chose me to go and fix these situations.' And he did. So, for him it was never about wins and losses, but about repairs and restitution. It's what he did—and he did it without complaint."

"His regimen was the same, no matter what. He took things as they came and handled the things he could, whether in the lockeroom, the office, or at the kitchen table. He also recognized the things that were not in his control. But Les was always constant by his attitude of remaining positive and his resolve to be strong. He never waivered."

Les could not have accomplished the program turn-arounds without Barbara's support, optimism, and input.

"It took a tremendous commitment from her to follow the ups and downs of my career," Les said in tones of respect. "A career like this takes two people. She always shared the burdens and bought into the program. A basketball wife committed to her husband's career is never a given. It's a hard life. She raised our children during my absenses, and then helped take care of the young players away from home for the first time. Her energy for our challenges was second to none.

"Barbara loved the sport of basketball. I doubt many have seen the hundreds and hundreds of games she has seen during our marriage. In addition, she became a person who understood things that coaches know—whether it be defensive changes, substitutions, or when to call a timeout. She really got into basketball," Les intimated. "I seriously doubt that there are many basketball wives ever that were as intensely involved into the Xs and Os of the game."

Barbara smiled.

The career took them places across the country, into Europe and Mexico, and into the room that selects the best teams in America to play in the #1 sports spectacle in America –*March Madness*. The unknowns of a young coach grew into the knowns of a career commitment shared by two. They were meant to be as one.

Sadly—on the day that midnight came near midday—Barbara Jean Simon Robinson passed away. A solar eclipse hid the sun. It was the rarity of two celestial objects aligned.

ACKNOWLEDGEMENTS

AND ARCHIVES

Les Robinson has an incredible memory of events, quotes, and circumstances. A fact-check on his stories would astonish a crowd at a magic show. He has amazing powers of recall. For this, the author is predisposed to thank him first and foremost before continuing on to others. Barbara Robinson once told the author that 'one could hear some story twenty years ago and again today and they would be exactly the same.' He never forgets the details. It is therefore with appreciation to the late Barbara Simon Robinson for her input and assistance with correcting what was written in error, usually an error by the author only.

Other appreciation goes to Andy Solomon, the former Associate Athletic Director at The Citadel, for providing so much from the media, including photographs, over the last few years. In addition, Solomon provided the condensed information of the Robinson career—as he has always done in a concise and factual manner. He's famous for that.

The author is thankful to acknowledge Ashley Perrucci, who served as Coach Bobby Cremin's executive assistant while he was coach at the College of Charleston. She transcribed audio and video recordings into print. It was a difficult chore, but Ashley was certainly up to the task. She never seemed to mind when more recordings were brought in with the colloquialism she did not recognize as *Robinson West Virginian dialectic*.

It is important to cite the family of Coach Les Robinson, who have been forthcoming with information and usually a family slant to a great story. They all seem to enjoy the experience—often many times over!

Trying to turn these scribbles into the King's English with punctuation placed correctly and redundancies redacted fell upon a long time Robinson family friend—Lynne McCombs. Of note, Lynne has spent her adult lifetime with another coach, Cal McCombs. Cal was head football coach at VMI and served as an assistant coach at the U.S. Air Force Academy and The Citadel. He spent five years as an NFL scout for the Denver Broncos. Meanwhile, Lynne taught the upper echelons of English students at every academic level. Her husband reports that earning a B in her class was as difficult as being a triathlete. Lynne McCombs proved to be an enormous enhancement to the book project. And she knew the stories, as well!

Coaches have a silent fraternity that few know about. One would think that they would mostly be unapproachable. But the opposite is true. It seems that they have all dealt with difficult administrations, out of control fans, demanding parents, eligibility snafus, et al. Coaches, with a few exceptions, are the kind of people you want to have in emergency situations. They know how to get through a crisis. The author acknowledges their input and insight as invaluable.

The coaches that came forward and assisted in this publication include Bobby Cremins, Mike Montgomery, Terry Holland, Dave Odom, Mike Krzyzewski, Richard Johnson, Randy Nesbit, Bill Foster, Fisher DeBerry, Cal McCombs, Duggar Baucom, Tom O'Brien, Bobby Johnson, Ralph Friedgen, Paul Scarpa, Ed Steers, Chuck Driesell, Alan LeForce, Dave Hanners, Jim Harrick, Butch Estes, Eddie Biedenbach, Ed Conroy, Buzz Peterson, Debbie Antonelli, Al Daniel, Greg Blatt, Mark Thompson, Jim Calhoun, and Roy Williams.

Several copy editors, photo editors, and publishing personnel were also called into service. The slick and correct print that resulted is much better than what was initially submitted. Their craft is most appreciated.

ABOUT THE AUTHOR
W. THOMAS MCQUEENEY

Author Tommy McQueeney has been a friend to the Robinson family for nearly fifty years. A 1974 graduate of The Citadel with a degree in English, McQueeney first met Les Robinson as a high school basketball player at a Citadel summer hoops camp run by Robinson. They remained steadfast friends throughout Robinson's remarkable career.

Around in Circles is McQueeney's ninth publication. His previous books included the genres of literature, history, humor, and fiction. McQueeney is married and has four children and four grandchildren. He is a 2009 recipient of The Order of the Palmetto, the highest award bestowed on a citizen of the State of South Carolina.